About the Editors

Prof. (Dr.) M.R. Biju, currently working as Dean, School of Social Sciences and Professor of Public Administration and Policy Studies, Central University of Kerala, Kasaragod. He has served the full term as Dean, School of Social Sciences (2017-2020), School of Legal Studies (2019-2022) and also a short span as Dean, Academic (2020). Prof. M.R. Biju is one of the widely cited writers in the field of Social Sciences with 161 citations and H-index of 6 and i10 index of 3.

Prof. Biju is the Editor of South Asian Journal of Socio-Political Studies (SAJOSPS), a UGC Listed Journal (No. 34425 Dated 11.01.2017 with an impact factor of 3.1028). He is also serving as Editor-in-Chief of International Journal of Political Science (IJOPS). He is a prolific writer on socio-political and developmental issues.

He has published Thirty five (35) books, One hundred and Seventy-Five (175) research papers, Seventeen (17) book chapters and 11 (Eleven) Seminar Proceedings. All the books were published by leading publishing houses in New Delhi. He has delivered 78 (Seventy-Eight) Invited Lectures, 16 (Sixteen) Key note addresses and reviewed over Nine Hundred books for South Asian Journal of Socio-Political Studies.

His teaching and research experience, spanning over three decades , includes several achievements such as completion of Three major research projects funded by Ministry of Panchayati Raj, Govt. of India and University Grants Commission, New Delhi and the post-doctoral fellowship awarded by the UGC in 2004-07. Prof. M.R. Biju has successfully guided doctoral students of University of Kerala and Central University of Kerala. Seven students are currently pursuing their doctoral studies under his supervision at CUK. He is consistently making professional academic contributions in the capacity of an Associate Board Member of Economics and Management, a prestigious journal published by the Technical University of Liberce, Czech Republic; as the Director and Member Secretary of the Asian Institute of Development Research (AIDR); and as a life Member of several Academic and Professional Bodies.

M.R.B. Anantha Padmanabha is currently serving as Deputy Editor of South Asian Journal of Socio-Political Studies. He has to his credit a sizeable number of publications in reputed research journals and he has presented papers in National Seminars and Conferences. He is a Doctoral Student in International Relations and Politics of Central University of Kerala, Kasaragod.

SUSTAINABLE DEVELOPMENT AND DIGITAL TRANSFORMATION

Edited by
M.R. Biju
M.R.B. Anantha Padmanabha

CONCEPT PUBLISHING COMPANY PVT. LTD.
NEW DELHI - 110059

ISBN: 978-93-5594-672-0

First Published 2025

Published and Printed by

Concept Since 1974

Concept Publishing Company Pvt. Ltd.
A/15-16, Commercial Block, Mohan Garden
New Delhi-110059 (India)
T: +91-11-41101460
E: publishing@conceptpub.com, *W*: www.conceptpub.com

Cataloging in Publication--Courtesy: D.K. Agencies (P) Ltd. <docinfo@dkagencies.com>

Sustainable development and digital transformation / edited by M.R. Biju, M.R.B. Anantha Padmanabha.
pages cm
Contributed articles.
Includes bibliographical references and index.
ISBN 9789355946720

1. Sustainable development--India. 2. Sustainable development--Technological innovations --India. I. Biju, M. R., 1965- editor. II. Anantha Padmanabha, M. R. B., editor.

LCC HC440.E5S87 2025 | DDC 338.95407 23

Preface and Acknowldgements

The pursuit of sustainable development has become increasingly intertwined with the rapid advancements in digital technologies, giving rise to the concept of digital transformation. This introductory note delves into the complex interplay between sustainable development and digital transformation, exploring their synergies, challenges, and potential implications. By examining key domains such as economic growth, social inclusion, environmental conservation, and governance, this presentation highlights the transformative power of digital technologies in advancing sustainable development goals. It underscores the importance of aligning digital transformation efforts with sustainable development principles to foster resilience, equity, and long-term well-being in a rapidly evolving digital era. The advent of digital technologies has brought about transformative changes in various facets of human life, including the realm of sustainable development. This note aims to unravel the intricate relationship between sustainable development and digital transformation, shedding light on how digital technologies can serve as enablers and catalysts for achieving sustainable development objectives. By exploring the domains of economic growth, social inclusion, environmental conservation, and governance, we gain insights into the potential benefits and challenges that arise from the intersection of these two spheres.

Keeping this background, an attempt has been made in this book to present an array of sixteen chapters which focuses on varied issues linked with the theme, viz. CSR and sustainable development, SDGs and good governance, democratic decentralisation and good governance, environmental, social and governance (ESG), Corporate Financial Performance (CFP), disaster management, Marxian perspective on environment, sustainable export of water intensive rice, armed conflicts and its environmental hazards, energy cooperation in Eastern South Asia, climate resilience and peace building practices, zero-waste management, theoretical developments in power and soft power, Digital India Initiatives, upsurge of Indian e-commerce industry and Neo-liberal instrumentality in governance.

Before conclude, the volume editors, would like to add that through these research papers and articles from the academics and researchers, they have tried to examine the varied aspects of sustainable development and digital governance in the context of contemporary India. Through their presentations, the contributors have submitted solid and practical suggestions to enrich the areas of sustainable development and digital transformation system, which may be useful for the students, researchers, practitioners and policy makers in the field. These prefatory remarks remain incomplete without expressing our gratitude to those who have been kind enough to help us in the preparation of this volume. First of all, we would like to thank our esteemed contributors to this anthology of articles. Similarly, we are extremely thankful to Shri Ashok Kumar Mittal, Managing Director of Concept Publishing Company Pvt. Ltd., New Delhi who brought out the volume in an elegant form.

M.R. Biju
M.R.B. Anantha Padmanabha

Contents

Preface and Acknowldgements v
Introduction ix
List of Contributors xxv

1. Corporate Social Responsibility and Sustainable Development: Lessons from India 1
   – *Mrutuyanjaya Sahu*
2. Sustainable Development Goals and Good Governance: The Agenda for Women Empowerment Through Quality Education: A Case Study of *Beti Bachao Beti Padhao* Scheme in India 25
   – *Neelima Deshmukh*
3. Democratic Decentralisation and Good Governance in the Context of Indian Urban Local Bodies: The Present Status 35
   – *Neelima Deshmukh*
4. Environmental, Social, and Governance (ESG) and Corporate Financial Performance (CFP): A Systematic Review using TCCM Approach 54
   – *Priyanka Aggarwal* and *Archana Singh*
5. Disaster Management and "Good Governance": Concerns and Strategies 98
   – *Santosh Kumar*
6. Environment and Society—A Theoretical Overview: Special Reference to Eco-Marxism 119
   – *Binu, K.*

7. Climate Crisis and Water Scarcity: Can Sustainable Practices Save India's Rice Exports? 130
– *Swati Pathak, Hitesh Solanki* and *Shefali Dani*

8. Armed Conflicts, Military Pollution and its Environmental Hazards: An Overview 154
– *O. Nirmala*

9. Energy Cooperation in Eastern South Asia to Strengthen Energy Security 164
– *Anita Elizabeth Mathew* and *Santhosh Mathew*

10. Does Awareness on Climate Resilience Promote Peace Building Practices in Adolescents? 172
– *Tara S. Nair* and *Anjali G.*

11. Zero Waste Management: A Key to Sustainable Development 179
– *Midatala Rani* and *Natasha Raikar*

12. Power and Soft Power: Theoretical Developments 194
– *S. Loganathan*

13. Digital India Initiatives in Transforming Governance to Achieve Sustainable Development Goals 224
– *Sanjeev Kumar Mahajan* and *Anupama Puri Mahajan*

14. Upsurge of Indian E-Commerce Industry in the Era of Post-Demonetisation 244
– *M. Sarngadharan*

15. E-Governance: An Indian Experiment with the MyGOV Application 254
– *Sudheesh Kumar J.*

16. Exploring Neoliberal Instrumentality in Governance 272
– *Arindam Roy*

Index 283

Introduction

The pursuit of sustainable development has become increasingly intertwined with the rapid advancements in digital technologies, giving rise to the concept of digital transformation. This introductory note delves into the complex interplay between sustainable development and digital transformation, exploring their synergies, challenges, and potential implications. By examining key domains such as economic growth, social inclusion, environmental conservation, and governance, this presentation highlights the transformative power of digital technologies in advancing sustainable development goals. It underscores the importance of aligning digital transformation efforts with sustainable development principles to foster resilience, equity, and long-term well-being in a rapidly evolving digital era. The advent of digital technologies has brought about transformative changes in various facets of human life, including the realm of sustainable development. This note aims to unravel the intricate relationship between sustainable development and digital transformation, shedding light on how digital technologies can serve as enablers and catalysts for achieving sustainable development objectives. By exploring the domains of economic growth, social inclusion, environmental conservation, and governance, we gain insights into the potential benefits and challenges that arise from the intersection of these two spheres. Some key areas which links sustainable development with digital transformation are given under:

Digital Transformation and Economic Growth: Digital transformation has the potential to spur economic growth by enabling innovation, entrepreneurship, and productivity gains. It fosters the development of digital infrastructure, e-commerce, and digital platforms that facilitate trade and investment. Moreover, it opens up new opportunities for job creation and economic diversification, particularly in sectors such as information technology, digital services, and advanced manufacturing. Harnessing digital technologies for sustainable economic growth requires addressing issues of digital divide, ensuring digital literacy, and promoting inclusive access to digital resources.

Social Inclusion and Digital Transformation: Digital technologies have the power to bridge societal divides and enhance social inclusion. They can improve access to education, healthcare, financial services, and other essential resources, particularly in underserved and remote areas. Through digital connectivity and mobile technologies, marginalized communities can participate in economic and social networks, access information, and voice their concerns. However, challenges such as the digital divide, affordability, digital literacy, and privacy and security concerns must be addressed to ensure equitable access and meaningful participation for all.

Environmental Conservation and Digital Transformation: The application of digital technologies can play a pivotal role in environmental conservation and sustainable resource management. For instance, the Internet of Things (IoT) and sensor-based technologies enable real-time monitoring of environmental parameters, leading to more efficient and targeted resource utilization. Big data analytics and artificial intelligence facilitate predictive modelling and decision-making for sustainable resource planning and management. Furthermore, digital solutions can promote sustainable practices in sectors like energy, transportation, agriculture, and waste management. It is crucial, however, to address the environmental impact of digital technologies themselves, including e-waste, energy consumption, and the carbon footprint of digital infrastructure.

Governance and Digital Transformation: Digital transformation can enhance governance systems by improving transparency, accountability, and citizen engagement. E-governance initiatives enable the delivery of public services, facilitate digital platforms for citizen participation, and streamline administrative processes. Digital technologies also enable data-driven decision-making and evidence-based policy formulation, fostering more efficient and effective governance. However, digital governance must ensure data privacy, cybersecurity, and protection of individual rights. It should also address the digital divide to ensure that marginalized communities are not further marginalized in the digital realm.

Challenges ahead: The intersection of sustainable development and digital transformation brings forth several challenges and considerations. Addressing the digital divide, ensuring digital literacy, and mitigating the risks of data privacy and cybersecurity are crucial. Ethical considerations surrounding the use of emerging technologies, such as artificial intelligence and automation, need to be carefully navigated. Additionally, fostering multi-stakeholder partnerships and global cooperation is essential to leverage the potential of digital technologies for achieving sustainable development goals and to address potential inequalities and disparities that may arise from digital transformation.

Furthermore, a holistic and integrated approach is needed to ensure that digital transformation efforts align with sustainable development principles. This entails considering the social, economic, and environmental dimensions of sustainability throughout the design, implementation, and evaluation of digital initiatives. Policymakers and stakeholders must promote responsible and inclusive digital innovation, taking into account the needs and aspirations of diverse communities and ensuring that no one is left behind. The intersection of sustainable development and digital transformation holds immense potential for driving positive change and fostering resilience in the face of complex global challenges. By harnessing the power of digital technologies, sustainable development goals can be advanced in domains such as economic growth, social inclusion, environmental conservation, and governance. However, to fully realize these synergies, careful attention must be paid to addressing challenges related to the digital divide, data privacy, cyber security, and ethical considerations. Policymakers, stakeholders, and technology innovators must collaborate to ensure that digital transformation is guided by sustainable development principles, leaving no one behind and promoting equitable access to the benefits of digital technologies. By embracing the opportunities offered by digital transformation while remaining mindful of its potential risks and challenges, we can pave the way for a resilient, inclusive, and sustainable future. Through continued research, dialogue, and informed policy-making, we can navigate the complexities of the digital era and shape a world where technology and sustainability go hand in hand, fostering the well-being of present and future generations.

Keeping this background, an attempt has been made in this book to present an array of sixteen chapters which focuses on varied issues linked with the theme, viz. CSR and sustainable development, SDGs and good governance, democratic decentralisation and good governance, environmental, social and governance (ESG), Corporate Financial Performance (CFP), disaster management, Marxian perspective on environment, sustainable export of water intensive rice, armed conflicts and its environmental hazards, energy cooperation in Eastern South Asia, climate resilience and peace building practices, zero-waste management, theoretical developments in power and soft power, Digital India Initiatives, upsurge of Indian e-commerce industry and Neo-liberal instrumentality in governance.

Content of the Volume

In the inaguaral chapter, **Mrutuyanjaya Sahu** presents a study on the linkages between "Corporate Social Responsibility and Sustainable Development based on India". According to the researcher, in the era of liberalization and globalization corporate social responsibility (CSR) has gained importance and has become a common concept whereby corporate sector companies consider the interests of society by taking responsibility for the impact of their activities. In India, CSR is in a flowering stage and facing daunting social and environmental challenges due to rapid economic developments, many Indian private sector companies have to go beyond their essential economic functions and to consider social and environmental aspects through CSR for their sustainability and development. CSR covers almost all issues like inequality of employment; environmental impact; involvement of civil society groups and local community; public safety; company cultures; brand image and reputation, etc. Recently, the Indian government has taken a number of regulatory measures to ensure firms, support to achieve sustainable development goals. The main objective of these rules and regulations is to achieve triple bottom line growth.

Further, through this study, Sahu highlights the relation between CSR and sustainable development in India in the context of mandatory CSR guidelines in the Companies Act, 2013 applicable for both public and private sector companies. This chapter is divided into the following sections. First, the literature on CSR is reviewed. Second, the sustainable and inclusive growth challenges of India are highlighted. Third, the chapter discusses the role of selected private sector companies as a case study and their related projects and investments at regional, national and global levels. Fourth, it highlights the key challenges in planning, implementing, monitoring and evaluating CSR projects. Finally, the chapter summarizes the findings, discusses their implication for all stakeholders and identifies possible future research.

Similar to the earlier chapter, **Neelima Deshmukh** tries to explore the relationship between "Sustainable Development Goals and Good Governance". Here, thc senior researcher focused her area of investigation on *Beti Bachao Beti Padhao* Scheme introduced by Government of India. According to her, the Millennium Declaration of United Nations (UN) set 2015 to provide quantitative benchmarks for 8 goals as, eradication of extreme poverty and hunger, Achieving universal Primary Education, promote gender equality and empowerment of women, reducing Child Mortality rates, Improve maternal health, Combat HIV, malaria and other diseases, ensuring environment sustainability, global partnership for the Development etc. Bold and transformative agenda 2030 for the Sustainable Development adopted by the world leaders at UN, also reaffirmed rationale for MSDGs to wipe out Poverty, Climate Change, Sustainable cities and Development, Gender equality, Fight inequality and emphasised their focus on Quality Education amongst the 17 measurable goals. The world is changing fast with the changing demands and needs of its population, their different kinds of requirements to cater and respond to the emerging situations and challenges are totally changed which has prioritized new agenda for the development of the country on the World canvass. The 2030 Agenda of SDGs is not about any individual country but the concentrated efforts of all the countries together creating the interlinked and globalised world, addressing the challenges of sustainable development from global to local, grass roots level. To see the visible results all through it calls for tailor made strategies, policies, programmes, with their effective and successful implementation, maximizing the synergies, convergence and impacts, across the society. Therefore, the good and smart governance is of crucial importance stressing upon the accountability, transparency, with the suitable regulatory mechanism needed to ensure human rights, equity, stability and long-term sustainability, safeguarding against the corruption and exploitation of vulnerable deprived societies at the time of crises, along with the Institution building and the strengthening of governance capacity is the only way to respond to these challenges of 21st century. The effective coordination between different levels of policy and sectors at vertical and horizontal levels calls for the imperative to initiate action towards key governance issues like rule based, quality administration, management with transparency, accountability and anticorruption mechanisms, with the effective use of public resources added with the improved governance for the realisation of SDGs in letter and spirit.

Neelima Deshmukh, in her second presentation to this volume, explores the connection between "Democratic Decentralisation and Good Governance in the context of Urban Local Bodies". In this context, it has to be noted that compared to rural local bodies, studies on urban local governments are quite limited in number. In this sense, Neelima Deshmukh's study has a special significance. According to the author, for Gandhiji, true independence for India meant a comprehensive transformation of Indian society and polity. He wanted political power to be distributed among the villages in "India" further he preferred the term "Swaraj" to describe what he called true democracy. 74th Constitutional amendment is a watershed in the policy of decentralisation in India. "Decentralisation is the process of redistributing or dispersing the functions, powers, people or things away from central location or authority." Decentralisation is a transfer of authority and responsibility for public functions from central government to intermediate and local government or quasi independent government organizations and/or the private sector. This is a complex multifaceted phenomenon. Different types of decentralisation should be distinguished because they have different characteristics, policy implementation, and conditions for success.

Neelima Deshmukh, further adds that urbanization and economic development have been two sides of the same coin, complementary to each other and necessary for raising the standard of life of its citizens. As globally observed governance is a soul of development, which is being instituted with well designed policies, programmes, schemes under Five Years Plans and taken to the grass roots level through various ministries and institutions efficiently, effectively with proper administration and governance. Moreover, India's economy, according to the author, is expanding rapidly and making steady shift from rural to urban and our cities need to be better managed and the special efforts are required to improve the governance. To this effect, government has rightly anticipated an ambitious Smart cities programme and Atal Mission for rejuvenation and urban transformation for better standard of living.

"Environmental, Social, and Governance (ESG) and Corporate Financial Performance (CFP): A Systematic Review" is the theme of discussion in Chapter four, by **Priyanka Aggarwal** and **Archana Singh**. According to the authors, although research on Environmental, Social, and Governance (ESG) is dispersed across numerous areas and dimensions of management, there is a paucity of reviews that synthesize the knowledge holistically in the context of its impact on Corporate Financial Performance (CFP). Using the Theory, Context, Characteristics and Methodology (TCCM) paradigm, this study employs a systematic review of 57 research articles published over a 9-year period (2014-2022) to resolve this gap. Consequently, the study seeks to address the following questions: (i) In order to explain the connection between ESG and CFP, what different theories or ideas have been considered?, (ii) In what contexts has the underlying research been conducted?, (iii) What features have been explored (i.e., independent, moderating, mediating, and dependent variables)?,

(iv) What methodologies were used to comprehend the underlying study topic? Our study reveals that these studies rely heavily on Corporate Governance theories to explain the impact of various factors on the ESG-CFP link; however, these theories are unable to capture the moderating role of "Innovation" in influencing corporate ESG-CFP decisions. We believe that "Innovation" is a significant factor in shedding light on the connection between ESG and CFP. As a result, the findings of our study give a conceptual framework in which the role of well-developed Corporate Governance theories must be investigated in the context of "Innovation", which would influence the decisions that firms make with ESG-CFP.

In Chapter five, **S. Santosh Kumar**, presents a debate on "Disaster Management and its linkage with Good Governance." He has focused both concerns and strategies linked with these two areas. According to the author, disaster are sudden, catastrophic, and unfortunate events that causes human and financial damages, destruction and devastation. Disasters also impede ongoing and impending development projects, and the impacts—outputs and outcomes—varies from geographies to geographies. Major reasons, as the literature suggests, are due to diversities and differences in the climatic and geo-spatial conditionalities which leads to the difference in the degrees of vulnerabilities caused to the physical environment and to the human resources. Disasters cause the adverse effects on the socio-economic, political and cultural dimensions of the affected area. A disaster can be due to human engagement or natural reasons. Given the capriciousness and unpredictability of the disasters, the states and the disaster mitigation machineries or communities to manage disasters need to be equipped and organised in advance, so as to minimise the aftereffects. The governments legislate, allocate resources and engage into the rational planning and sustainable development. Disaster Management and Planning is a significant and critical part of governments' myriad responsibilities and a subject to be addressed earnestly by the concerned authorities.

The author further says that governance processes play a vital role in managing disaster with 3-E's, i.e., efficiency, effectiveness and economical mitigation process, helps to synchronize political, economic and administrative activity in the management of disaster.

It comprises mechanisms, processes and institutions through which citizens and groups articulate their interests, exercise their legal rights, meet their obligations and mediate their differences to overcome the crisis, whether by the private sector and civil society organizations. This chapter explores the various aspects of the governance of disaster management mechanisms, majorly in India, with the help of the selected case studies.

Binu K. in chapter six, submits a study on the "Marxian theoretical view on environment and society". According to Binu, environmental sociology deals with social, cultural, and ecological areas of human life. This area of research is very useful for the development of environmental policies and the process of equitable development of a nation. It also helps to cultivate environmental awareness and a new sociological outlook to the learners and administrators. It is an attempt to understand various epistemological views related to the interrelationships between sociology and environment but mainly focuses on the eco-Marxism. As a new theoretical outlook Eco Marxism explores the interaction between people and environment with the motive of maximization of profit and the intuition of exploitation of nature and natural recourses. In modern times, the effect of unlimitedness in human motives and the crises of technological domination converts human into more utilitarian towards nature. It reflects all sorts of environmental crises and ecological problems in the modern society. Eco Marxism as the central concern of this chapter highlights the inherent social division in the society on the basis of the possession of wealth and material and how it leads to fundamental reason of ecological crisis and issues. Overexploitation of the nature and material resources for economic and developmental purposes results the condition of the alienation of people from the harsh realities of life. This study also discusses the alienation of people within the framework of modern industrial and socio-cultural transactions.

In chapter seven, three environmental scientists, **Swati Pathak, Hitesh Solanki** and **Shefali Dani**, dwells into an issue titled, "Does Sustainable Export of Water Intensive Rice in India depend on Climate Change and Water Scarcity?" According to them, Rice, a highly water intensive crop not only contributes large to India's GDP in terms of export revenue, but about 8% of total water for agricultural irrigation is used to produce rice. Therefore, this is an emerging concern to understand and conduct in-depth analysis about the sustainability of rice production and export from India within the constraints of climate change and acute water crisis in India. Climate change impact various sectors, the most vulnerable sectors being water bodies and agriculture in India. This study is an attempt to analyze the causal relationship between water usage for export of rice and climate factors and available water resources in India.

The study is based on government reports, websites and peered reviewed journal articles. Compilation of time series data for a period of thirty-two years (1986-2018) was done on climate parameters namely temperature, rainfall, special events, economic variables, quantity of export in India, domestic production, yield and irrigated area for rice and hydrological variables, water availability, water needed for irrigations and water usage for export of rice.

Our analytical findings indicate: First, average surface temperature is increasing over the years combined with declining trend of rainfall and more frequent natural calamities such as floods, droughts etc. Second, water availability rate is significantly low compared to water needed for agricultural irrigation. Third, substantial exploitation of groundwater triggers depletion of water tables which in turn causes huge financial burden on farmers in terms of irrigation cost. Fourth, significant causal relationship exists between water availability and water used for producing exportable amount with climate parameters.

O. Nirmala, in chapter eight, tried to explore, the relationship between armed conflicts, military pollution and its environmental hazards. To her, Conflicts especially Armed Conflict or War is always a threat to human survival. It not only affecting the relationship among nations but also affects the relationship between the man and the nature. The environmental hazards before, during and after conflicts has to be critically examined in order to protect the environment otherwise pose a serious threat to particular people, group or entire regions. This chapter tries to explore the relationship between armed conflict and its environmental impacts.

Anita Elizabeth Mathew and **Santhosh Mathew**, in their chapter, titled "Energy Cooperation in Eastern South Asia to Strengthen Energy Security" reviews the existing energy sector of the

BBIN countries on an individual basis and then intends to explore the prospects and benefits of sub-regional cooperation in the energy sector in a multilateral arrangement among the four countries—Bangladesh, Bhutan, India and Nepal. To them, Regional Cooperation in South Asia has been a slow-moving process due to numerous reasons, the most prominent of which is the India-Pakistan conflict. This has led scholars to explore new ways of cooperation. One such concept is the concept of sub-regional cooperation excluding either of the two conflicting countries.

Energy, according to the authors, is one of the basic needs for development of any country. Being developing nations, Bhutan, Bangladesh, India and Nepal face a growing demand for energy. All the four countries are heavily dependent on energy. Energy holds a prominent position in their EXIM trade basket. Constant increase in imported energy sources such as coal, gas and oil have an adverse impact on the energy security of the sub-region. The energy demand in the region is expected to grow at an annual rate of 5%. (Rahman *et al.*, 2012) This sub-region is equipped in producing almost all kinds of energy (hydro, thermal, wind, solar). Some of these energy generation is affected seasonally. But the sub-region has the geographical advantage of being contiguous in nature. The willingness of sub-regional political regime is the most significant factor for enhancing sub-regional cooperation in supply of fossil fuel and energy trading.

In chapter ten, **Tara S. Nair** and **Anjali G.** presents a paper titled, "Does Awareness on Climate Resilience Promote Peace Building Practices in Adolescents?" This study is an attempt to examine the role of Political Science Education to facilitate holistic learning experiences that contribute to learners' resilient and peace building attitude as a lens to explore one and relationships so that chances to build capacity and respond critically and positively to these issues could be identified. The sample size was 400 higher secondary school students taken from different schools of Alappuzha and Pathanamthitta districts in Kerala. Test of Awareness on Climate Resilience and Scale of Attitude towards Peace Building Practices were the tools used to collect data. The results indicate a positive relationship between the variables studied which serves as a pointer to introduce resilient and peaceful practices in educational practices that favour agreeable ideologies that promote collective capacities for nation building.

"Zero Waste Management as a tool to sustainable development" is the focus of attention in chapter eleven which is presented by **Midatala Rani** and **Natasha Raikar**. According to the authors, Waste management for any city is a Herculean task. It is the duty of the City Corporations to provide clean and healthy environment to their residents. Various aspects of waste management including collection of waste, recycling, disposal, energy, environment, NIMBY syndrome are attracting global attention. In recent times, the Supreme Court of India has also intervened on issues of waste management. Increasing urbanisation contributes to waste generation. It leads to many crucial issues pertaining to the national and global economies. Adopting traditional techniques in waste management have proved a futile exercise. New initiatives are needed. In this context, Zero Waste Management (ZWM) has proved to be an effective alternative. The objectives of the chapter are to understand the importance of ZWM as a key to Swachh Bharat launched by Government of India to fulfil the vision of 'Clean India'; to find out the effectiveness of various measures launched by Mysore City Corporation with regard to ZWM as Mysore City is tagged as the Second Cleanest City in the Country; to manage ZWM more effectively leading to environmentally sustainable city.

"Theoretical developments in power and soft power" is the topic of discussion in chapter twelve. According to the author, **S. Loganathan**, the concept of power is primitive in nature. The power is endless phenomenon and where it starts and where it ends is altogether unfathomable. The search for single conceptualisation of power will become completely illusory and parochial. From birth to death, human existence is driven by endless power relationships. Every human encounter is made up of power. Identifying and observing, evaluating and estimating, comparing and controlling and contemplating the power and its different nuances is really enigmatic. The subtlest and least observable character of power is most effective. Power cannot be compared or equated with any concept or material (animate or inanimate resources) because power is beyond the material wealth, that is, power is a capacity of actors who he involved in the process.

Thinkers like Foucault, Pareto, Boulding and Lukes have tried to unfold the subtle aspect of power into practical reality, actuality, specificity, observability and usability. Since 1990s, the subtle aspect of power became very dominant in international relations which was identified as soft power by Nye in the form of inanimate resources. He compared soft power as non-material resources which end up with vehicle fallacy or resource fallacy. To overcome this vehicle fallacy in soft power analysis, Vuving has come out with power currency approach to end all kinds of confusion which arise from resource driven approach of soft power.

In chapter thirteen **Sanjeev Kumar Mahajan** and **Anupama Puri Mahajan** presented a study on “Digital India Initiatives”. In this study, the researchers examine the impact of Digital India initiatives in transforming the governance to achieve the sustainable development goals. Sustainable Development Goals (SDGs), according to the authors, have an agenda to achieve social, economic and environmental goals by 2030. 196 member nations of the United Nations pledged to work according to the 17 SDGs with proper procedures and processes of implementation and monitoring. This monumental task can be broken down into achievable targets and activities by the nations according to their ecosystem. The one solution to achievement of SDGs that emerges is digital efforts in transforming governance. India has become the leading emerging and fastest economy of the world with the youngest population as its driving force which is empowered by digitalization. The Digital India initiatives have yielded promising results leading an increase in production, ease of doing business and ramping up of government procedures and processes. Its digitally monitoring systems of projects in the infrastructural areas has led to their speedier completion and commencement. India has finally come out of the colonial set up of policymaking trends and administrative procedures by adopting new methods in utilizing the ICTs. It is pushing the manufacturing industry to transform from Industrial Revolution 4.0 to 5.0 which ensures human touch via artificial intelligence to the machines. The manufacturing sector has come to binding machines and intelligent devices through smart networks that are enabled to control each other. However, India has enhanced its basic administrative structure by digitalizing it at the grass roots level with active involvement of local bodies besides the higher levels of administration.

M. Sarngadharan, a senior researcher and professor in Commerce, presents a study titled "Upsurge of Indian E-Commerce Industry in the Era of Post-Demonetisation". The chapter attempts to examine the enrichment of e-commerce industry in India, consequent on the decision for demonetization. The required data, congregated from the research reports and articles published in research journals were bestowed for drawing conclusions of the study. According to the author, the aftermaths of demonetisation in 2016 are positive as well as negative in the Indian economy, when viewed from social, economic, political and legal dimensions However, the economic impact on e-commerce industry is considered momentous on account of the boost foreseen in digital deals and online payments. It is a universally accepted fact that technology enabled innovations like digital payments, hyper-local logistics, analytics driven customer engagement and digital advertisements are prone to support the growth of e-commerce industry unquestionably. The growth in e-commerce sector would boost employment, increase revenues from export, boost tax collection by exchequer, and provide better products and services to customers in the long run.

In chapter fifteen, **Sudheesh Kumar J**, explores a study on "E-governance with special focus on MyGOV application". According to Sudheesh Kumar, governance is emerging as a game-changer in public administration. The tools and techniques used in e-governance have great potential in transforming organizational behaviour in the public sector (UNDESA, 2020, p. xxviii). Today, the people as beneficiaries of the e-services fall dependent on digital governance. The chapter examines the features of e-governance concept and the levels of its implementation in India. India has developed its digital administrative ability from the initial provisions of e-services to complex projects like citizen-government interaction tools. The staging of an application called myGov by the government of India is an attempt to promote virtual democracy at least as an opening attempt. The features and content of the application are examined in the chapter.

In the concluding chapter, **Arindam Roy**, views that the origin, maturation, trepidation and ramifications of the concept of governance is inherently associated with neoliberalism. Hence, the time has come to demystify the concept of governance and interrogate the neoliberal motives before adopting it. To the author, unlike most of the literatures which primarily concentrate on what is governance, how better it can be conceptualized/managed, and what are the parameters of it; the present chapter moots a rather unsettling existential question as to why governance came into being in the first place. In course of analysis the chapter argues that the concept of governance, especially the way it is understood by the donee countries, is a neoliberal construction of furthering its dream of unification of global markets by downsizing state on the one hand, and establishing mechanism for ensuring the repayment of loan amounts from the regions suffering the 'failed state syndrome' on the other, without strengthening the structure or institution of state.

M.R. Biju
M.R.B. Anantha Padmanabha

List of Contributors

Anita Elizabeth Mathew (Dr.), Assistant Professor in Political Science, St. Mary's College, Sultan Bathery, Kuppadi P.O. Wayanad District, Kerala.
Email: anita.elizabeth@gmail.com, anitha.elizabeth@stmarysbathery.ac.in

Anjali, G., M.Ed. Scholar, N.S.S. Training College, Pandalam.
Email: tharasnair@gmail.com

Anupama Puri Mahajan (Dr.), Researcher & Book Author based at Shimla. **Email:** mahajan4949@gmail.com

Archana Singh (Dr.), Associate Professor, Delhi School of Management, Delhi Technological University, Shahbad, Daulatpur Village, Rohini, NewDelhi.
Email: archana.singh@nls.ac.in

Arindam Roy (Dr.), Associate Professor of Political Science, The University of Burdwan, Golapbag, Bardhamah, West Bengal.
Email: arindambu.du@gmail.com

Binu, K. (Dr.), Assistant Professor, Department of Sociology, Vimala College, Thrissur. **Email:** bijuk@vimalacollege.edu.in

Hitesh Solanki (Dr.), Department of Climate Change and Impact Management, Gujarat University, Ahmedabad.
Email: husolanki@yahoo.com

M. Sarngadharan (Dr.), Senior Fellow-ICSSR, Gulati Institute of Finance and Taxation, Thiruvananthapuram.
Email: msarngadharan@hotmail.com

Midatala Rani (Dr.), Professor of Political Science and Director UGC-Human Resource Development Centre (Retd.), University of Mysore, Manasagangotri, Mysore.
Email: mallirani@yahoo.co.in

Mrutuyanjaya Sahu (Dr.), Assistant Professor, Department of Humanities and Social Sciences, Birla Institute of Technology & Science, Pilani. **Email:** m.sahoo@dubai.bits-pilani.ac.in

Natasha Raikar (Dr.), Completed MA in Public Administration, University of Mysore, Manasagangotri, Mysore.
Email: mallirani@yahoo.co.in

Neelima Deshmukh (Dr.), Former Head & Professor of Public Administration and Local Government, RTM Nagpur University & Senior Fellow ICSSR.
Email: neelimadeshmukh87@yahoo.in

O. Nirmala (Dr.), Assistant Professor, Department of Defence and Strategic Studies, Gurunanak College, Anna Garden, Velachery, Chennai, Tamil Nadu.
Email: nirmala.o@gurunanakcollege.edu.in

Priyanka Aggarwal (Dr.), Research Scholar, Delhi School of Management, Delhi Technological University, Shahbad, Daulatpur Village, Rohini, NewDelhi.
Email: agarwal.priyanka021@gmail.com

S. Loganathan (Dr.), Research Scholar, Centre for South Asian Studies, Pondicherry University, Kalapet, Puducherry.
Email: loguhere@gmail.com

Sanjeev Kumar Mahajan (Dr.), Ex-Dean, Faulty of Social Sciences, Himachal Pradesh University, Shimla.
Email: mahajan4949@gmail.com

Santhosh Mathew (Dr.), Associate Professor, Centre for South Asian Studies, Pondicherry University, Kalapet, Puducherry.
Email: santhoshveranani@gmail.com

Santosh Kumar (Dr.), Professor and Dean, Public Policy, Adamas University, Kolkata. **Email:** kumar.santhosh@flame.edu.in

Shefali Dani (Dr.), Director, GLSBBA, GLS University, Ahmedabad, Gujarat. **Email:** shifalira@gmail.com

Sudheesh Kumar J. (Dr.), Assistant Professor, Political Science, Mahatma Gandhi College, Thiruvananthapuram.
Email: sudheeshjanan@gmail.com

Swati Pathak (Dr.), Doctoral Student, GLS University, Ahmedabad.
Email: husolanki@yahoo.com

Tara S. Nair (Dr.), Assistant Professor, Postgraduate Department of Education, N.S.S. Training College, Pandalam.
Email: tarasnair@gmail.com

1
Corporate Social Responsibility and Sustainable Development
Lessons from India

Mrutuyanjaya Sahu

Introduction

Corporate Social Responsibility (CSR) has emerged an important topic of discussion in the public and private sector, and international business forums due to its multidimensional benefits. Today, as people are getting more conscious about climate change and ethical business practices, it is expected from the companies that they become seriously worried about their liability for the local people and the society as a whole. Hence, CSR has emerged as an inevitable concern in the business firms in recent times. India is a prominent South Asian country with a population of more than 1.2 billion inhabitants. According to the International Monetary Fund (IMF), India will be the fastest growing major economy by 2030. Through its enormous manpower potential and natural resources, the country has secured a prominent position in the world economy. However, the socio-economic conditions of the majority of the people are still severe. According to the World Bank (2016) nearly 31.4% of the entire Indian population live in poverty. This widespread poverty is also closely related to gender inequality, illiteracy, and poor health conditions of the majority of Indian people. Furthermore, India is being crippled by environmental issues like deforestation, loss of biodiversity, air and water pollution, illegal wildlife trading, and the vulnerability of ordinary people to natural disasters. Hence, there are ample opportunities for the Indian companies to come forward and to contribute unselfishly to the welfare of society.

In India, public and private organizations have also started to realize the importance of CSR as a vital partof attaining sustainability in a highly competitive business organization. Multinational companies are increasingly pressured by numerous stakeholders to engage in social and environmental responsibility. According to the *Stern Review on the Economics of Climate Change (2006),* environmental sustainability could become the central social responsibility challenge for business. Thus, managers must be able to determine how their companies can become more socially responsible, ecologically sustainable, and economically competitive. In short, business executives must become more adept at integrating their organization's market and non-market strategies (Desjardins, 2007). The growing pressure towards meeting social and economic performance demands from a wide variety of stakeholders raises important research questions, crossing numerous fields in business administration and several related social science disciplines. Specifically, two research questions that, for the most part, have remained unanswered in this increasingly important field of inquiry are: how can social and environmental responsibilities be implemented more effectively through the integrated market and non-market strategies? Second, how can the various business organizations contribute to our understanding of the determinants of superior financial, social, and environmental performance?

To address these unresolved research questions, the chapter is structured in the following manner. In the first section, the literature on CSR is reviewed. Second, the sustainable and inclusive growth challenges of India are highlighted. Third, the chapter discusses the role of selected private sector companies as a case study and their related projects and investments at regional, national and global levels. Fourth, it highlights the key challenges in planning, implementing, monitoring and evaluating CSR projects. Finally, the chapter summarizes the findings, discusses their implication for all stakeholders and identifies possible future research.

Corporate Social Responsibility: Conceptualization

Corporate Social Responsibility has gained much prominence over the past decades in academic literature.There is no single invariably gained definition of CSR, each definition that currently available underpins the impact that businesses have on society at large and the societal expectations of them. Inconsistencies and debates regarding the proper definition of CSR have hampered scientific progress in understanding the antecedents and consequences of this activity. The notion of CSR is a comprehensive one—encompassing the various dimensions of the business. Society and business, social issues management, public policy and business, stakeholder management and corporate accountability are just some of the terms used to describe the phenomena related to corporate responsibility in society (Garriga & Mele, 2004). Although the roots of CSR lie in philanthropic activities (such as donations, charity, relief work, etc.) of corporations. Globally, the concept of CSR has evolved and now encompasses all related concepts such as triple bottom line, corporate citizenship, philanthropy, strategic philanthropy, shared value, corporate sustainability and business responsibility.

The academic literature provides various definitions of the concept of corporate social responsiveness, and it is argued that business and society are interlinked: society has an undeniable belief regarding business, and therefore the companies have responsibilities towards the development of the society. CSR can be defined as the "economic, legal, ethical, and discretionary expectations that society has of organizations at a given point in time" (Ghulliani, 2013). Naylor (1999) defined it as "the obligation of managers to choose and act in ways that benefit both the interests of the organization and those of society as a whole." The European Commission defines "CSR as the responsibility of enterprises for their impacts on society and to meet their social responsibility, enterprises should have in place a process to integrate social, environmental, ethical human rights and consumer concerns into their business operations and core strategy in close collabouration with their stakeholders." The World Business Council for Sustainable Development defines that "CSR is the continuing commitment by business to behave ethically and contribute to economic development while improving the quality of life of workers and their families and the local community and society at large" (World Bank, 1999).

Carroll (1979) describes CSR as a multi-layered concept that can be differentiated into four interrelated aspects—economic, legal, ethical and philanthropic responsibilities. Carroll presents these different responsibilities as consecutive layers within a pyramid, such that "true" social responsibility requires the meeting of all four levels consecutively. The model probably is the most accepted and established. Carroll makes clear that various aspects such as philanthropic, ethical, economic and legal to be considered by the organizations while framing their CSR report. According to the UNIDO (2001), "CSR is a management concept whereby companies integrate social and environmental concerns in their business operations and interactions with their stakeholders". CSR is generally understood as being the way through which a company achieves a balance of economic, environmental and social imperatives (Triple-Bottom-Line Approach), while at the same time addressing the expectations of shareholders and stakeholders. In this sense, it is important to draw a distinction between CSR, which can be a strategic business management concept, and charity, sponsorship or philanthropy. Even though the later can also make a valuable contribution to poverty reduction, will directly enhance the reputation of a company and strengthen its brand, the concept of CSR clearly goes beyond that.

Therefore, the meaning of CSR is two-folded. First, it presents ethics that an organization should practice for its internal as well as external employees. On the other hand, it means that the responsibility of an organization for the environment and the society in which it operates. CSR needs to address the well-being of all stakeholders and not just the companies shareholders. CSR is considered as a mean or a medium by which companies give something back to society. Philanthropic activities are only a part of CSR, which otherwise constitutes a much broader set of activities entailing strategic business benefits. Its mission is to provide innovative solutions for social and environmental challenges. But the challenge for business and professional community is to identify priorities and areas of CSR interventions that are important in the context of achieving sustainable development goals. Therefore, it is necessary to study and understand how companies are using their CSR initiatives or what is the impact of social responsibility activities in the socio-economic development of the rural population.

Understanding CSR in India

Historically, CSR has been seen as events for developed countries. Having a large body of literature has amalgamated the practices of CSR in the context of developed countries, however the literature on the theory and practice of CSR in developing countries remains still low (Belal, 2000). Only a few studies are carried out which have examined the CSR practice in India. Though various investigations in different parts and the time period and also in classical literature of India have shown the practice of CSR in various corporations. In India, corporate philanthropy has by now become an integral component of normal business operations. It is also embedded in corporate policies and practices. CSR in India has traditionally been seen as a philanthropic activity. And in keeping with the Indian tradition, it was an activity that was performed but not deliberated. As a result, there is limited documentation of specific activities related to this concept. However, what was clearly evident that much of this had a national character encapsulated within it, whether it was endowing institutions to actively participating in India's freedom movement, and embedded in the idea of trusteeship. One of the earliest and the most prominent theories of CSR was put forward by Mohandas Karamchand Gandhi (Mahatma Gandhi, 1931) as the 'Trusteeship' model, that he described as 'India's gift to the world' that provided a means of transforming the capitalist order of the society into an egalitarian one. It did not recognize any right of private ownership of property except so far as it may be permitted (deemed harmless) by society (social organization). He exhorted businessmen to regard themselves as trustees and servants of the poor and therefore, to regulate their commerce for toiling millions and be 'satisfied with earning an honest penny' (Premlata & Agarwal, 2013).

The evolution of CSR development in the corporate culture of India can be traced back to pure philanthropy and charity during the industrialization process (1850–1914) then to social development during independence (1914–1960). As some observers have pointed out, the practice of CSR in India still remains within the generous space but has moved from the institutional building (educational, research and cultural) to community development through various projects. As industrialization gained momentum in the post-independence period, the family-owned business units such as the Tatas, Birlas, and Mafatlals lost the pre-eminent position they once occupied in the industrial landscape of India. The arrival of professionally managed groups like the Larsen & Toubro and Hindustan Unilever made this change in the tenor and tone of corporate philanthropy more perceptible (Sundar, 2013). The concept of CSR gained currency and when this concept gained ground, the focus shifted to more tremendous and broader, social and environmental issues. The canvas became wider. The emphasis thus shifted from the religious and the spiritual to the social and humanistic aspects. Also, with global influences and with communities becoming more active and demanding, there appears to be a discernible trend, that while CSR remains restricted mainly to community development, it is getting more strategic in nature (that is, getting linked with business) than philanthropic, and a large number of companies are reporting the activities they are undertaking in this space in their official websites, annual reports, sustainability reports and even publishing CSR reports (Sharma, 2015).

In the age of globalization, companies in India have also started to understand the immense benefits of being involved with CSR activities. It is clear to the top management that strong CSR programmes are indispensable ingredients for being good corporate citizens and enhancing the overall image of their company. According to a recent study conducted by Mitra (2007) 97% representatives of 63 companies of the city of Madhya Pradesh in India agreed with the concept that "CSR enhances an organization's corporate image", while 91% were of the opinion that "CSR increases visibility as a community leader and ensures sustainable development of both the organization and the community in the long-run". Furthermore, nearly 77% of the respondents agreed that "CSR contributes to the welfare of employees" and 63% of the respondents agreed that "CSR is a business obligation". In the past, Indian companies were involved with CSR activities by the sole intention of getting tax exemptions and other incentives from the government. However, they are today far more motivated by the desire for social services. Due to the increasing awareness of the people regarding the societal responsibilities of companies, they have started to voluntarily undertake CSR activities (Narayan, 2014). Finally, a globalized world in a 'confused state' characterized partly by traditional philanthropic engagements and partly by steps taken to integrate CSR into a sustainable business strategy (1980 until the present) (CSR Compendium, 2013) came to stay.

CSR and Sustainable Development in India

As both businesses, as well as governments, have existed on earth since ancient times, why are the terms like 'CSR' and 'sustainable development' being talked of now only for the last decade? The answer lies in the growing sizes of businesses and the corresponding shrinking roles of governments. There are many companies in the world whose annual sales are more than the Gross National Products (GNP) of many countries. The total annual revenue receipt of the retail chain, Wal-Mart, is greater than the economies of all but 30 of the world's nations. In India too, there is a growing number of companies (in the private sector) whose revenue receipts are much more than Rs.10,000 crore, led by Reliance Industries Limited (RIL), which has crossed the figure of Rs. 90,000 crore (Agarwal, 2008). These companies control a large part of the earth's resources, the price of which is paid in the form of sacrifices by different sections of society. On the other hand, governments are redefining their roles and are limiting themselves to governance and facilitation. This development is sometimes dubbed as symbolizing a shift from state-centred polity to the market-centred polity. People in a democratic state expect the government to fulfil their basic needs. In the new envisaged scenario, the private sector would increase its role in the economy, while the government would take care of services such as basic education, public health, and basic medical care. As success brings with it responsibility, the growing size and clout of corporate houses have led to growing expectations as also to a growing need for regulations. The reason why CSR has assumed so much importance today is because corporate houses intervene in so many areas of social life, they must be responsible towards society and the environment (Mitra & Schmidpeter, 2017).

The corporate sustainability is derived from the concept of sustainable development which is defined by the Brundtland Commission (1990) as "development that meets the needs of the present without compromising the ability of future generations to meet their own needs." Corporate sustainability essentially refers to the role that companies can play in meeting the agenda of sustainable development and entails a balanced approach to economic progress, social progress, and environmental stewardship.The CSR is more often used interchangeably with the term 'corporate citizenship' and further linked with the concept ofTriple Bottom Line (TBL) reporting, a term which is used to denote framework for measuring company's performance against economic, social and environmental parameters. The concept of TBL which interprets as profit, people, and people has two more aspects included namely social and environmental concerns. An organization wishing to follow up on TBL would imply a CSR activity. The TBL reporting makes companies accountable for economic, social and environmental effects of doing business. This helps to create commitment towards the sustainability venture undertaken by the corporate. It is recommended that the TBL concept can be constructive and beneficial to corporate implementing CSR activities (Carroll, 1979). Social and environmental performances and preferences are today considered to be as significant as financial performance. Increasingly, organizations around the world are recognizing the value of demonstrating transparency and accountability beyond the traditional domain of financial performance. The measurement of the success of any business has moved far away from merely bloating bottom lines to its all-around sustainability in terms of its environmental and social performance. In the new global economy, companies that are responsive to the demand of all their stakeholders are arguably better positioned to achieve long-term sustainability.

CSR in India tends to focus on what is done with profits after they are made. On the other hand, sustainability is about factoring the social and environmental impacts of conducting business, that is, how profits are made. Hence, much of the Indian practice of CSR is an essential component of sustainability or responsible business, which is a larger idea, a fact that is evident from various sustainability frameworks. In a country like India, which is highly populous and is predicted to have one of the world's youngest and thereby the most significant working population by 2026. Yet, it still ranks 130 among 189 countries in the Human Development Index (HDI) (Human Development Report, 2017). India as a country is rich in natural resources and has a highly knowledgeable populace, but the people living in it are poor due to a gap between the rich and the poor—a gap which is increasing day-by-day, leading to new types of social problems. The economic inequality has increased and with that the government is aiming at achieving a consistent annual growth rate of 7 per cent has brought environment and social risks (Premlata & Agarwal, 2013). The conventional economic development through industrialization leads to loss of agriculture and forest land as well as traditional occupation putting stress on women and children. For example, the diverting of river water and heavy industrial usage of water leads to groundwater depletion causing water scarcity drinking water. The women then travels miles to get their drinking water and they would carry their children along with them for security. Thus lack of sustainable water usages policy in industrial policy in the region creates pressure among vulnerable groups like women and children who miss out on their education and health. Without education and health, the future generation is excluded from many development programmes and opportunity. It is important to understand this interrelation of these factors that is industry, water, education and gender to sustainable development with CSR. In the last 70 years, the Indian companies have spent on education, health, water, and infrastructure as part of their CSR even though not much evidence and documentation exists whether such interventions has brought any significant difference (Urmila, 2011).

Perhaps, the above discussion can help to develop a framework for how CSR can lead to sustainable development in emerging economies around the world. Environmental processes follow no national borders. We live in a global ecosystem in which the actions of Indian companies (just as with all other countries) have a domino effect on social, economic and environmental systems around the world. Considering the magnitude of India's population and relatively untapped social potential, it is of utmost importance that local companies should focus on providing the local people with opportunities for the development of skill sets that positively impact not only their own quality of life but that of all lives on the planet (Mitra & Schmipeter, 2017). As per the recent Companies Act, 2013, around 8,000 companies are likely to spend $ 3 to $ 4 billion annually on peripheral development as part of their CSR activities. This presents a huge opportunity for financial and otherwise to link CSR with sustainable development goals in India. A compelling case in point is the National Voluntary Guidelines for social, environmental and economic responsibilities of business issued by the Ministry of Corporate Affairs in June 2011. Principle eight relating to inclusive development encompasses most of the aspects covered by the CSR clause of the Companies Act, 2013. However, the remaining eight principles relate to other aspects of the business. The UN Global Compact, a widely used sustainability framework has 10 principles covering social, environmental, human rights and governance issues, and what is described as CSR is implicit rather than explicit in these principles.

CSR and New Law & Regulations in India

Traditionally 'social' has been the domain of the governments in India. However, corporations have been doing philanthropy on different scales depending upon their urge and resources at different times. The initial paternalistic approach of the corporations towards the employees got extended into a trusteeship approach after India's independence. The present form of CSR, initially showcased by the public sector enterprises, percolated down to the corporations only after the liberalization reforms of 1992. The boom in the economy during the last decade and rising global concerns about corporate social irresponsibility triggered the debate about public policy on CSR. In this sense, CSR is new to the Indian policy and law discourse. The Government of India, through the recently passed Companies Act, 2013 has replaced the previous 57-year-old Act of 1956. The new Act has very clearly articulated under Section 135 on the eligibility criteria; the processes to be followed in terms of composition of a CSR Committee; the CSR activities, which qualify under Schedule VII and so on for companies having a net worth of Indian Rupees (INR) 5 billion or more, or a turnover of INR 10 crore more, or a net profit of INR 50 million or more during any financial year. This Act hopes to initially target more than 16,237 companies mandated to report on

CSR spent, with an approximate amount of INR 200 billion each year.

This law requires the companies to be actively involved in the following categories of CSR, as outlined in Schedule VII (Appendix C) of the Act (came into effect from April 1, 2014). The law also requires the companies to establish CSR committees for devising, monitoring, and recommending CSR activities. The CSR committees will be comprised of board members, at least one of which must be an independent director. Some of the other striking features of this new Act are mentioned below (PwC 2013):

Surplus arising out of CSR activities will have to be reinvested into CSR initiatives, and this will be over and above the 2% figure. The company can implement its CSR activities through the following methods:

- Directly on its own.
- Through its own non-profit foundation set-up so as to facilitate this initiative.
- Through independently registered non-profit organizations that have a record of at least 3 years in similar such related activities.
- Collabourating or pooling their resources with other companies.
- Only CSR activities undertaken in India will be taken into consideration.
- Activities meant exclusively for employees, and their families will not qualify.
- A format for the board report on CSR has been provided which includes amongst others, activity-wise, reasons for spends under 2% of the average net profits of the previous 3 years and a responsibility statement that the CSR policy, implementation and monitoring process is in compliance with the CSR objectives, in letter and spirit. This has to be signed by either the CEO or the MD or a Director of the company [7].

Subsequently, with more corporations aligning themselves towards the CSR agenda, the number of corporations in the CSR space is expected to increase manifold and raise the community investment capital. It is expected that the new CSR law would bring about significant changes in the attitudes of large business organizations in India. Companies which were previously reluctant to spend money on societal causes would come forward and make significant contributions. As India is a country that is desperately in need of funding for development, the new CSR mandate can be hugely beneficial for the country. Companies are required to contribute to the public good by spending a good portion of their profit for CSR initiatives. An assessment of CSR expenditure of 5,097 companies in India for the year 2015-16 indicates that 172 public sector undertakings (PSUs) and 4,925 private corporate companies together have spent Rs. 9,822 crores during the year 2015-16.

Table 1.1: Development Sector-wise CSR Expenditure during Financial Year 2015-2016

Sl. No.	The subject in Schedule VII	CSR Expenditure in Indian Rupees (Crores)
1	Health/Eradicating Hunger, Poverty and Malnutrition	3,117.27
2	Education/Livelihood/Differently Abled	3,072.62
3	Gender Equality/Women Empowerment/ Old age homes	212.85
4	Environment & Animal Welfare	922.84
5	Heritage/Art & Culture	89.53
6	Encouraging Sports	94.68
7	PMs National Relief Fund	135.71
8	Rural Development	1,050.91
9	Slum Development	9.08
10	Swacch Bharat Kosh	355.06
11	Clean Ganga Fund	3.01
12	Any Other Fund	261.87
13	Other Sector	496.64
	Total	**9,822.08**

Source: Ministry of Corporate Affairs, Government of India, 2017.

According to the data available for 224 companies for the year 2018-19, against a required CSR spend of Rs. 4,366.8 crore, the firms spent an aggregate of Rs. 3,994 crore or 91.5% of the requirement. The percentage stood at 79% in FY'16, 83.8% in FY'17 and 83.2%

in FY'18. Data further shows that both the number of companies eligible for mandatory CSR spending and their total spend have shown a significant rise. While the amount stood at Rs. 6,446 crore in FY'15 for 849 companies, it was Rs. 10,115 crore in FY'18 for 1,077 companies. While data is available only for 224 companies as of now for 2018-19, and they have spent Rs. 4,525 crore.

Table 1.2: CSR spend by NSE listed companies over last 5 years

No of companies considered for the analysis	2018-19	2017-18	2016-17	2015-16	2014-15
Required CSR spends	4,366,82	10,364,78	9,668,51	9,088,06	8,201,51
Shortfall in spends	372,56	1,740,91	1,565,06	1,883,41	2,444,63
CSR spends as a per cent of required CSR	91.47	83.20	83.81	79.28	70.19

Firms listed on NSE and obligated to spend on CSR and for which CSR details were available in Annual Reports.
CSR spend figures in crore (Indian Rupees).
Source: Prime Database.

However, with this growing expenditure, it will be difficult for authorities to monitor the implementation of CSR initiatives taken by the Indian companies, as no indicator is set for measuring the impact of CSR in the new CSR mandate of the Companies Act, 2013. It may be the case that a company spends a required amount on CSR indiscriminately, rendering the target of bringing happiness and success to the familiar people impossible to achieve. CSR activities should be tailored to the needs of local communities and the Indian culture; otherwise, the result could be disastrous for the company in terms of its reputation. Another limitation of the new CSR law is that no incentives will be provided to companies which spend more than 2% of their net annual profit. This may limit them to spend only this fixed amount, and they will not be encouraged to go further. Apart from that, companies may consider mandatory CSR as a "check the box" exercise rather than finding ways for innovation and generating returns from CSR. Furthermore, as there are more than 3.3 million non-governmental organizations (NGOs) working in India, companies may not work diligently to find credible, high-impact organizations capable of managing large projects effectively that can have a large-scale impact on the common good (GoI, 2017). Sometimes, the CSR law may also drive companies to engage in philanthropic activities that do not have any direct or indirect business implications. However, CSR should also be considered a social investment, by which CSR activities are included in a company's core business strategies.

In addition to this, companies may start hiding their annual profit amount if they are compelled to spending a fixed part of it on CSR. This may open up ways of unfair practices. Hence, a CSR law should not be the only driving force for companies to go for CSR activities. A law has particular implications, but companies need to come forward and engage themselves for CSR activities voluntarily so that their actions can have more positive impacts on the poor people in India. As commented by Rahul Bajaj, Chairman of the National Council of Corporate Governance and Regulatory Affairs: "If you are mandating conscience and generosity, it is not generosity anymore" (Bose, 2015).

Recent Private Corporates Initiatives: Setting the Context

To study and understand the CSR initiatives taken by some private Indian enterprises and its impact on socio-economic measures, 8 private Indian companies/firms have been selected. While the selection of these companies, efforts were made to select a variety of sectors for a full & bright image. Therefore, the selected companies are from different industrial sectors such as pharmaceuticals (Mr. Reddy's Lab, Lupin, India), metals (Vedanta Aluminum Ltd.), Tata Steel, financial institution (ICICI Bank), chemicals & fertilizers (Ambuja Cement Ltd.), InfoTech (Satyam PC), consumer durables (Coca-Cola India, Inc.), manufacturing company (Asian Paints). The methodology of this study is based on internet-based research; literature review seems to understand the practice of CSR in the context of sustainable development in India. For purposes of analysis of CSR initiatives for sustainable development have been divided into five areas: livelihoods, health, education, environment, and infrastructure.

The study shows that all the companies presented themselves as they have CSR policies and also practice at the ground level. A large number of companies reflect their CSR philosophy or social, environmental and ethical objectives and their mission, vision documents, organizational policy and plans. However, even if surveyed firms have CSR policies and objectives but there was no relationship between the agenda of the company and the sustainable development goals (SDGs). The companies are adopting CSR initiatives for rural development in India. From the study, it can also be noted that education is the priority for many companies which were taken, followed by health and improving standards of livelihoods.

About 50% of companies take CSR initiatives in the infrastructure and 57% in the environment sector which includes events like tree planting, the awareness creation among the masses on the environmental issues, etc. It is also surprising that even if the Central Govt. and the State Govt. have separate departments for education and health sector, these two are the priority issues for the firms and are often under the banner of CSR in both public and private companies in India. The study shows that out of the 8 companies surveyed, 2 companies implemented their CSR initiatives directly by divisions dedicated to CSR that are responsible for planning and executing these activities. In other companies, CSR initiatives are applied through local management of the factory and Human Resources Department (HRD). Many companies as Tata Steel, India's Lupin, Dr. Reddy s' Laboratories, Satyam Computers, Ambuja Cement Ltd., establish foundations dedicated to the implementation of CSR rural development initiatives. Most of these foundations promote the participation of communities in planning and implementing their CSR activities. It is also interesting to note that these foundations which has implemented its programmes in collabouration with government departments are a good example of public-private partnership (PPP). For example, Dr. Reddys' foundation is in collabouration with the Ministry of Rural Development Department, Government of India. Similarly, Satyam Foundation is also working with the Government of Andhra Pradesh (GoAP). The study also found that four companies who have or do not have their own foundations are partners with NGOs to implement CSR initiatives. In the agreement for the above, the company provides funds, infrastructure, while NGO provides base level support for the implementation of CSR activities. The impact of CSR programmes resulted in a sample of 8 leading private companies in India has been classified into five areas: livelihood, health, education, environment, and infrastructure.

Livelihoods: The Grameen-LABS is a programme implemented by Dr. Reddys' Foundation in collabouration with the Rural Development Department, Government of India has provided livelihood opportunities to around 35,000 youths in rural India between the ages of 18-25 years in 7 states of India. Outcomes of livelihood support programmes by Dr. Reddy Foundation shows that SHG members are in the stable income group with INR 2,000 p.m. and members of the banana plantations and poultry are working to earn extra income of INR 7000-8000 p.a.The livelihood initiatives certainly helped the local people to develop a safety net for long-term asset creation and livelihood promotion.

Health: The study shows that many companies organize a series of health camps to create health awareness and education on health on various issues such as vaccination, blood donation, water purification pills, condom distribution, etc. Till 2007-08, Vedanta Aluminium Ltd. conducted 267 health camps for the benefit of over 4.5 lakh people. In Lanjigarh (Odisha) Vedanta Aluminium Ltd. covers 53 villages with 32,000 inhabitants, providing free medicine, treatment, and referral service on their mobile units. Also it has launched projects like "Sakhi", "Mamta", "Bhagyalaxmi" for skill development which will benefit 2.37 million people form 1,759 villages. Tata Family Health Initiatives Foundation (TSFIF) has established "Lifeline Express" Wheeled Hospital has helped more than 50,000 patients in Jharkhand, Odisha, and Chhattisgarh.

Education: Aditya Birla Group provided education to 62,000 children living near the plants by running 26 regular schools. Asian Paints establishment of "Shree Gattu Vidyalaya", a school providing education to 25,000 children from class I to X, by this effort formal education have reached rural areas in Gujurat and helped the children there. Similarly, Satyam Computers have developed 170 modern schools benefiting 40,000 rural children. Schools "Project Smiles" with the support of Coca-Cola India Inc. was started and completed in 20 schools. It left its impact on the lives of approximately 10,000 children.

Environment: Towards sustainable development and management of the natural resources, many companies have been working on tree plantation, watershed management, and waste management, wind firms, etc. for example, Tata Steel has planted 13.5 million trees in and around the steel plants or mines till date. Watershed Development Programme by Ambuja Cement Ltd. has covered 9,000 hectares in the last four years. Sustainable water management continues to lead the priority list of Coca-Cola India Inc. So far, the company's water conservation initiative has improved the lives of more than 1,40,000 people and created social awareness on the essential importance of water conservation among the millions of people.

Infrastructure: Of the 8 companies available data shows that only six companies offer different infrastructures facilities such as construction and road development, installation of electricity, water, sanitation, schools, health center, community, etc. Welfare Lupin, Human Welfare, and Research Foundation initiated the scheme "Apna Gaon Apna Kam". This scheme covered 38,000 villages in Rajasthan, and almost all areas have the school buildings, potable water, ponds, connecting roads, community centers, and electricity. Tata Steel has participated in the construction and repair of 33 km of pucca roads per year, providing nearly two lakh people in 435 villages to access the modern infrastructure each year. In Andhra Pradesh in collabouration with Hyderabad Urban Development Agency, local rural communities, and NGOs, Coca-Cola India has helped around 16 thousand people of "Saroor Nagar" to restore existing check dam in the water catchment areas.

The study shows that all companies surveyed appear to have policies and practices of CSR. Most companies design and implementation of CSR initiatives in the area of work cover the entire community. A broad range of CSR initiatives ranging from income generation subsistence activities, the health check-up camps, mobile health services, education, adult literacy, agriculture development, provision of drinking water management and natural resources development, infrastructure services are developed by these companies. Although the way of working is switching from philanthropic development to sustainable welfare, there was no association between company CSR Agenda and the sustainable development goals. It has also been revealed during the study that many companies promote and implement CSR initiatives through the companies human resources department and foundation or in collabouration with local NGOs, but there is a lack of full-fledged CSR department. CSR initiatives are undertaken by Indian companies for rural development have a positive effect and impact on the overall development of society and business.

Issues and Challenges

Many private corporations such as the Tatas, Wipro and TVS have undertaken many notable projects which benefit not only the local community in the areas surrounding their workplaces and factories but also the society on a much larger scale. While these trends are welcome, they should not lull us into complacency. We have a long way to go. One cannot venture to state that corporate citizenship has taken deep roots in the Indian economy. A purely qualitative assessment suggests that even corporate social responsibility has yet to take strong roots in the country. There are a few deficiencies, which need to be made right in order to make the industry socially more responsible.

Lack of Capacity Building: A significant obstacle that Indian companies are facing quite regularly while implementing CSR initiatives is the lack of expertise. The absence of enthusiasm, knowledge, and skills to deal with CSR issues and practices often prevent companies from making positive impacts on society and the environment. Companies could make a positive difference to society and environment if they create the enthusiasm, knowledge, and the skills to deal with CSR issues. Also, the government could drive development by providing statutory guidelines for leading companies into a definite direction for their CSR efforts in all the areas, where improvement is necessary.

Lack of Sufficient Funding: A lack of sufficient funding often hinders Indian companies to devote to CSR activities. It has been identified that many small and medium-sized enterprises (SMEs) in India do not have any sort of budget allocated to CSR, and so their contribution to society often remains negligible (Sundar, 2013). Ordinary people in India often remain uninterested to get involved in CSR initiatives. Hence, they do not feel the urge to put pressure on companies in order to get them actively engaged in CSR initiatives. This factor often creates severe challenges for CSR efforts by Indian companies. In India, CSR has evolved to encompass employees, customers, stakeholders and notions of sustainable development or corporate citizenship. In transnational companies, the approach to CSR typically emerges from one of three elements including a decentralized strategy (which might examine human rights), a centralized strategy (which would be company-wide) or a globally integrated strategy.

Family Feuds: Family feuds continue to plague the private sector even today. The disputes among many eminent Indian business families bear ample testimony to this statement. The differences within the families, which lead to severe erosion of the credibility of the companies concerned, militate against the principle of corporate social responsibility and have had adverse repercussions on the national economy.

Lack of Community Participation: There is a lack of interest in the local community in participating and contributing to CSR activities of companies. The situation is further aggravated by a lack of communication between the company and the community at the grassroots. As there is no availability of well-organized NGOs in remote and rural areas that can assess and identify the real needs of the community and work along with companies to ensure successful implementation of CSR activities. In this case, the role media in highlighting good cases of successful CSR initiatives are welcomed as it spreads good stories and sensitizes the local population about various ongoing CSR initiatives of companies. NGOs and Government agencies usually possess a narrow outlook towards the CSR initiatives of companies, often defining CSR initiatives more donor-driven than local in approach.

Government's Interference in the Private Sector: The private sector alone cannot be found faulty with for want of professionalism. The private sector also suffers from the deficiency for instances where the local representatives and Ministers have treated the private sector enterprises as their personal interest continue to be reported even today despite all proclamations of conferring autonomy to the public sector in a deregulated economy. The Companies (Amendment) Bill, 2019 highlights that the unspent CSR amount would be transferred to an escrow account for three financial years. Subsequently, if the amount remain unspent then the same would be moved to funds specified in Scheduled VII of the Companies Act. Under the Act, certain class of profitable companies are required to shell out at least two per cent of their three-year annual average net profit towards CSR activities. Section 135 of the Act was being also amended to provide for specific penal provision in case of non-compliance of CSR provisions.

Inadequate and Weak Regulatory Framework: The regulatory framework in India is also not sufficiently reliable. The Competition Commission Act whose objective is to replace the Monopolies and Restrictive Trade Practices Commission is yet to become operational.

Way forward

1. The company must align with the objectives of CSR national targets under the sustainable development goals (SDGs).
2. The company must have a division dedicated to CSR well-trained, qualified and experienced professionals from social science or social work, sociology, rural development and development studies and experience in management for better planning, implementation, and evaluation of CSR initiatives.
3. CSR programmes implemented by the Indian companies must be based on the felt needs of the local population so as their participation in the programme can be improved. It is also necessary to create jobs and economic activity in the rural community to uplift the masses.
4. Social audits should be conducted by an external source agency to evaluate the performance of CSR of a company.
5. The government can encourage the big players of the business world to take into account the ethical, social and environmental issues of the country. The government should play the role of motivator, catalyst, facilitator rather than the director of corporate social responsibility.
6. An annual report on social responsibility must be prepared to highlight the company committed to sustainable community development.

Conclusion

Indian companies need to engage proactively in CSR activities, as through CSR initiatives they will be able to earn their customer's trust. The immense value of CSR is universally recognized, and so these companies should come forward to find out the best possible ways to spend money on CSR. The CSR monitoring team must ensure that CSR initiatives do not only bring immense reputation and success for the company but are equally helpful for society and the environment as a whole. If this money is used illegally or for corrupt practices, it would ultimately be disastrous for the company. Another important initiative that the Government of India and business organizations need to take into account is to create a pool of skilled manpower with people who will have in-depth knowledge about CSR and will be able to guide the companies so that they can achieve the goals of their CSR efforts. For this purpose, companies need to arrange appropriate training programmes to those who will look after CSR projects. Also, the government's role is essential in this regard because the government can make necessary arrangements to send people abroad for proper training, who can positively contribute to the success of CSR initiatives when they return.

Companies should also come forward and put more efforts in organizing seminars, symposiums, conferences, etc. in order to make more people skilled and knowledgeable about CSR issues. Strong budgetary support should be accompanied by these proactive efforts. In addition to this, companies need to make necessary amendments to their corporate policies so that a strong partnership with their stakeholders can be developed. This would ultimately improve their brand images and render them into socially responsible companies. Indian companies are still not very serious about CSR reporting on an annual basis. Therefore, the Indian government should make it mandatory for them to publish CSR reports regularly. This would ensure accountability and sincerity of those companies in terms of their CSR commitments. Companies should extend their CSR activities in less privileged states rather than concentrate on resource-rich states. It is essential that companies develop a compelling value chain system of their products through their CSR activities, which is essential for competing in the global market. It will give better results if activities are based on a more participatory approach and touch the grassroots level. Voluntarism among employees should be encouraged and institutionalized through recognition and incentives. There is also a need for a public-private partnership with well-defined controls and process for the best use of resources for social change.

Considering the economic outcome of CSR initiatives, companies in India must come forward to look after their communities and the environment in order to gain the societal acceptance of their business operations. Neglecting the need for familiar people will cause detrimental effects on the overall reputation of those companies. It is highly expected that the new CSR law will make Indian companies more socially responsible, and also bring them closer to the needs of ordinary people. In the Indian poverty-stricken society, CSR initiatives can be considered as immensely beneficial. Only the joint collabouration of authorities, civil society, and business organizations will lead CSR initiatives to result in happiness and success for the poor people in India.

References

Baron, David P. (2001). "Private Politics, Corporate Social Responsibility, and Integrated Strategy", *Journal of Economics and Management Strategy*, Vol. 10, pp. 7-45.

Belal, A. (2000). Environmental Reporting in Developing Countries: Empirical Evidence from Bangladesh. *Eco-Management and Auditing*, Vol. 7, No. 3, pp. 114-121.

Bose, R. (2011). Mandatory CSR: India Inc bristles, but has little options. First post. Retrieved November 20, 2015, from http://www.firstpost.com/business/mandatory-csr-india-inc-bristlesbut-has-little-options-83310.html (2011)

Carroll, A.B. (1979). A three-dimensional conceptual model of corporate social performance. Academy of Management Review, Vol. 4, pp. 497-505.

Desjardins, J.R. (2007). *Business, ethics, and the environment: Imagining asustainable future*. Upper Saddle River, NJ: Pearson Prentice Hall. Economy and Business, Vol. 8, pp. 1132-1139.

Garriga, E., and D. Melé (2004). Corporate social responsibility theories: mapping the territory, *The Journal of Business Ethics*, Vol. 53, pp. 51-71.

Ghulliani, C. (2013). India Companies Act 2013: Five key points about India's "CSR Mandate". *Business for Social Responsibility* (*BSR*). Retrieved November 20, 2015, from http://www.bsr.org/en/our-insights/blog-view/india-companies-act-2013-five-key-points-about-indias-csrmandate.

Government of India (2011). National Voluntary Guidelines on social, environmental and economic responsibilities of business. Ministry of Corporate Affairs, GoI.

Government of India (2017). Corporate Social Responsibility Report, Ministry of Corporate Affairs, GoI.

Mark S. Schwartz and Archie B. Carroll (2003). Corporate Social Responsibility: A Three-Domain Approach, *Business Ethics Quarterly*, Vol. 13, No. 4. pp. 503-530.

Miluwi, J.O. (2013). Corporate social responsibility: Global idea and national importance in the 21st Century. *International Journal of Advanced Research in Management and Social Sciences*, Vol. 2, No. 3, pp. 92-116.

Mitra, M. (2007). *Its only business! India's corporate social responsiveness in a globalized world*. New Delhi: Oxford University Press.

Narayan, A. (2014). Being a corporate citizen in India: History and situation today. *Journal of Economy and Business*, Vol. 8, pp. 1132-1139.

Nayan Mitra and Rene′ Schmidpeter (2017). *The Way, What and How the CSR Mandate: The India Story, Corporate Social Responsibility in India*, Eds. Switzerland: Springer International Publishing.

Naylor, J. (1999). *Management*. Pitman Publishing. London.

Premlata & Agarwal (2013). A Corporate social responsibility: An Indian perspective. *Journal of Business Law and Ethics*, Vol. 1, pp. 27-32.

Sharma, R. (2015). India's economy is surpassing China, so investors should look at these funds. *The Street*. Retrieved November 20, 2015, from http://www.thestreet.com/story/13161402/1/indias-economy-is-surpassing-china-so-investors-should-look-at-these-funds.html.

Stern, N. (2006). *Review on the economics of climate change*. London, UK: HM Treasury Cabinet Office.

Sundar, Pushpa (2013). *Business and Community: The Story of Corporate Social Responsibility in India*, Sage Publications Pvt. Ltd., New Delhi, p. 408.

United Nations Industrial Development Organisation http://www.unido.org/what-we-do/trade/csr/what-*is-csr.html#pp1[g1]/0/*(2001).

Urmila, M. (2011). Corporate social responsibility in India. Babasaheb Gawde Institute of Management Studies. Retrieved November 20, 2015, from http://www.mmbgims.com/docs/full_paper/36_Urmila%20Moon_ab.pdf.

World Bank (1999). http://www.wbcsd.org/work-program/business-role/previous-work/corporate-social-responsibility. aspx.

World Bank (2011). *Poverty and equity*. Retrieved February 22, 2016, from http://povertydata.worldbank.org/poverty/country/IND (2011).

2

Sustainable Development Goals and Good Governance: The Agenda for Women Empowerment Through Quality Education

A Case Study of *Beti Bachao Beti Padhao* Scheme in India

Neelima Deshmukh

The Millennium Declaration of United Nations (UN) set 2015 to provide quantitative benchmarks for 8 goals as, eradication of extreme poverty and hunger, Achieving universal Primary Education, promote gender equality and empowerment of women, reducing Child Mortality rates, Improve maternal health, Combat HIV, malaria and other diseases, ensuring environment sustainability, global partnership for the Development etc. Bold and transformative agenda 2030 for the Sustainable Development adopted by the world leaders at UN, also reaffirmed rationale for MSDGs to wipe out Poverty, Climate Change, Sustainable cities and Development, Gender equality, Fight inequality and emphasised their focus on Quality Education amongst the 17 measurable goals. The world is changing fast with the changing demands and needs of its population, their different kinds of requirements to cater and respond to the emerging situations and challenges are totally changed which has prioritized new agenda for the development of the country on the World canvass. The 2030 Agenda of SDGs is not about any individual country but the concentrated efforts of all the countries together creating the interlinked and globalised world, addressing the challenges of sustainable development from global to local, grass roots level. To see the visible results all through it calls for tailor-made strategies, policies, programmes, with their effective and successful implementation, maximizing the synergies, convergence and impacts, across the society. Therefore, the good and smart governance is of crucial importance stressing upon the accountability, transparency, with the suitable regulatory mechanism needed to ensure human rights, equity, stability and long-term sustainability, safeguarding against the corruption and exploitation of vulnerable deprived societies at the time of crises, along with the Institution building and the strengthening of governance capacity is the only way to respond to these challenges of 21st century. The effective coordination between different levels of policy and sectors at vertical and horizontal levels calls for the imperative to initiate action towards key governance issues like rule based, quality administration, management with transparency, accountability and anticorruption mechanisms, with the effective use of public resources added with the improved governance for the realisation of SDGs in letter and spirit.

National Institution for Transforming India **(NITI AYOG)** with the Prime minister of India as its chairperson has been assigned the responsibility ensuring the implementation of SDGs in the country. Considering the Indian scenario some notable schemes and the interventions like Make in India, Digital India, Skill India, Swacch Bharat Abhiyan, Beti bacaho Beti Padhao, Pradhanmantri Jan Dhan Yojna, Mudra Bank yojna, Atal Mission for Rejuvenation and Urban Transformation (AMRUT), Smart Cities, Soil Health Card scheme, Ujjawala Yojana, Mission Indradhanush, Namami Gange, Rashtriya Gram Swaraj Abhiyan etc. have been undertaken for supporting the advancement of SDG s in India. Out of these Beti Bacaho Beti Padhao scheme is the direct intervention for ensuing women empowerment through the emphasis of Quality education. As the education and empowerment of women is directly correlated this ambitious programme has been pivotal in shaping the destiny of the country to the great extent. Therefore, it is thought pertinent to discuss and deliberate on the scheme of Beti Bacaho Beti Padhao with the positive hopes about its governance aspect in details. AS Quality Education has been identified as an engine of wealth production and needs to be instituted and strengthened at all the strata's of the society so as to raise the standards of living of the citizens. Despite the frantic efforts of the Government to impart quality education to children in particular, still much needs to be done to achieve the targets. Empowerment of underprivileged needs to be seen from the Systems perspectives as outcome of the interdependent factors, of extreme poverty, hunger, illiteracy and diseases interacting impact fully, hampering the basic objective of the development. The situation becomes further more alarming when the issues of gender bias and typical Indian psyche of the society discriminates men and women differently leading to gender disparity where women are the worst sufferers. Same is the fate of girl-child as the most underprivileged, whose basic child rights are jeopardized because of the strongly interacting factors at every level of society and governance.

Conceptualizing Empowerment of Women

Women's economic empowerment is a prerequisite for sustainable development and pro-poor growth. Achieving women's economic empowerment requires sound public policies, a holistic approach and long-term commitment and gender-specific perspectives must be integrated at the design stage of policy and programming. Women must have more equitable access to assets and services; infrastructure programmes should be designed to benefit the poor, both men and women, and employment opportunities must be improved while increasing recognition of women's vast unpaid work. Innovative approaches and partnerships include increased dialogue among development actors, improved co-ordination amongst donors and support for women organizing at the national and global level.[1] Measuring social processes such as empowerment is a complex task, which makes it difficult to deliver exact results.

Determinants of Empowerment

According to our understanding, empowerment is determined by the interaction of agency, access to resources and opportunity structures. Exercising agency is closely related to the individual or collective access to resources. This access refers to both tangible resources, such as material and financial assets, and intangible resources, including education, skills, knowledge, expertise and participation in networks. The framing institutions, rules, norms, social relationships and power relations that constrain and structure agency and access to resources make up the opportunity structures of empowerment (Kapitsa, 2008).[2] Based on these general assumptions, it is believed that empowerment processes occur through changes along four different pathways. Analyzing empowerment from this angle allows for a more structured look at change processes (Chen & Mahmud, 1995)[3]:

- The material pathway involves changes in access to and control over material resources. Changes in income, ownership of assets, fulfilment of basic needs and earning capacities are included here.
- The perceptual pathway encompasses changes in the self-perception of women (e.g., self-esteem, self-confidence, visions and plans for the future) as well as changes in how women are perceived by others (e.g., visibility, respect, recognition).
- Changes at the level of knowledge, skills and awareness of the wider environment are associated with the cognitive pathway.
- The relational pathway considers changes relating to social interaction (e.g., decision-making, bargaining power, participation, self-reliance, organizational strength and mobility).

Although these four pathways are listed separately here for conceptual clarity, it is important to note that these pathways are interdependent. Hence, changes along the different pathways are related to and mutually affect one another. Or, to put it differently, empowerment processes are expected to occur through changes in different aspects along various pathways. The numerous aspects of change can be thought of as ingredients for empowerment.[4]

The changing rigid gender roles and the unequal distribution of power that favors men in all areas requires time, awareness and effort. For example, husbands normally serve as guarantors for female clients in case of repayment problems. It is possible that this fact further reinforces women's dependency on men instead of diminishing it.[5]

Along with the above mentioned factors setting the chain reaction, there is one more crucial issue in case of girl-child, that is ensuring their safety and security, particularly that of the adolescent girls. Right from their birth, female foeticide, infanticide, females ranging from 2-80 years of age are being beaten, brutally raped, kidnapped, molested, dragged into trafficking, forced to the prostitution, harassed at the work place and exploited in various ways, due to the lack of formal education, which practically moulds the very personality of the person. The situation is worst in some parts of Indian states and in the rural areas where along with many other factors the lack of proper infrastructure to meet the feminine demands of these adolescent girls deters their formal education, affecting the drop-out rate which definitely hampers their empowerment through the engine of education. Of late with the introduction of skill development and various vocational training programmes/schemes by the government, seems to be a good take off.

In the background of the various issues, problems, challenges, and the multiple factors, affecting process of empowerment of the girl child from the underprivileged lower strata of the society and the popular government scheme **"Beti Bacaho, Beti Padhao"** (means save girl child and educate the girl child) educating her to be confident and self-dependent citizen of new immerging nation of India assumes greater importance.

International Women's Day Theme For The Year 2014 said –

"Equality for women is progress for all"

Economic empowerment and economic development are closely related. There is a bi-directional relationship between economic development and women's empowerment. Empowerment with respect to women can be defined as "improving the ability of women to access the constituents of development—in particular health, education, earning opportunities, rights and political participation". Education has direct correlation with women empowerment at large.

Women's Rights to Health care, right to health and reproduction Right to education, right to employment, registration of marriages, protection of women from violence, domestic violence, accountability for women's rights conventional mechanism to monitor and protect women's rights, women's rights to information technology come under single gamut, affecting the entire process of empowerment of women in various fields, yet there are disturbing trends of gender discrimination, sexual and gender based violence, lack of opportunities and participation of women in education, employment, decision making have been reported on large scale from across the globe. Here the role of government comes into picture. Today's girls are tomorrows' women forming the society. Therefore, there is acute need to care and do the needful for their empowerment since their childhood itself.

The state is supposed to ensure not only safety and security of women but create a conducive environment where they are at peace & bliss through various measures support system aimed at their peaceful co-existence, as a mark of indicator of national development at large which ultimately revolves around effective policies pro women programmes calling for its implementation through the capacity building of the institutions. Identifying this crucial point off late various new schemes have been launched, out of which Beti Bachao Beti Padhao (save daughter, educate daughter), seems to be most effective in handling the challenges of major issues related to women's lives making headway through.

Beti Bachao, Beti Padhao Yojana: BBBP Scheme (Save Daughter, Educate Daughter Scheme)

In July 2014, the Government has introduced a new scheme called Beti Bachao, Beti Padhao. Significantly, which was launched at the hands of Prime Minister Shri Narendra Modi chose to launch the scheme from Haryana, in January 2015 which has one of the worst sex ratios in the country—the lowest being Mahendragarh, Distt. Where there are only 775 girls per 1000 boys. For every 1000 boys only 918 girls are born and survive in India (Census, 2011). This imbalance can lead to undesirable consequences, which are becoming alarming. Census (2011) confirmed the unabating decline in the Child Sex Ratio (CSR) between the 0-6 age group with an all-time low of 918. The SRB for the period 2010-12 was 908 as per SRS Statistical Report-2012, which is quite low as against the internationally observed normal SRB of 952 clearly pointing out to lesser number of girls born than the boys in India.[6]

A decline in the CSR is a major indicator of women's disempowerment: Which reflects

(a) Pre-birth discrimination (sex selective abortion),
(b) Post-birth discrimination (limited access to health, nutrition and education).

At the heart of India's declining CSR lies in son preference and daughter aversion resulting in the Girl Child's increasing exclusion from life itself. Strong socio-cultural religious biases, the easy availability, affordability and misuse of diagnostic tools have accentuated the problem in the last five decades. These challenges raise questions about the multiple deprivations faced by women and girls over their life-cycle continuum. Urgent coordinated action is required to empower the girl-child. Beti Bachao Beti Padhao (BBBP) was launched by the Prime Minister on 22 January 2015 as a comprehensive scheme that promotes the girl-child's empowerment, with Pan-India expansion in March 2018 to all 640 Districts (Census, 2011). It aims at preventing gender based sex selective elimination and ensuring the survival, protection, education and participation of the Girl Child Anchored by the Ministry of Women & Child Development (MWCD), it is a tri-ministerial effort with the Ministries of (a) Health & Family Welfare (MoHFW), and (b) Human Resource Development (MoHRD) with the following objectives:

(a) Prevent gender based sex selective abortion,
(b) Ensure the survival and protection of the girl-child,
(c) Provide education and promote the participation of the girl-child.

The scheme has a two-pronged strategy comprising:

(a) Media, Advocacy and Outreach,
(b) Multi-Sectoral Action that is planned and executed at the District level to achieve specific monitorable targets.

BBBP's first approach to transformative change through 'Media, Advocacy and Outreach' is a nation-wide 360° programme that aims to create awareness by changing mindsets. This is a prerequisite to end discrimination meted out to the Girl Child and bring about a positive change in CSR. The Media Campaign focuses on questioning socio-cultural norms. By encouraging girls to grow into empowered citizens of the country, it links National, State and District level interventions implemented at the community level that bring together different stakeholders for accelerated impact. Social media is being effectively used to enhance outreach especially among the youth.[7]

(a) Need and rationale for this programme: The sharp decline as pointed by Census 2011 data is a call for urgent action, as it highlights that the girl-child is increasingly being excluded from life itself. Coordinated and convergent efforts are needed to ensure survival, protection and education of the girl-child. The Government has announced Beti Bachao, Beti Padhao (BBBP) Scheme to address the issue of decline in CSR through a mass campaign across the country, and focused intervention & Multi-Sectoral Action in 100 gender critical districts. The District Collectors/Deputy Commissioners (DCs) would lead and coordinate action of all departments for implementation of BBBP at the District level.

The **first section** of this Scheme comprises of Innovative Activities that Districts have designed and programmed to promote the 'survival of girls'. BBBP addresses this aspect of the Girl Child's development by ensuring for the effective implementation of the Pre Conception & Pre-Natal Diagnostic Techniques (PC & PNDT) Act that bans gender-based sex selection. In addition, a reduction in the Under Five Child Mortality Rate and increase in:

(a) Institutional deliveries, and
(b) First trimester ante-natal care registrations are also areas that BBBP actively promotes interventions in. In order to achieve these monitorable targets, Districts have implemented several initiatives that address the 'survival' of the Girl Child at the grass roots level like 'Daughters' Clubs' that comprise parents who have only daughters, honoring Gram Panchayats that have achieved a high Sex Ratio at Birth over the last few years and initiatives like 'Bitiya Aur Birwa', which recognize families that have daughters, to name a few activities. This section provides an overview of such interventions.[8]

The **second section** of this scheme revolves around providing an account of activities that Districts have implemented in relation to the 'protection of girls'.

(b) The **third section** addresses a key area that BBBP is also a strong advocate of—the **'education of girls'.** The scheme promotes active enrolment, retention, transition and completion of secondary school education for girls, in addition to re-enrolling drop-outs. It also encourages District Administrations to ensure that every school has a separate functional toilet for girls. Innovative Activities that Districts have initiated revolve around the creation of adolescent girls clubs like 'Balika Manches', promoting a dialogue between District Collectors/ Magistrates/Commissioners and adolescent girls such as 'Collector ki Class', encouraging girls to understand the functionality of police stations through initiatives like Bal Mitra Police and campaign like 'Aao School Chale' to encourage girls to attend school. Most importantly, emphasis has been laid on providing knowledge about hygiene, menstruation to girls in schools through initiatives like campaign, which have been an empowering and enriching source of information.

(c) The **fourth section** of this report emphasizes the need to encourage the effective 'participation of girls' in society. In order to address this need, District Administrations have creatively demonstrated community-level activities that raise awareness about promoting an enabling environment to empower girls. Initiatives like 'Saas Bahu Sammelan' (Mother and daughter In law convention) which brings mothers-in-law together, 'Women's Parliaments', the gender sensitization of men, 'Jan Sabhas', the holding of Special Gram Sabhas on International Girl Child Day and solidarity displayed through human chains are examples of Innovative Activities that have been executed to encourage people from different walks of life to come together in encouraging the 'participation of girls'.

The thematic classification the survival, protection, education, participation and valuing of girls is not standardized, as BBBP addresses the empowerment of women and girls on a life cycle continuum—activities may transcend themes. This aspect serves as a base upon which new ideas can be explored, implemented and replicated. The adoption of Innovative Activities by Districts in accordance with their local needs, contexts and sensibilities makes a huge difference by enacting change at the grass roots level in innovations under *Beti Bachao Beti Padhao*

To sum up, Overall Goal of the scheme is to: Celebrate the Girl Child & Enable her Education with the objectives of Preventing gender biased sex selective elimination, Ensuring the survival & protection of the girl-child and to ensure education of the girl-child enabling her to live dignified life. In addition to the earlier phase, this ambitious programme under SDG through the remarkable scheme has been extended to all the 35 districts of Maharashtra state in 2018 as a welcome step with the sizable achievement of the goal in near future.

Notes

1. *Poverty Reduction and Pro-Poor Growth: The Role of Empowerment*— © OECD 2012, pp. 2-3.
2. Larissa M. Kapitsa, *Women's Economic Empowerment, Division for the Advancement of Women*, p. 14, November, 2008, p. 23.
3. Chen, Martha A. and Simeen Mahmud (1995). *Assessing Change in Women's Lives: A Conceptual Framework*, Bangladesh, p. 345.
4. Bennet, L., (1988). *Women, poverty and productivity in India*, Washington, DC, Economic Development, Institute of the World Bank, p. 9.
6. Chen, Martha & Mahmud, Simeen (1995). *Assessing Change in Women's Lives: A Conceptual Framework*, Bangladesh, p. 455.
7. *Women & Men in India-2014*, Central Statistics office of the Ministry of Statistics and Implementation, Press Information Bureau, Government of India.
8. *BETI BACHAO BETI PADHAO*, Ministry of Women & Child Development, Government of India, Scheme https://wcd.nic.in/BBBPScheme/Implementation guideline BBBP for State Government and UT May 2019.

3

Democratic Decentralisation and Good Governance in the Context of Indian Urban Local Bodies

The Present Status

Neelima Deshmukh

For Gandhiji, true independence for India meant a comprehensive transformation of Indian society and polity. He wanted "political power to be distributed among the villages in India", further he preferred the term 'Swaraj' to describe what he called true democracy. "74th Constitutional amendment is a watershed in the policy of decentralisation in India". "Decentralisation is the process of redistributing or dispersing the functions, powers, people or things away from central location or authority."[1] Decentralisation is a transfer of authority and responsibility for public functions from Central Government to intermediate and local government or quasi-independent government organizations and/or the private sector. This is a complex multifaceted phenomenon. Different types of decentralisation should be distinguished because they have different characteristics, policy implementation, and conditions for success.[2]

Urbanization and economic development have been two sides of the same coin, complementary to each other and necessary for raising the standard of life of its citizen. As globally observed governance is a soul of development, which is being instituted with well designed policies, programmes, schemes under Five Year Plans and taken to the grass roots level through various ministries and institutions efficiently, effectively with proper administration and governance.

India's economy is expanding rapidly and making steady shift from rural to urban and our cities need to be better managed and the special efforts are required to improve the governance. To this effect government has rightly anticipated an ambitious Smart cities programme and Atal Mission for rejuvenation and Urban transformation for better standard of living.

Development of the country is fostered by its efficient governance. To ensure betterment of their citizens, governments over the world have accepted Sustainable Development Goals (SDGs), announced by the United Nations Development Programme (UNDP) in the year 2015, as acceptable governance targets for all. Information and Communication Technologies (ICTs) serve as meaningful contrivances to engage with all the cross-currents linking the 17 SDGs together. Digital technologies were initially deployed in the early1990s as means of dissemination of public services and information. Presently, these digitalization programme with its technologies have been accepted and implemented for citizen centred participatory models of the governance too. Based on the analysis of the relevant academic literature and the extensive field experience of practical working and association of the researcher with the local government institutions there seems to be a direct link for achieving targets of Sustainable Development Goals and strengthen the relationship between state and its citizenry through the efficient and successful e-Governance. Hence, the role of e-Governance becomes very important in this Present electronic era.

AMRUT and Smart Cities Mission uses Information and Communication Technologies to further enhance the quality of performances of urban services to reduce the cost and resource consumption and to engage more effectively. The focus is on its core infrastructure services like adequate and clean water supply sanitation, and solid waste management, efficient urban mobility and public transportation, affordable houses for poor, power supply, robust IT Connectivity, governance especially e-governance citizen participation.

The Local governance comprises of set of institutions, mechanisms, and processes through which citizens, pressure groups articulate their interest, needs and mediate their differences, exercise their rights and obligations at the local level. The building blocks of good local governance are many: such as citizen participation, Partnership amongst the key actors at a local level capacity of the local actors across all the sectors, multiple flows of information institutions, of accountability, and pro poor orientation. Local governance emphasises the need to look beyond the narrow perspectives of legal frameworks and the local government entities which pertains more to supporting the creation of the enabling environment where multi-stakeholder's processes including public and private sectors as well as civil society interact to foster effective local development processes.

The local economic development is a transformation process of the way economic and political decisions are made at local level with the objective of improving the standards of the local society in an inclusive manner through efficient and sustainable use of the existing and potentially available resources, aspire to build up socio-economic opportunities such as creation of employment and incomes and tries to strengthen the good local governance aiming to enhance the competitiveness and encourage inclusive sustainable development establishing the close linkage between local economic development with its reliance on SMART governance which is key component of its local governance through its public participation and democratic decentralisation with the basic principles of accountability, transparency, non-discrimination, participation and efficiency.

As emphasised repeatedly the administration doesn't function in isolation but in a complex supra environmental system responding to the ever changing demands and challenges from the emerging situations in the society. The process of governance and the policy framing in the public interest calls for the micro level planning focus for making the changes effective needs to be transparent and sensitive to the crucial demands of people from legal provisions and Human rights perspectives also. These working principles are based on age old premises of administrative theories which became obsolete in the era of LPG and are not proving effective and fruitful. Hence, there is an acute need of reinventing the new theories which would cater to the demands and expectations of the desired kind of governance to meet the challenges of raising common man's standard of life and the objectives of national development which are intertwined together.

Challenges of MDGs & SDGs before the Local Government

The Millennium Declaration of United Nations (UN) set 2015 to provide quantitative benchmarks for 8 goals as, eradication of extreme poverty and hunger, achieving universal Primary Education, promote gender equality and empowerment of women, reducing Child Mortality rates, improve maternal health, Combat HIV, malaria and other diseases, ensuring environment sustainability, global partnership for the Development etc. Bold and transformative agenda 2030 for the sustainable Development adopted by the world leaders at UN, also reaffirmed rationale for MSDGs to wipe out Poverty, Climate Change, Sustainable cities and Development, Gender equality, Fight inequality and emphasised their focus on Quality Education amongst the 17 measurable goals. The world is changing fast with the changing demands and needs of its population, their different kinds of requirements to cater and respond to the emerging situations and challenges are totally changed which has prioritized new agenda for the development of the country on the World canvass. The 2030 Agenda of SDGs is not about any individual country but the concentrated efforts of all the countries together creating the interlinked and globalised world, addressing the challenges of sustainable development from global to local, grass roots level. To see the visible results all through it calls for tailor-made strategies, policies, programmes, with their effective and successful implementation, maximizing the synergies, convergence and impacts, across the society.

Therefore, the good and smart governance is of crucial importance stressing upon the accountability, transparency, with the suitable regulatory mechanism needed to ensure human rights, equity, stability and long-term sustainability, safeguarding against the corruption and exploitation of vulnerable deprived societies at the time of crises, along with the Institution building and the strengthening of governance capacity is the only way to respond to these challenges of 21st century. The effective coordination between different levels of policy and sectors at vertical and horizontal levels calls for the imperative to initiate action towards key governance issues like rule based, quality administration, management with transparency, accountability and anticorruption mechanisms, with the effective use of public resources added with the improved governance for the realisation of SDGs in letter and spirit.

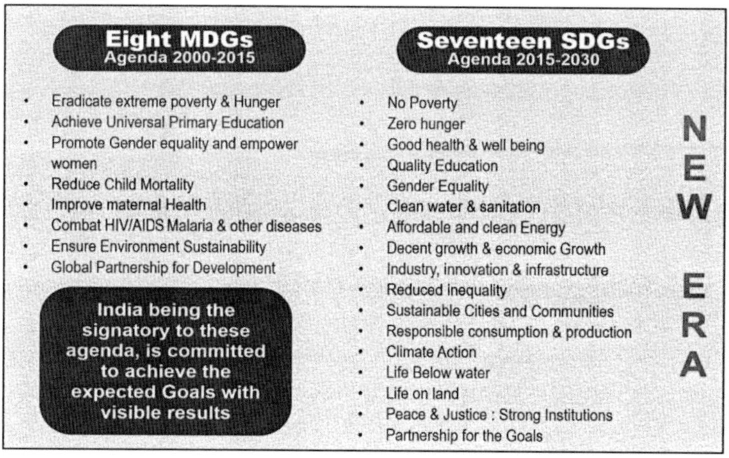

Fig. 3.1: Millennium Development & Sustainable Development Goals.

In order to handle multiple challenges of emerging situations, the local government machinery has to be strengthened and empowered calling for its capacity building to respond to the dynamic demands and requirement of the society. Local government at local level is supposed to take care of development and befitting service delivery issues both in rural as well as in urban areas through their respective institutions of Panchayati Raj and Municipalities Municipal Corporations and other allied agencies. In order to face the challenges of the herculean multidimensional tasks, the administrative machinery needs to be strengthened and empowered appropriately with not only good but smart governance which plays the major role in the implementation of plans, policies, programmes designed to be responsive catering to the requirements and needs of the hour.

After the in-depth studies about the Major Challenges before Urban Local Bodies in dealing with the development of the city, key issues calling for Urgent Attention are found to revolve around, growing urbanisation, implementation of e-Governance, Rural Industrialization, Fiscal decentralisation and Policies, Disempowerment of the local institutions, Core service delivery, Restructuring and redesigning 73rd and 74th CAA to suit the changing needs and scenario, using the unused proviso in letter and spirit for the practical purposes in addition to the natural corollaries arising from System's perspectives.

Key Indian Agencies at Work on SDGs

Given India's federal structure of governance, the focus has been on common understanding, coordination and designing monitoring and reporting mechanisms at all levels. Responsibilities have been divided among various bodies which require the efforts of implementing ministries, departments and agencies at central and state levels as illustrated in the flowchart (Fig. 3.1).

The National Institution for Transforming India (NITI Aayog), with the Prime Minister of India as its chairperson, has been assigned the responsibility for overseeing the implementation of the SDGs in India. As part of this implementation process, NITI Aayog has carried out a detailed mapping of the 17 Goals and 169 targets to Nodal Central Ministries, Centrally Sponsored Schemes and major government initiatives. The results of the mapping exercise were circulated to the Central Ministries and placed on the NITI Aayog website to facilitate better awareness, common understanding and faster implementation of the SDGs. Most sub-National Governments have carried out a similar mapping of the SDGs. Under this scheme of Ministry of Urban Affairs, Govt. of India with fast emerging as metro city facing the various challenges for the local bodies.

Most sub-national 24/Good Governance and United Nations Sustainable Development Goals governments have carried out a similar mapping of the SDGs and targets to the departments and programmes in their respective states. The NITI Aayog has initiated a series of national and regional consultations in collabouration with the other organizations to deepen dialogue on the SDGs with states and stakeholders including experts, academia, institutions, civil society organizations, international organizations and Central Ministries.

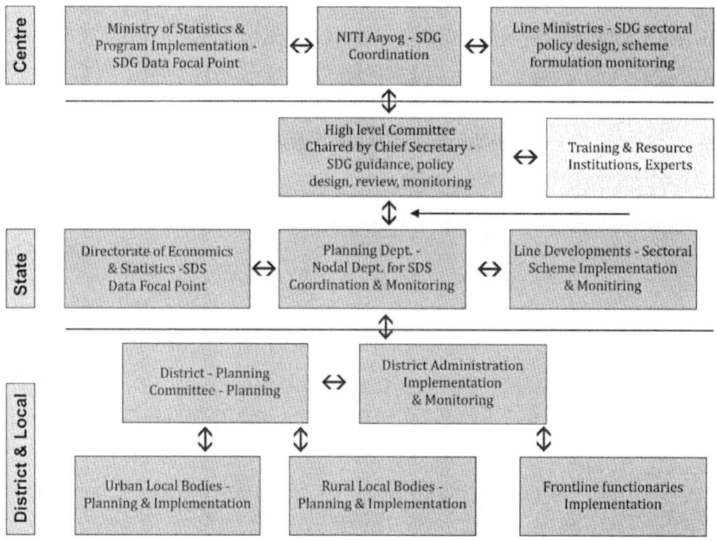

Fig. 3.2: Flowchart depicting the Agencies contributing to the implementation of SDGs.

Source: Localizing SDGs NITI Aayog Report, 2019.

After substantial financial devolution to the PRIs under 14th Finance Commission, the Ministry of Panchayati Raj (MoPR) is supporting village-level PRIs in planning and implementing development initiatives in their respective areas. The national development agenda covering the SDG framework guides the capacity building of the PRIs as well as the actual planning process. The District Administration plays an important role in scrutinising and endorsing Local Government plans. India, having a federal governance structure, most of the functions that have a bearing on SDGs fall within the purview of the State Governments. The commitment of the Government of India in achieving the Sustainable Development Goals can be realised only if actions at the national level are complimented by initiatives of the State Governments and the Union Territories (UTs). Further, the focus of SDGs on equality, inclusion, justice and the core principle of 'Leave No One Behind' makes the participation and contribution of states imperative in the pursuit of SDGs. In the context of India, there are strong Local Governments; Panchayati Raj Institutions (PRIs) in rural areas and Urban Local Bodies (ULBs) in urban areas.

As a result, awareness of the District Administration on SDGs assumes importance. Several states have either entrusted the District Planning and Development Councils (DPDC)(a Constitutional body for district level planning and monitoring of programmes) with the responsibility of coordinating SDG implementation or have created district level structures—District SDG Cell) under the leadership of the District Collector for the purpose. The MoPR has been advocating integrating SDGs within the local plans (known as the Gram Panchayat Development Plans -GPDP) and have prepared guidelines to support this integration. Since GPDPs are to be prepared in a participatory manner and also approved by the village council (gram sabha), integrating SDGs into these plans is an important step to effect change on ground and ensure transformative impact. Effective localization of SDGs requires linking budgets to the local plans which in turn requires an approach that promotes vertical as well as horizontal convergence. It also requires devising strategies for effective monitoring to allow course correction at the local levels. The process of recognising local contexts in the achievement of the 2030 Agenda can be attained through localising the SDGs.

Concept of Governance

The concept of governance came into present parlance reflecting the changes which occurred in the role and nature of the State during the era of post public sector reforms of 1980-1990s witnessed during the regime of Margaret Thatcher led Britain and Ronald Region led USA. It was coined for the first time by World Bank in its report of Sub-Saharan Africa in 1989 mentioning "underlying the litany of Africa's Development problems is the crises of governance. By governance it meant the exercise of political powers to manage the nation's affairs."[3] Governance traditionally refers to form of political system and the manner in which administrative power is exercised in utilizing country's economic and social resources for development. It also includes the capacity of government to design political and administrative system to formulate policies and to implement those policies effectively and efficiently.

Governance is all about the process of decision making and the process by which the decisions are implemented. Governance is a value laden and relates to the type of relationship between the government and citizens to whom government serves and protects. Governance is an exercise done jointly by economic, political and administrative authority to manage nation's affairs. Government is one of the actors in governance. Other actors involved in governance vary depending upon the level of government, e.g. local, municipal, landlords, farmers, NGO, political and religious leaders, financial institutes etc. The moral and natural purpose of governance is assuring on behalf of those governed, a worthy good pattern. Politics provides a means by which the governance process operates.

The governance needs to be seen in the perspectives of development administration for the implementation of programmes and policies for a cause, care and concern of human beings through the Human Rights, the basic tenet itself is a very vast subject involving. Various intricacies and problems affecting the dignity of the human life. There has been plethora of programmes, policies, evaluation, and analysis of various critical and demanding issues trying to raise a standard of life of a common man for almost last 50 years.

Good Governance

Governance is a mechanism of effective use of resources and deliverance of services to citizens. "Good governance" denoted the better standards of such formulation and hence the imperative to achieve them. Formulation of various policies for rural development and provision of budget outlay for implementation of those policies is the job of government. However, it is imperative that these policies and programmes are put to implementation in such a way that it reaches to the target population in full and within time. Management of public service delivery is sub-optimal; efficiency of public expenditure is affected; and finally, it impacts the effective management of natural resources which are sovereign wealth under sovereign ownership. Good governance that ensures effective implementation of plans and programmes. Good governance is critical to translating Plan outlays into significant outcomes on the ground. It is critical because without good governance, resources that are allocated are not efficiently utilized.

As defined by UNDP, Good governance is .... "among the other things participatory, transparent and accountable. It is also effective and equitable. And it promotes the rules of law." UNDP views 'good governance' as participatory, transparent, accountable which includes State Institutions with Private Sectors and civil society organization. UNDP Human Development Report (2002) reported the concept of 'democratic governance' with central objective s of promoting political freedom, human Rights and removal of discrimination which would ultimately promote human development.[4]

As per United Nations Development Program (UNDP), governance as the exercise of political, economic, and administrative authority in the management of country's affairs at all levels. It is the complex mechanisms, processes and institutions through which citizens and groups articulate their interests, exercise their legal rights and obligations, and mediate their differences. This definition indicates two major components of governance, a country and its citizens. Governance is how a state organizes and administers its functions through exercising power through its agencies.[5]

Table 3.1: Principles of Good Governance under UNDP Framework

Legitimacy and Voice	**Participation:** All men and women should have voice in the decision making
	Consensus Orientation: To reach a broad consensus on what is in the best interest of group
Direction	**Strategic Vision:** To have the long-term perspectives on good governance and human development
Performance	**Responsiveness:** Institutions and processes try to serve all the stakeholders **Effectiveness and Efficiency:** Processes and institutions produce results that meet needs while making the best use of the resources
Accountability	**Accountability:** Decision makers are accountable to public as well as the institutional stakeholders **Transparency:** Built on free flow of information **Equity:** All men and women have opportunities to improve and maintain their well-being
Fairness	**Rule of Law:** legal framework should be fair and enforced impartially, particularly the laws on human rights.

Source: India Governance Report 2012, p. 4.

Good Governance with democracy or democratic good governance refers to political regime with the liberal democratic polity which protects human and civil rights with non-corrupt and accountable Public Administration (Chalker, 1991).[6]

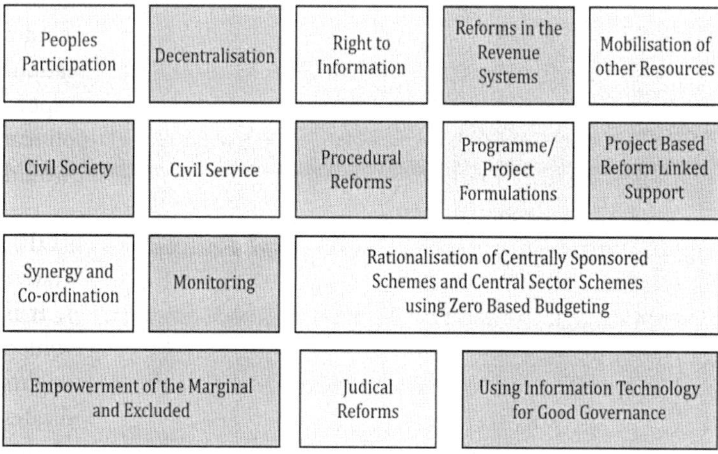

Fig. 3.4: Issues and Strategies for Improving Governance.
Source: India Governance Report 2012.

Indian response to the good governance was visible in the first published document on governance, "Governance for the Human Development" was included as a chapter in Planning Commission first ever Human Development Report (2001)[7] which concluded with agenda ahead underscoring the devolution of power in the decentralised frame, followed by the inventory of functions, funds and functionaries devolved to urban as well as rural local bodies along with the status of decentralised Planning etc. Good governance is aimed at tackling three basic problems in governance which are, systemic improvement in effectiveness of government's planned expenditure on new programmes, improvement in customer satisfaction on delivery of services and means and ways to combat corruption.

The World Bank[8] has identified three discrete aspects of governance which needs to be emphasized for reform:

"(i) The form of political regime;

(ii) The process by which authority is exercised in the management of a country's economic and social resources for development; and

(iii) The capacity of government to design, formulate and implement policies and discharge functions."

Agenda for National Human Development Report, 2002

- Devolution of powers to manage local affairs and decentralisation in decision making.
- Civil service reform aimed at the improving transparency, accountability, efficiency and sensitivity in Public Administration at all levels.
- Enforcing incentive/disincentive structures that truly reflect social values and norms.
- Procedural reforms covering all aspects of governments interface with public.
- Empowerment, particularly of women, marginal and excluded.[9]

Government of India in its Twelfth Five Year Plan 2012-2017 has identified this problem in governance and has put emphasis on good governance and corrective measures for following identified activities have been planned to improve the quality of governance so that the schemes and programmes can be implemented in effective and efficient manner for the benefit of rural population of India :

(a) Strengthening of Local Institutions,
(b) Re-structuring of centrally sponsored schemes,
(c) Independent evaluation of offices,
(d) Improving public system delivery,
(e) Dissemination of Information,
(f) Combating corruption, and
(g) Civil services reforms.

E-Governance, Good Governance & Smart Governance

Information & Communication Technology (ICT) is globally used to deliver services to its citizens in most effective, efficient and transparent manner. India being a land of diversity spanning across culture, traditions, languages and uneven economic conditions needs effective governance as a tool particularly for the rural population for all-round development of Rural Society. Application of e-governance in the recent past have demonstrated surprising results in terms of quality services, data bank creation, tracking and monitoring system, interacting with departments and related organizations. If the attributes of good governance are transparency, efficiency, responsiveness and accountability, e-governance is the means to attain these attributes through application of technology in the Indian history. But still there remains a gap between the expected and existing desired targets ensuring a palatable life of a common man for various reasons, unequal treatments to human lives at various social stratification level. The situation particularly worsens when it comes to Women's issues and the discrepancies and imbalances arising out of gender equations and bias prevailing in the society makes it more precarious.

The overall views expressed by the various scholars discussed the trends of administration of the present era calling for the de-bureaucratization process and bureaucracy less governance. Hierarchy became too rigid, network becomes administration apparatus as in the period of pre bureaucracy followed by bureaucracy as which was comparatively secured. In place of tall hierarchy, the pattern of horizontal bureaucracy is the need of the hour and the Weberian model be discarded and there is need for the reforms in administration theories by non private sector. NPM philosophy has also failed, Public Choice Theory also failed the bureaucracy with its rigid approach and concentration of power has helped to maximize interest of the bureaucrats and not a common man.

They are self-centred and there is nothing like public service but their own, their interest is in the large budgets, supervisory positions increase power position tangents producing self-interest in the budget so as to have larger hierarchies quality-wise and will give more quantity. Public Choice theory also cautions the agenda of state civil society asserting upon the strong and powerful contacts amongst themselves, market based criteria, charter spirit be absorbed through legally enforceable documents.

Good Governance and New Public Management

Concept & Importance of Good Governance for the Development

In simplest terms, New Public Management (NPM) is an application of Private sector management principles to the public sectors for effective delivery of services to the citizens. New Public Management represents an approach in public administration that employs knowledge and experiences acquired in business management and other disciplines to improve efficiency, effectiveness, and general performance of public services in modern bureaucracies.[10] The New Public Management (NPM) can be seen as an attempt to reengineer relationships between politicians, bureaucrats, and the public.[11]

"The UK played an important role in developing the concept of New Public Management (NPM) and can claim to have been its birth place" (McLaughlin *et al.,* 2002). Indeed, the seminal paper which coined the term NPM was the product of the UK experience (Hood,1991). The work done by Osborne & Gaebler (1992) also contributed considerably in the elabouration of the concept. It soon spread to the United Nations circles, Australia and New Zealand and then further to Scandinavia and Continental Europe.

Good Governance conceptualized in the past as ideal state of Ram Rajya has suddenly entered into the vocabulary of Public Administration since 1990s. Traditionally, the governance refers to the form of political system and the manner in which the power is exercised in utilizing country's economic and social resources for the development. Good governance is associated with efficient and effective administration in a democratic framework. It is purposive and the development oriented administration which is committed to the improvement of the quality of life of the people. It implies high level of organisational effectiveness and also relates to the capacity of centre of power of political and administrative system to cope with the emerging challenges of the society. It refers to the adoption of new values of governance to establish the efficiency, legitimacy and credibility of the system. In simple terms good governance can be considered as citizen friendly, citizen caring and responsive administration.

Good and humane governance is the most important issue faced by the country today which is tottering under the weight of political and bureaucratic corruption. Good governance implies gearing up of the government machinery and administrative structure to provide, responsive, transparent, clean, and people friendly administration. Further it is also considered as an act or manner of governing the way of control. It is linked up with the role of the state what it can do or cannot do matching its capacity and the resources to undertake the task assigned for itself.

According to the Public Management Committee of the OECD (1995)

The NPM is aimed at fostering a performance-oriented culture in a decentralized public sector having the following features:

(a) Attention to results in terms of efficiency, effectiveness, and quality of service;
(b) Replacement of highly centralized, hierarchical structures by decentralized management whereby service organization can be made closer to the point of delivery enabling quicker feedback;
(c) Flexibility to explore alternatives to direct public provision and regulation that are cost-effective;
(d) Insistence on efficiency in the services provided directly by the public sector; and
(e) Strengthening of strategic capacities at the center to guide the entire process in a cost-effective way.

According to Pollitt (1995) NPM is made up of eight main elements

1. Cost cutting; capping budgets and greater transparency in resource allocation;
2. Disaggregating traditional bureaucratic organizations into separate agencies;
3. Decentralized management within public agencies;
4. Separating the function of providing for public services from their purchase;
5. Establishing market and quasi-market mechanisms;
6. Emphasizing performance management targets, indicators and output objectives;

7. Introducing term contracts, performance-related pay and local determination of pay and conditions; and
8. Increasing emphasis on service quality, standard setting and customer responsiveness.

The various ideas and themes of NPM may be categorised broadly into two strands. On the one hand, there are those ideas that derive from managerialism, i.e. emphasising management in government. These include management decentralisation, desegregation and downsizing of government, creating leaner and flexible organisational structures and systems, and giving managers more freedom to manage. On the other hand, there are ideas emanating from new institutional economics that emphasise markets and competition as a way of giving choice and "voice" to users and promoting efficiency in service delivery, i.e. the use of market mechanisms such as franchising, vouchers, contracting out, internal markets, user fees and customer orientation.[12]

NPM for Local Administration in the Context of Issues and Problems

Being a vast country and comprising mostly of the rural population residing in villages, Indian administrative system is also equally complex and difficult to manage with the traditional forms of administrative techniques. Disadvantages of traditional bureaucratic form of administration like red-tapism, corruption and political interference have been main responsible causes for the poor delivery of services to the rural citizens. The policies and programmes implemented for the benefit of poor hardly reach to the end user defeating the whole purpose of those programmes. e-Governance programmes are aimed at eliminating these hurdles on the way of effective service delivery by bringing in transparency, accuracy, accountability and speedy delivery of services. e-Governance will enable implementation of concepts of New Public Management in rural administration in particular.

Contextualizing Public Administration in India, the scholars were of the opinion LPG has influenced many countries since 1990, i.e. After New Economic Policies, reflecting market as a forceful instruments, followed by state failures. Private pillars are glorified for quality and effectiveness, private sector not able to take care of all these issues of common man. Executive arms of withering of states. Counter agreement, of New Economic Policy, economic recession has forced the government to rethink with the compulsions of IMF, SAIF (Structural Adjustments).

Mismatch Between Functions Assigned and the Available Resources

With the rapid urbanization process, the demographic, technological, socio-economic, financial, environmental challenges for the growing cities are posing the tough challenges before the governance but the approaches to deal with them remains fragmented. With this background, this chapter attempts to understand and analyse the responsibilities for managing these cities, which are divided between the centre, state, and local government for the practical purposes, the matching well coordinated governance at the institutional levels is still not visible. Ever since the implementation of 74th Amendment practically much has been written about the failures of the State government to implement the implied provisions during last 30 years but now with Smart cities project the situation is all the more unsatisfactory owing to the creation of another independent development body with the overlapping of the functions and powers of its elected representatives in particular. "The implementation failure narratives tend to focus upon how the local governments are financially constrained and do not have the administrative capacity to carry out its functions."[13]

The Constitution of India provides Functional domain through Schedule XII, of CAA under Article 243G indicates list of 18 functions assigned to municipalities and have been classified by XI-Finance Commissions as, Core Functions, Developmental Functions, Welfare Functions, and Agency Functions. As observed by the various committees and Commissions local government of majority of cities also remains in fiscal stress as a routine feature.

On one hand these bodies have very limited fiscal autonomy on the other hand the citizens expectations to get the services of quality and quantity increases with the passage of time and the technologies. As these institutions remain stressed and dependent for their fiscal devolutions, it is pertinent to understand how their fiscal capacity could be improved upon so that they may augment their own resources to discharge their responsibilities. These local bodies with the constitutional status engaged in providing variety of civic amenities and infrastructures, CAA has assigned enormous responsibilities to them including the preparation of the economic development that needs technical competency and social justice. In order to perform these tasks, the municipal government has to be financially sound with commensurate amount of powers for raising the resources. While the constitution has specified and listed expenditure responsibilities it does not provide clear regime taxes and revenue resources of the municipal Government. As such it is clearly observed there is a mismatch of the resources and responsibility because of which most of the times it fail to deliver the expected results. Since the CAA 1992 does not empower them with any defined own sources of Finance they are dependent at rationality of their respective states. Strengthening these local government bodies in terms of their fiscal capacity is a very critical issue in discharging their mandated responsibilities keeping in mind the changing situations.

While the 74th Amendment has become a pivotal foundation for civic activism in many cities, it has certain inherent limitations as mentioned in the earlier elabourations. As the cities struggle to meet the basic needs of their inhabitants there is an urgent need to re-examine the existing modes of organising the power in urban India. Unlike 73rd Amendment which provides for three levels of Panchayats (Village, taluk and district level) power in urban area is concentrated in a single municipal body, whether it is Municipal Corporation, Municipal Council or Nagar Parishad. However due to heavy urbanization trends all over country majority of the cities have grown exponentially over last 30 years with crossing minimum of 10 million population mark, there is an acute need for rethinking about the present model of urban governance that vests power in a single authority of Municipal Corporation neglecting the other units at the appropriate levels. While urban governance reforms can take multiple shapes they must be fore-grounded in the political empowerment of local government which will enhance further local democratic accountability.

Notes

1. Definition of decentralisation, retrieved from the Free Dictionary.com, accessed on 4-2-2013.
2. World Bank definition of Decentralisation, retrieved from http://www.worldbank.org/publicsector/decentralisation /what.htm, 25-09-2014.
3. As quoted by Leftwich in States of Development, chapter five, p. 104 also World Bank 1989: 60.
4. UNDP Human Development Report 2002.
5. *Ibid.*
6. Chalker (1991), as cited in Leftwitch, Adrian (1993), *op. cit.,* p. 6.
7. Human Development Report 2001 : Planning Commission, Government of India.
8. D. Bandyopadhyay (1996), Administration, Decentralisation and Good Governance. *Economic and Political Weekly*, Vol. 31, No. 48 (November)
9. National Human Development Report, 2002.
10. Eran Vigoda, *New Public Management Encyclopaedia of Public Administration and Public Policy*, p. 812.
11. Scott Fritzen, Bureaucrats and Politicians in Southeast National University of Singapore, *Encyclopaedia of Public Administration and Public Policy*, p. 42.
12. http://siteresources.worldbank.org/INTROADSHIGHWAYS/Resources/338993-1115316483571/3-public_sector_mgmnt_reform.pdf State of e-governance in Maharashtra 2013, Directorate of Information and Technology, Govt. of Maharashtra, p. 11.
13. Mathew Idicula: *The Hindu*, p. 8, dated 14 June, 2018.

4

Environmental, Social, and Governance (ESG) and Corporate Financial Performance (CFP)

A Systematic Review using TCCM Approach

Priyanka Aggarwal and *Archana Singh*

Introduction

Sustainable management is a long debating issue in business research and is currently understood in three pillars of environment, social, and governance (ESG) (Ma & Park, 2021; Liu *et al.*, 2022; Velte 2016; Oh *et al.*, 2020). ESG is a movement that underscores to maximize corporate financial performance (CFP) and non-financial values including "green practices", "social and ethical values", and "improvement of corporate governance" simultaneously (Broadstock *et al.*, 2021; Zhou *et al.*, 2022; Li *et al.*, 2021; Huang, 2022). ESG-style management proponents frequently pitch it as something new, revolutionary, and novel. Yet, they rarely cite the long history of its antecedent theories, including "corporate social responsibility", "corporate social performance", "socially responsible investing", "stakeholder capitalism", "shared value creation", the "triple bottom line", and "impact investing" among others (Competitive Enterprise Institute, n.d.; Fama 2020; Shahrokhi *et al.*, 2022). The United Nations' 2006 report on the Principles for Responsible Investment (PRI), which encompassed the Freshfield Report (Freshfields Bruckhaus Deringer,

2005) as well as "Who Cares Wins" (United Nations Department of Public Information, 2004) was the beginning of the discussion of ESG issues. Environmental, Social, and Governance (ESG) refer to the three central factors in measuring the sustainability and societal impact of an investment in a corporate entity (Friede *et al.*, 2015; Ketter *et al.*, 2020; van Duuren *et al.*, 2015). The ESG perspective emphasizes social objectives beyond the traditional financial objectives of the companies and has a great impact not just in production but more importantly on supply chain, resources allocation, marketing channels, and customer networking within and across global markets (Drempetic *et al.*, 2019). The three-factor ESG has been considered salient in the entire society, including policymakers and social activists, but has become particularly critical in the area of investment (Al-Shaer & Zaman, 2019; Benlemlih *et al.*, 2018). ESG metrics have been derived from reports and news articles, evaluating the company in different sustainability and social impact aspects (Benlemlih *et al.*, 2018; Drempetic *et al.*, 2019; Friede *et al.*, 2015; van Duuren *et al.*, 2015). Financial performance, which assesses the fulfilment of the firm's economic goals, has long been a central focus in management research on firm performance (Combs *et al.*, 2005; Richard *et al.*, 2009). Financial performance can be classified as "financial visibility, or the extent to which a company achieves its economic goals" (Orlitzky *et al.*, 2003).

Despite the growing literature on ESG-CFP, one of the major issues has been to establish a clear picture of the correlation between them. The academic studies suggested conflicting results with regard to the impact of incorporating ESG issues on the firm's financial performance, with studies suggesting a positive (Orlitzky *et al.*, 2003; Allouche & Laroche, 2005; van Beurden & Gössling, 2008; Busch & Friede, 2018), negative (Brammer *et al.*, 2006; Hoepner & McMillan, 2009; Revelli & Viviani, 2014; Nollet *et al.*, 2016; Duque-Grisales & Aguilera-Caracuel, 2019) or a neutral (Aupperle *et al.*, 1985; Griffin & Mahon, 1997; Jha & Rangaranjan, 2020)relationship. Studies in the area of ESG-CFP decisions have covered a variety of theories, contexts, characteristics, and methods. As a result, high level conclusions cannot be drawn that can provide a bird's eye view of the ESG-CFP field to the interested academic or practitioner. Taking all of this into consideration, the purpose of this review is to supplement and expand upon previous assessments of the ESG-CFP by (i) providing a holistic view of both empirical as well as theoretical aspects of the ESG-CFP relationship, and (ii) outlining future research directions that will aid in the advancement of the field. Thus, the study aims to systematically review 57 research articles published in the past 9 years (2014-2022). For this purpose, the study employs the TCCM framework (Paul & Criado, 2020; Paul & Rosado-Serrano, 2019) which outlines both empirical as well as theoretical aspects of a specific research domain. Consequently, the chapter attempts to answer the following questions: (i) What theories have been used to explain the connection between ESG and CFP?, (ii) In what contexts has the underlying research been conducted?, (iii) What features have been explored (i.e., independent, moderating, mediating, and dependent variables)?, and (iv) What methodologies were used to comprehend the underlying study topic?

The study contributes in the following ways. To begin, this chapter provides a comprehensive analysis of the ESG-CFP connection based on the most recent research. Till date, to the best of our knowledge, a comprehensive picture of the factors influencing the company's ESG-CFP actions is still expected so that future study directions can be proposed. Following the TCCM framework, our study demonstrates that majority of the studies have applied Corporate Governance theories rather than multidisciplinary theories to explain the ESG-CFP decisions by corporates. The majority of research studies pertaining to the underlying topic are conducted in the United States of America and only concentrate on non-financial companies. In terms of the characteristics, our research reveals that the majority of research studies have focused their attention on analysing the influence of ESG activities on the financial performance of corporations, with the implicit premise that the causality cannot flow in the other direction. Second, based on our review, we provide a theoretical framework and lay out a future research agenda in the field of ESG-CFP. Our study presents a conceptual framework offering the future direction to the research academics, to discover—How do "Innovation" mend the ESG-CFP relationship? We hypothesise that the moderating role of "Innovation" is a crucial feature to be considered while determining the ESG-CFP relationship. Further, it is noticed that the existing Corporate Governance models are unable to capture the characteristics of ESG-CFP interaction. Therefore, future partnerships spanning management, finance, accounting, marketing, sociology, psychology, philosophy, anthropology, economics and political science theories have the prospects to extend our grasp of the intricate trade-offs arising from undertaking ESG activities.

Methodology

The research endeavours to utilize a two-step methodology encompassing PRISMA guidelines (Moher, 2009) and TCCM framework for systematically reviewing the research articles. The systematic literature review (sometimes known as "structured literature review" or "SLR") has entered management research as a viable tool for analysing prior literature to bring the various aspects of the management field closer together (Tranfield *et al.*, 2003; Paul & Criado, 2020). The systematic literature review is a repetitive process directed to identify the significant studies to answer defined research questions (Singh *et al.*, 2020; Srivastava *et al.*, 2020). Such analyses attempt to synthesise, assess, and draw conclusions from the existing literature. Replicable and reliable findings are the end consequence of a comprehensive literature study. At the first stage, the study employs PRISMA protocol to systematically select research articles from Web of Science database (Shamseer *et al.*, 2015). Web of Science is considered the greatly reputable resource for bibliometric investigations because it is free of bias towards any publisher (Falagas *et al.*, 2006), as well as further, ensures the inclusion of the most influential journals (Kullenberg & Kasperowski, 2016). The second step involved the application of TCCM methodology for synthesising the previously published work in the underlying field. Understanding the current state of the underlying research stream, locating knowledge gaps, and suggesting potential directions for future study are all products of a well-executed systematic literature review.

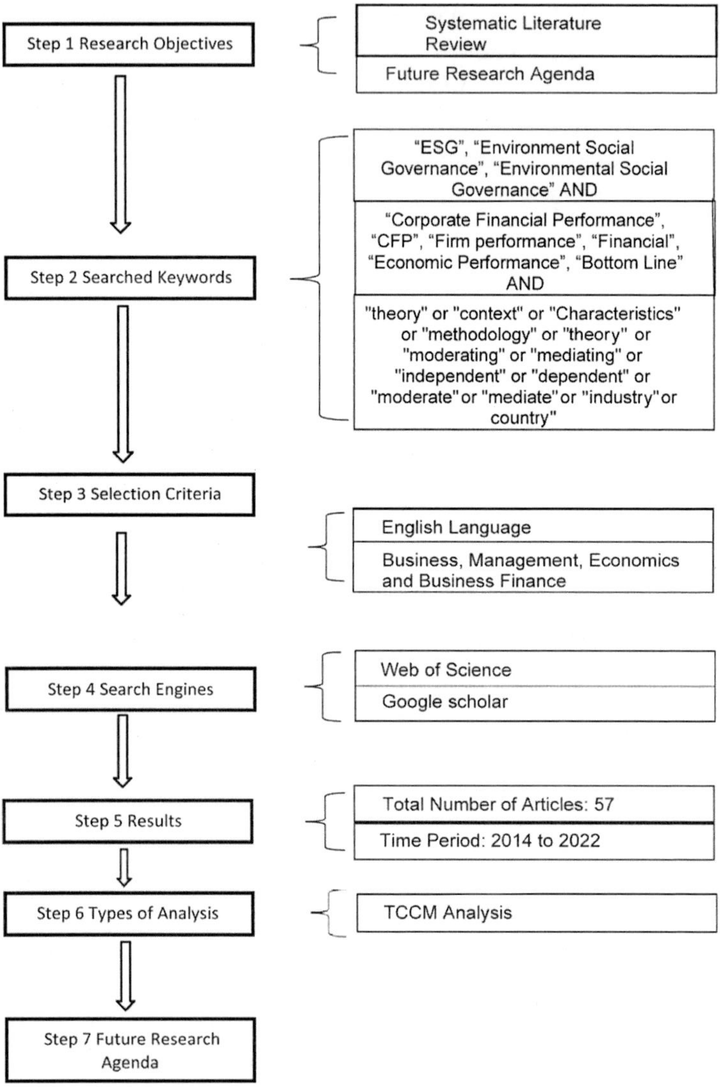

Fig. 4.1: Review Methodology.

The PRISMA Protocol

Various researchers in the past have proposed different steps for the process of systematic literature review (Vásquez-Carbonell, 2022; Tranfield *et al.*, 2003). For ensuring the selection of articles in an unbiased and transparent manner, PRISMA guidelines consisting of a four-phase paradigm (identification, screening, eligibility, and inclusion) were being followed. This resulted in more comprehensive and trustworthy results (Fig. 4.2). Web of science (WOS) was selected as search database for the study. It was chosen because of being a comprehensive pan-disciplinary database and a well-accepted, established and highly recommended approach for such studies in management area (Snyder, 2019). It is cleaner, has better coverage of research articles than Scopus database and has been extensively used in various published studies making significant impact in their respective domain (Agarwal and Kumar, 2020). Further, WOS includes impactful and quality publications from various fields such as social science, science, arts and humanities (Goswami & Goswami, 2022; Mahadevan and Joshi, 2021) and from various key databases such as Social Science Citation Index (SSCI), Science Citation Index (SCI), Emerging Sources Citation Index (ESCI) and Arts and Humanities Citation Index (AHCI) databases. The study adopted the following process for extracting articles from WOS: (i) We searched for the combination of the following words in the topic (title, abstract and keywords)—"ESG" or "Environment Social Governance" or "Environmental Social Governance" (Topic) and "corporate financial performance" or "CFP" or "Firm performance" or "financial" or "economic performance" or "bottom line" (All Fields) AND "theory" or "context" or "Characteristics" or "methodology" or "theory" or "moderating" or "mediating" or "independent" or "dependent" or "moderate" or "mediate" or "industry" or "country" (All Fields); (ii) the time period criteria was left open-ended, and we received papers from 2014 to 2022; (iii) the disciplines taken into account were business, management, economics, and business finance; and (iv) only publications published in English were taken into account. Using the aforementioned parameters, we were able to draw from the WOS database a total of 223 research publications. Furthermore,

155 pertinent articles in the underlying research field were gathered after carefully reviewing the abstract, title, keywords, and in certain cases, introduction (where applicable). After reading all the research publications, we were able to cut the sample down to 57 studies that were actually relevant to the study question (Table 4.1). Also, Fig. 4.2 depicts that these research articles have been published over a period of 9 years starting from 2014 till 2022 (the year 2022 has been taken till the month of July).

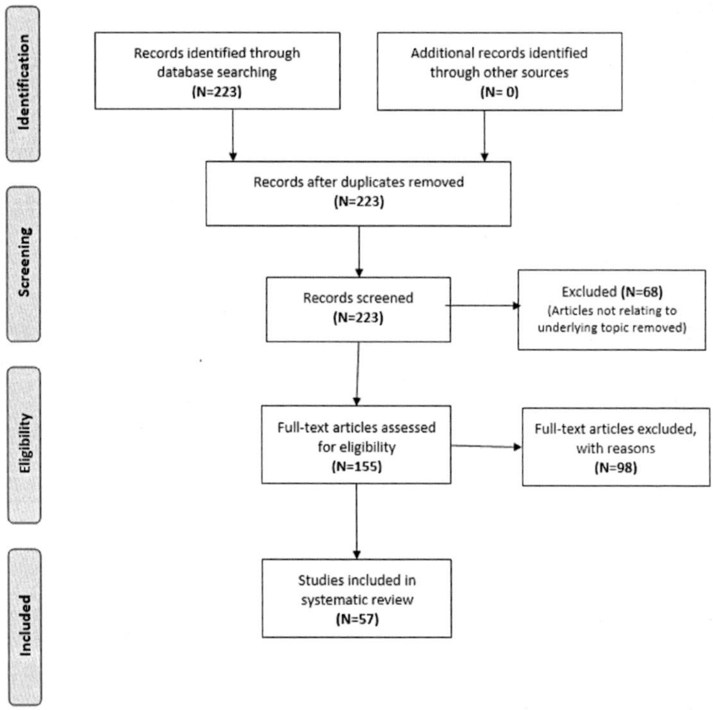

Fig. 4.2. Methodology for Data Collection following PRISMA Guidelines.

Table 4.1: Top Journals in ESG-CFP research

Sources	Articles
Sustainability	7
Corporate Social Responsibility and Environmental Management	6

(*Contd.*)

Sources	Articles
Business Strategy and the Environment	4
Sustainability Accounting Management and Policy Journal	4
Journal of Business Ethics	3
Accounting and Finance	2
Corporate Governance—An International Review	2
Journal of Business Economics and Management	2
Management Decision	2
Academia-Revista Latinoamericana de Administracion	1
Agricultural Economics—Zemedelska Ekonomika	1
Borsa Istanbul Review	1
Business & Society	1
Critical Perspectives on Accounting	1
Economic Research—Ekonomska Istrazivanja	1
Energy Policy	1
International Journal of Bank Marketing	1
International Journal of Emerging Markets	1
International Journal of Human Resource Management	1
International Review of Finance	1

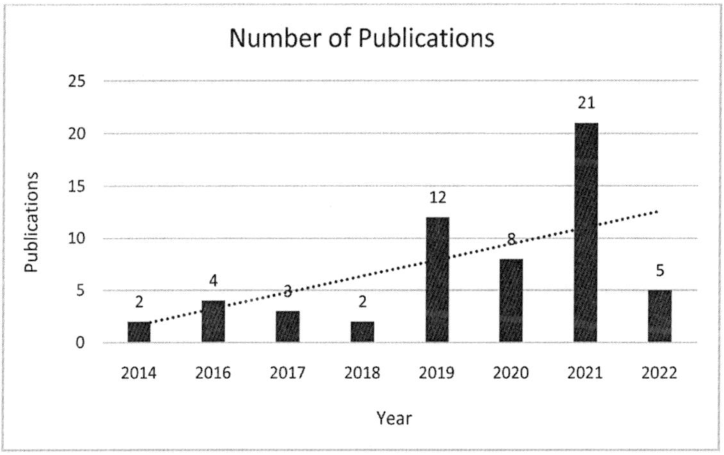

Fig. 4.3: Publication Trend in ESG-CFP research area.

TCCM Framework

We systematically review the literature on ESG-CFP following the TCCM framework (Paul *et al.*, 2021; Paul & Criado, 2020; Paul & Rosado-Serrano, 2019). TCCM analysis helps in bridging the gaps identified in the previous studies and offers pathways for further scope (Sharma *et al.*, 2020). This analysis identifies the prominent TCCM elements, paving the way for further research into the uncharted or understudied territories. Additionally, it paves the way for the construction of theoretical models from the perspective of less-explored countries and industries, allowing for a broader scope of study in the field. Further, the study provides a synopsis of the gaps found in the existing literature on responsiveness in the form of TCCM and the future research agenda for advancement in this area. As a first step, we take a look at the most popular theories in the field of ESG-CFP, including the Legitimacy theory, the Stakeholders theory, the Shareholder theory, the Resource-based View theory, the Agency Cost theory, and the Institutional theory. We then go on to talk about the environment in which ESG-CFP studies are conducted, including the various sectors and nations in which they are conducted. We then looked at the factors (i.e., independent, moderating, mediating, and dependent variables) that influence the ESG-CFP link. Finally, we evaluate the primary methodological features, such as research approach, analytic techniques, data sources, and sample characteristics, that have been used to the ESG-CFP literature. After doing a comprehensive analysis, we make suggestions on where future studies should go.

TCCM Framework

Theory

The development of theoretical underpinnings in the context of ESG-CFP has been significantly improved. Table 4.2 provides an overview of the frequently used theories in the ESG-CFP research. The two theories that monopolize the study on the importance of ESG-CFP are stakeholder theory (Freeman, 1984; Donaldson & Preston, 1995) and legitimacy theory (Tavares & Dias, 2018; Scherer & Palazzo, 2007, 2011). Freeman (1999) advocated the stakeholder theory, which proposes that a firm's prime objectives be engaged to all stakeholders (customers, employees, society, government, investor, regulators) and not limited to shareholder wealth maximization, which was the prime goal of the finance literature (Battisti *et al.*, 2019, 2022; Jensen, 2001). This broader perspective of stakeholder engagement boosts integrated Corporate Social Responsibility practices in the early days (Belyaeva *et al.*, 2020; Rey-Martí *et al.*, 2016) and ESG practices in the modern world and their impact on firm value (Buallay, 2019). The legitimacy theory states that companies disclose sustainability information to stakeholders to reiterate an organization's commitment towards society in support of the stakeholder theory. According to the legitimacy theory, firms' disclosures towards ESG enable the firm's commitment towards society and generate a sustainable pool of profit. Firms and stakeholders believe that these investments generate long-term benefits (Behl, *et al.*, 2021). Firms require legitimacy to sustain their long-term viability. "A broad assumption or perception that an entity's behaviours are acceptable, reasonable, or relevant within some socially constructed system of standards, values, assumptions, and definitions", illustrates (Suchman, 1995). Firms involved in disputes have their organisational legitimacy questioned when they are viewed as lacking acceptable credibility (Palazzo & Scherer, 2007). Stewardship, Institutional, Slack Resource, Good Management and Information Asymmetry theories also support ESG-CFP relationship. Stewardship theory views management as stewards of all organisational assets and capitals for the purpose of preserving the interests of all stakeholders. Hernandez (2007) states that stewardship theory promotes "the long-term best interests of a group ahead of personal goals that serve an individual's self-interests." According to institutional theoretical theory, corporate legitimacy gives several economic and non-economic advantages like a lower risk of incurring legal or social sanctions and better access to resources (Claassen & Ricci, 2015). To seize these advantages, firms need to protect or enhance their legitimacy, which is possible by meeting the expectations of institutions and stakeholders (Scott, 2005). These economic and non-economic advantages might then improve the firms' long-term financial performance (Berrone & Gomez-Mejia, 2009). According to good management theory (Waddock & Graves, 1997), if stakeholders perceive a company to have a good social performance, it will lead to an improvement of the company's reputation among its main stakeholders. In turn, the company will find it easier to achieve better CFP. This is in line with stakeholder theory (Freeman, 1999). In addition, more profitable corporations, which in line with the resource slack theory, invest more in social duties than their counterparts. As a result, companies with more financial resources tend to invest more in ESG. ESG disclosure helps companies decrease information asymmetries.

After reviewing the articles, it also appears that many scholars based on Agency theory and Trade-off theory have argued that sustainability efforts are waste of company's resources (Nguyen, 2020). Agency theory focuses on risk sharing and agency problems between shareholders and management by suggesting that the interests of principals (owners) and their agents (executives) are often not aligned (Fama & Jensen, 1998). The early thinking of ESG activities is that it is an agency problem that leads to wealth deterioration. This is clearly demonstrated by (Friedman, 1970) who argues that the corporate manager, as the agent, should conduct the business activities in accordance with the shareholders' desire for wealth maximisation. In other words, he advocated that firms should not spend corporate resources on things such as environmental, social or good governance activities as they will ultimately lead to deterioration of shareholder's wealth and are generally not in the interest of shareholders (Masulis & Reza, 2014). Based on the trade-off theory, fulfilling ESG responsibilities could negatively impact financial performance in the short run. Friedman (1970) pointed out that costs tend to increase with the investment in ESG.

Table 4.2: Theories used to explain ESG-CFP Relationship

Theory	**Articles**	**Articles (%)**	**Examples**
Stakeholder Theory	27	47%	Saygili, *et al.*, 2022; Linnenluecke, 2022; Li *et al.*, 2021; Profitlich *et al.*, 2021; Eliwa *et al.*, 2021; Huang, 2022; Kabir Hassan *et al.*, 2021; Sepulveda-Alzate *et al.*, 2021; Qureshi *et al.*, 2021; Garzón Jiménez & Zorio-Grima, 2021; Buallay *et al.*, 2021;

(Contd.)

Theory	Articles	Articles (%)	Examples
			Daszynska-Zygadlo *et al.*, 2020; Nirino *et al.*, 2021; Pirtea *et al.*, 2021; Nekhili *et al.*, 2021; Vural-Yavas, 2021; Shahbaz *et al.*, 2020; Kim & Lee, 2020; D.Z.X. Huang, 2021; Minutolo *et al.*, 2019; Nekhili, Boukadhaba, Nagati, *et al.*, 2021; Brogi & Lagasio, 2019; Xie *et al.*, 2019; Garcia-Blandon *et al.*, 2019; Kolbel *et al.*, 2017; Araissi *et al.*, 2016; Girerd-Potin *et al.*, 2012
Legitimacy Theory	9	16%	Eliwa *et al.*, 2021; Sepulveda-Alzate *et al.*, 2021; Reber *et al.*, 2021; Garzón Jiménez & Zorio-Grima, 2021; Shakil *et al.*, 2021; D.Z.X. Huang, 2021; Minutolo *et al.*, 2019; Aboud & Diab, 2019; Giannarakis *et al.*, 2014
Agency Theory	8	14%	Dong *et al.*, 2022; Garzón Jiménez & Zorio-Grima, 2021; Buallay *et al.*, 2021; Melis & Rombi, 2021; Nekhili *et al.*, 2021; Shahbaz *et al.*, 2020; Araissi *et al.*, 2016; Girerd-Potin *et al.*, 2012
Institutional Theory	5	9%	Eliwa *et al.*, 2021; Sepulveda-Alzate *et al.*, 2021; Melis & Rombi, 2021; Araissi *et al.*, 2016; Li *et al.*, 2021
Good Management Theory	4	7%	Daszynska-Zygadlo *et al.*, 2020; Vural-Yavas, 2021, Brogi & Lagasio, 2019; Isaksson & Woodside, 2016
Theory of Asymmetric Information	3	5%	Feng & Wu, 2021; Reber *et al.*, 2021; Garzón Jiménez & Zorio-Grima, 2021
Slack Resource Theory	3	5%	Chen *et al.*, 2021; Chams *et al.*, 2021; Qureshi *et al.*, 2021
Trade-Off Theory	3	5%	Qureshi *et al.*, 2021; Buallay *et al.*, 2021; Chen *et al.*, 2021
Stewardship Theory	2	4%	Tilba, 2022; Garzón Jiménez & Zorio-Grima, 2021
Other Theories			
Theory of Sustainable Development	1	2%	Zhou *et al.*, 2022
Absolute Valuation Theory	1	2%	Zhou *et al.*, 2022

(*Contd.*)

Theory	Articles	Articles (%)	Examples
Theory of Relative Valuation	1	2%	Zhou *et al.*, 2022
Theory of Firm	1	2%	Huang, 2022
Transparency Fallacy	1	2%	Reber *et al.*, 2021
Impression Management Theories	1	2%	Reber *et al.*, 2021
Corporate Culture Theory	1	2%	Yoon *et al.*, 2021
Managerial Opportunism Hypothesis	1	2%	Qureshi *et al.*, 2021
Negative Synergy Theory	1	2%	Qureshi *et al.*, 2021
Theory of Planned Behaviour	1	2%	Sultana *et al.*, 2018
Goal Setting Theory	1	2%	Sultana *et al.*, 2018
Behavioural Asset Pricing Model	1	2%	Sultana *et al.*, 2018
Financial Theory	1	2%	Chan *et al.*, 2017
Complexity Theory	1	2%	Isaksson & Woodside, 2016
Political Cost Theory	1	2%	Giannarakis *et al.*, 2014
No Theory	15	26%	Jitmaneeroj *et al.*, 2016; Busch *et al.*, 2016; Limkriangkrai *et al.*, 2017

Context

Table 4.3 summarise our findings regarding the contexts investigated in ESG-CFP relationship. Our analysis clearly indicates that most of the reviewed studies are conducted in United States of America (23%) and Europe (18%). The review suggested that the literature on motivations for greater ESG-CFP relationship has traditionally been linked to advanced economies only (Bassen *et al.*, 2006; Cheng *et al.*, 2013). However, emerging markets, despite being a major contributor of businesses around the world, have not yet find significant place in the current ESG-CFP literature (Baughn *et al.*, 2007; Dobers & Halme, 2009; Chauhan and Kumar, 2018; Daugaard, 2019). Further, the analysis revealed that almost all the studies were conducted within a single country. There are few studies (Eliwa *et al.*, 2021; Kabir Hassan *et al.*, 2021; Sepulveda-Alzate *et al.*, 2021; Buallay *et al.*, 2021; Miralles-Quiros *et al.*, 2019) that undertakes a multi-country analysis. The issue of data collecting and data comparison in the cross-national examination may be a possible cause. Since the results of the single-country study cannot be compared, they offer only preliminary insights. Further with respect to industries, most of the papers focused on non-financial listed firms (Dong *et al.*, 2022; Saygili, *et al.*, 2022; Eliwa *et al.*, 2021; Kabir Hassan *et al.*, 2021; Melis & Rombi, 2021) with few exceptions (Daszynska-Zygadlo *et al.*, 2020; Shakil *et al.*, 2021; Miralles-Quiros *et al.*, 2019).

Table 4.3. Countries Investigated in the Review Articles

Country	Articles	Articles (%)	Examples
North America			
United States of America	13	23%	Tilba, 2022; Feng & Wu, 2021; Kabir Hassan *et al.*, 2021; Reber *et al.*, 2021; Kim & Lee, 2020; Qureshi *et al.*, 2021; Melis & Rombi, 2021; Shakil *et al.*, 2021; Miralles-Quiros *et al.*, 2019; Minutolo *et al.*, 2019; Tilba, 2022; Feng & Wu, 2021; Kabir Hassan *et al.*, 2021; Reber *et al.*, 2021; Kim & Lee, 2020; Qureshi *et al.*, 2021; Melis & Rombi, 2021; Shakil *et al.*, 2021; Miralles-Quiros *et al.*, 2019; Chan *et al.*, 2017; Eliwa *et al.*, 2021; Sepulveda-Alzate *et al.*, 2021; Reber *et al.*, 2021; Garzón Jiménez & Zorio-Grima, 2021; Shakil *et al.*, 2021; D.Z.X. Huang, 2021; Minutolo *et al.*, 2019; Aboud & Diab, 2019; Giannarakis *et al.*, 2014
Europe	10	18%	Eliwa *et al.*, 2021; Buallay *et al.*, 2021; Melis & Rombi, 2021; Nirino *et al.*, 2021; Vural-Yavas, 2021; Miralles-Quiros *et al.*, 2019; Lagasio & Cucari, 2019; Isaksson & Woodside, 2016; Girerd-Potin *et al.*, 2012; Profitlich *et al.*, 2021
Latin America	5	9%	Sepulveda-Alzate *et al.*, 2021; Garzón Jiménez & Zorio-Grima, 2021; Duque-Grisales & Aguilera-Caracuel, 2021; Martinez-Ferrero *et al.*, 2020; Lagasio & Cucari, 2019

(*Contd.*)

Country	Articles	Articles (%)	Examples
Africa	3	5%	Kabir Hassan *et al.*, 2021; Daszynska-Zygadlo *et al.*, 2020; Lagasio & Cucari, 2019
Asia			
China	4	7%	Dong *et al.*, 2022; Zhou *et al.*, 2022; Chen *et al.*, 2021; Buallay *et al.*, 2021
Japan	2	4%	Buallay *et al.*, 2021; Miralles-Quiros *et al.*, 2019
India	1	2%	Buallay *et al.*, 2021
Korea	1	2%	Yoon *et al.*, 2021
No specific country	19	33%	Jitmaneeroj *et al.*, 2016; Busch *et al.*, 2016

Characteristics

Our review indicates that researchers have investigated a variety of variables in ESG-CFP research. Table 4.4 provides an overview of the variables that have been examined in the underlying research. We have classified these variables according to their role in each study, i.e. independent, moderating, mediating, and dependent variables.

Independent Variables

The independent variable is the variable the experimenter manipulates or changes and is assumed to have a direct effect on the dependent variable. In most of the studies, ESG has been taken as independent variable (Dong *et al.*, 2022; Zhou *et al.*, 2022; Chen *et al.*, 2021; Eliwa *et al.*, 2021; Feng & Wu, 2021; Kabir Hassan *et al.*, 2021; Reber *et al.*, 2021; Yoon *et al.*, 2021; Kim & Lee, 2020; Buallay *et al.*, 2021; Daszynska-Zygadlo *et al.*, 2020). Thus, the focal point of the bulk of research studies has been on analysing the impact of ESG activities on Corporate's Financial performance, with an implicit assumption that the causality cannot flow the other way.

Moderating Variables

The existing body of work around ESG and CFP mainly focuses on explaining the direction of the relationship without getting to the factors affecting it. Regarding moderating variables, the study indicate that 21% of the studies consider moderating effects. Business scholars have been paying a lot of attention to the use of moderation in model creation and testing (Farooq & Vij, 2017). The impact of a third variable on the relationship between two variables is referred to as moderating effect (Dawson, 2013). The third variable is known as a moderator, and it determines when particular impacts will persist (Baron & Kenny, 1986). The moderating impacts emerge both internally and externally in general, albeit moderators differ depending on the theoretical backgrounds of the researchers. The influence of an independent variable (predictor) on a dependent variable (criterion) as a function of a third, moderating variable is interpreted as moderation (Baron & Kenny, 1986). As a result, the moderator influences the direction as well as the strength of the predictor-criterion association. Most of the past researchers have considered the moderating effects of board diversity (Campanella *et al.*, 2020; Qureshi *et al.*, 2019), employee board representation (Nekhili *et al.*, 2020), financial slack (Aguilera-Caracuel *et al.*, 2014; Surroca *et al.*, 2009; Waddock & Graves, 1997), international diversification and total quality management (Duque-Grisales & Aguilera-Caracuel, 2021) while analysing the ESG-CFP linkages.

Mediating Variables

The transmission of the criterion's effect on the predictor through one or more additional variables (mediators), is referred to as mediating effects. Mediators describe how external physical events take on internal psychological significance and discuss how and why such effects happens (Baron and Kenny, 1986). There is only one study that considered the mediating impact of Corporate Social Responsibility (CSR) Committee (Martinez-Ferrero *et al.*, 2020).

Dependent Variables

Finally, since the objective of the study is to determine the ESG-CFP relationship, the dependent variable in most of the studies is CFP (Dong *et al.*, 2022; Saygili, *et al.*, 2022; Zhou *et al.*, 2022; Chen *et al.*, 2021; Daszynska-Zygadlo *et al.*, 2020). The dependent variables is the variable being tested and measured in an experiment, and is 'dependent' on the independent variable.

The choice of firms to integrate ESG practices often has positive effects in terms of reduced costs, improved product quality and higher customer satisfaction (Magon *et al.*, 2018). These benefits often lead to improved firm performance; in fact, some studies have found that ESG practices have a positive and significant impact on return on assets (Almeyda and Darmansya, 2019) as well as on competitive advantage and corporate reputation (Alsayegh *et al.*, 2020; Chen *et al.*, 2015; Zhai *et al.*, 2018). According to others, however, integrating ESG practices does not necessarily improve corporate profitability, due to the high investment costs in R&D that the path to sustainability requires (Buallay, 2019).

Table 4.4: Variables Investigated in the Review Articles

Characteristics/ Variables	**Articles**	**Articles (%)**	**Examples**
Independent Variables			
ESG Related			
Environmental Social Governance Composite Scores	21	37%	Dong *et al.*, 2022; Zhou *et al.*, 2022; Chen *et al.*, 2021; Eliwa *et al.*, 2021; Feng & Wu, 2021; Kabir Hassan *et al.*, 2021; Reber *et al.*, 2021; Yoon *et al.*, 2021; Kim & Lee, 2020; Buallay *et al.*, 2021; Daszynska-Zygadlo *et al.*, 2020; Pirtea *et al.*, 2021; Nekhili *et al.*, 2021; Shahbaz *et al.*, 2020; Miralles-Quiros *et al.*, 2019; Minutolo; Nekhili, Boukadhaba, Nagati, *et al.*, 2021; *et al.*, 2019; Aboud & Diab, 2019; Brogi & Lagasio, 2019; Xie *et al.*, 2019; Sultana *et al.*, 2018; Limkriangkrai *et al.*, 2017
Environmental Social & Governance Scores (Individually)	5	9%	Yoon *et al.*, 2021; Kim & Lee, 2020; Buallay *et al.*, 2021; Shahbaz *et al.*, 2020; Limkriangkrai *et al.*, 2017

(Contd.)

Characteristics/ Variables	Articles	Articles (%)	Examples
Firm Performance Related			
Free Cash Flows	1	2%	Chams *et al.*, 2021
Tobin's Q	2	4%	Chams *et al.*, 2021; Qureshi *et al.*, 2021
Market-to-book Ratio	1	2%	Qureshi *et al.*, 2021
Book Value Per Share of Stocks	1	2%	Miralles-Quiros *et al.*, 2019
Financial Leverage	2	4%	Giannarakis *et al.*, 2014
Earnings Per Share	1	2%	Miralles-Quiros *et al.*, 2019
Return on Equity	1	2%	Qureshi *et al.*, 2021
Return on Assets	1	2%	Qureshi *et al.*, 2021
Other Variables			
Board Diversity	3	5%	Shahbaz *et al.*, 2020; Dong *et al.*, 2022; Martinez-Ferrero *et al.*, 2020
Sustainability Scores (Different 21 parameters like Environmental Disclosure Score, Stakeholder policy, Stakeholder participation in management, Human resources policy, Relations with customers and suppliers)	1	2%	Saygili, *et al.*, 2022

(*Contd.*)

Characteristics/ Variables	**Articles**	**Articles (%)**	**Examples**
Chief Financial Officer Compensation	1	2%	Profitlich *et al.*, 2021
Director's Liability and other related variables	1	2%	Melis & Rombi, 2021
Corporate Controversies	1	2%	Nirino *et al.*, 2021
Percentage of Women Directors	2	4%	Shakil *et al.*, 2021; Araissi *et al.*, 2016
Religiosity	1	2%	Terzani & Turzo, 2020
Materiality/ Immateriality of ESG	1	2%	Kim & Lee, 2020
Corporate Social Irresponsibility Coverage	1	2%	Kolbel *et al.*, 2017
Altman's Z Score	1	2%	Chan *et al.*, 2017
CEO Duality	1	2%	Giannarakis *et al.*, 2014
Greenhouse Gas Emissions	1	2%	Giannarakis *et al.*, 2014
KZ Index	1	2%	Chan *et al.*, 2017
Economic Policy Uncertainty	1	2%	Vural-Yavas, 2021
Moderating Variables			
Total Quality Management	1	2%	Chams *et al.*, 2021
Environmental Social Governance Composite Scores	1	2%	Qureshi *et al.*, 2021

(*Contd.*)

Characteristics/ Variables	Articles	Articles (%)	Examples
Environmental Social & Governance Scores (Individually)	1	2%	Qureshi *et al.*, 2021
Financial Slack	1	2%	Duque-Grisales & Aguilera-Caracuel, 2021
Geographical International Diversification	1	2%	Duque-Grisales & Aguilera-Caracuel, 2021
ESG Controversies	1	2%	Shakil *et al.*, 2021
Labour board representation and Employee-shareholder board representation	1	2%	Nekhili *et al.*, 2021
Competition	1	2%	Vural-Yavas, 2021
Franchising Strategy	1	2%	Kim & Lee, 2020
Employee Board Representation	2	4%	Nekhili, Boukadhaba, Nagati, *et al.*, 2021
Investment Horizon	1	2%	Sultana *et al.*, 2018
Mediating Variables			
CSR Committee	1	2%	Martinez-Ferrero *et al.*, 2020
Dependent Variables			
Firm Performance Related			
Tobin's Q	11	19%	Dong *et al.*, 2022; Saygili, *et al.*, 2022; Zhou *et al.*, 2022; Chen *et al.*, 2021; Daszynska-Zygadlo *et al.*, 2020; Nekhili *et al.*, 2021; Shahbaz *et al.*, 2020; Kim & Lee, 2020; Miralles-Quiros *et al.*, 2019; Nekhili, Boukadhaba, Nagati, *et al.*, 2021; Xie *et al.*, 2019

(*Contd.*)

Characteristics/ Variables	**Articles**	**Articles (%)**	**Examples**
Return on Assets	12	21%	Saygili, *et al.*, 2022; Chen *et al.*, 2021; Kim & Lee, 2020; Buallay *et al.*, 2021; Chen *et al.*, 2021; Daszynska-Zygadlo *et al.*, 2020; Pirtea *et al.*, 2021; Shahbaz *et al.*, 2020; Miralles-Quiros *et al.*, 2019; Aboud & Diab, 2019; Brogi & Lagasio, 2019; Xie *et al.*, 2019
Return on Equity	3	5%	Chen *et al.*, 2021; Buallay *et al.*, 2021; Pirtea *et al.*, 2021
Return on Net Assets	1	2%	Chen *et al.*, 2021
Return on Invested Capital	1	2%	Chen *et al.*, 2021
Cost of Debt	2	4%	Eliwa *et al.*, 2021; Feng & Wu, 2021
Market Risks -Total Market Risk, Idiosyncratic Risk, Systematic Risk	1	2%	Kabir Hassan *et al.*, 2021
Volatility -Total Volatility, Idiosyncratic Volatility	1	2%	Reber *et al.*, 2021
Degree of Tax Avoidance -BTD (Difference between net income and taxable income)	1	2%	Yoon *et al.*, 2021
Customised Credit Rating Scale	1	2%	Kim & Lee, 2020

(*Contd.*)

Characteristics/ Variables	Articles	Articles (%)	Examples
Compensation - Total compensation, Performance based compensation	1	2%	Melis & Rombi, 2021
Financial Risk	1	2%	Kolbel *et al.*, 2017
Corporate Financing decisions	1	2%	Limkriangkrai *et al.*, 2017
Stock Returns	2	4%	Limkriangkrai *et al.*, 2017; Araissi *et al.*, 2016
EBIT	1	2%	Pirtea *et al.*, 2021
Stock Prices	1	2%	Miralles-Quiros *et al.*, 2019
Bid-Ask Spread	1	2%	Aboud & Diab, 2019
Corporate Efficiency	1	2%	Xie *et al.*, 2019
Investment Decision	1	2%	Sultana *et al.*, 2018
Not Specified	1	2%	Nirino *et al.*, 2021
ESG Related			
Environmental Social Governance Composite Scores	8	14%	Profitlich *et al.*, 2021; Chams *et al.*, 2021; Shakil *et al.*, 2021; Martinez-Ferrero *et al.*, 2020; Terzani & Turzo, 2020; Vural-Yavas, 2021; Shahbaz *et al.*, 2020; Giannarakis *et al.*, 2014
Environmental Social & Governance Scores (Individually)	4	7%	Chams *et al.*, 2021; Vural-Yavas, 2021; Shahbaz *et al.*, 2020; Giannarakis *et al.*, 2014
CSR	1	2%	Chan *et al.*, 2017

Methodology

In this section, we assess the methodological aspects of the research articles studying the ESG-CFP relationship, in terms of the research approach undertaken (quantitative or qualitative) and the analytical methods that have been employed to investigate the relationship between the variables. Table 4.5 and 4.6 present the overview of the findings. Our review indicates that more than 80% of the studies are based on quantitative approaches. Furthermore, very few studies have used qualitative approaches (Table 4.5). Our review further indicates that regression analysis is the most used analytical method such as multiple regression.

Table 4.5: Research Approach Employed in the Review Articles

Research Approach	Articles	Articles (%)	Examples
Quantitative	48		
Secondary Data	46	81%	Dong *et al.*, 2022; Saygili, *et al.*, 2022; Zhou *et al.*, 2022; Linnenluecke, 2022; Profitlich *et al.*, 2021; Chen *et al.*, 2021; Eliwa *et al.*, 2021; Feng & Wu, 2021; Kabir Hassan *et al.*, 2021; Sepulveda-Alzate *et al.*, 2021; Chams *et al.*, 2021; Reber *et al.*, 2021; Yoon *et al.*, 2021; Kim & Lee, 2020; Qureshi *et al.*, 2021; Garzón Jiménez & Zorio-Grima, 2021; Buallay *et al.*, 2021; Melis & Rombi, 2021; Daszynska-Zygadlo *et al.*, 2020; Pirtea *et al.*, 2021; Shakil *et al.*, 2021; Martinez-Ferrero *et al.*, 2020; Terzani & Turzo, 2020; Nekhili *et al.*, 2021; Shahbaz *et al.*, 2020; Uyar *et al.*, 2020; Kim & Lee, 2020; Miralles-Quiros *et al.*, 2019; Minutolo *et al.*, 2019; Aboud & Diab, 2019; Giese *et al.*, 2019; Nekhili, Boukadhaba, Nagati, *et al.*, 2021
Survey (Primary)	1	2%	Isaksson & Woodside, 2016
Mix (Both Primary and Secondary)	1	2%	Cubas-Díaz & Martínez Sedano, 2018
Qualitative	9	16%	
Primary Data	2	4%	Khemir, 2019; Eccles *et al.*, 2020
Secondary Data	7	12%	Tilba, 2022; Li *et al.*, 2021; D.Z.X. Huang, 2021; Lagasio & Cucari, 2019; Busch *et al.*, 2016; Gillan *et al.*, 2021; Huang, 2022

Table 4.6. Research Methods Employed in the Review Articles

Research Method	Articles	Articles (%)	Examples
Linear Regression	4	7%	Zhou *et al.*, 2022; Buallay *et al.*, 2021; Melis & Rombi, 2021; Xie *et al.*, 2019
Multiple Regression	15	26%	Profitlich *et al.*, 2021; Kim & Lee, 2020; Daszynska-Zygadlo *et al.*, 2020; Duque-Grisales & Aguilera-Caracuel, 2021; Daszynska-Zygadlo *et al.*, 2020; Pirtea *et al.*, 2021; Shakil *et al.*, 2021; Martinez-Ferrero *et al.*, 2020; Vural-Yavas, 2021; Shah; Kim & Lee *et al.*, 2020; Uyar *et al.*, 2020; Miralles-Quiros *et al.*, 2019; Minutolo *et al.*, 2019; Brogi & Lagasio, 2019; Kolbel *et al.*, 2017
Generalised Method of Moments	5	9%	Dong *et al.*, 2022; Garzón Jiménez & Zorio-Grima, 2021; Nekhili *et al.*, 2021; Nekhili, Boukadhaba, Nagati, *et al.*, 2021;
Panel Vector Autoregressive Model	2	4%	Chen *et al.*, 2021; Qureshi *et al.*, 2021
Pooled Ordinary Least Squares Regression	5	9%	Eliwa *et al.*, 2021; Kabir Hassan *et al.*, 2021; Yoon *et al.*, 2021; Nirino *et al.*, 2021; Aboud & Diab, 2019
Logistic Regression	3	5%	Feng & Wu, 2021; Melis & Rombi, 2021; Chan *et al.*, 2017
Principal Component Analysis	3	5%	Sepulveda-Alzate *et al.*, 2021; Terzani & Turzo, 2020; Girerd-Potin *et al.*, 2012
Structural Equation Modelling	2	4%	Pirtea *et al.*, 2021; Sultana *et al.*, 2018
Distributed Lag Regression Methodology	1	2%	Chams *et al.*, 2021
Regression Residual	1	2%	Reber *et al.*, 2021
Barra Long-Term Global Equity Model (GEMLT)	1	2%	Giese *et al.*, 2019
Pearson correlation	1	2%	Garcia-Blandon *et al.*, 2019
Kruskal-Wallis and Mann-Whitney tests	1	2%	Garcia-Blandon *et al.*, 2019
Data Envelopment Analysis	1	2%	Xie *et al.*, 2019

(*Contd.*)

Research Method	Articles	Articles (%)	Examples
Non-Parametric Regression	1	2%	Xie *et al.*, 2019
Expectation Maximization (EM) clustering and the Bayesian Network classifiers with Tree Augmented Naïve Bayes (BN-TAN) Partial Least Square (PLS)	1	2%	Jitmaneeroj *et al.*, 2016
Fama and French 3-factor model in realized	1	2%	Araissi *et al.*, 2016
Hausman-Taylor	1	2%	Saygili, *et al.*, 2022
Conceptual Papers	7	12%	Tilba, 2022; Gillan *et al.*, 2021; Khemir, 2019; Eccles *et al.*, 2020; D.Z.X. Huang, 2021; Lagasio & Cucari, 2019; Busch *et al.*, 2016

Future Research Agenda

The above review has improved our understanding as to how the literature on ESG-CFP has evolved over the past 9 years. Based on this systematic literature review, we now propose the future research agenda within each domain of TCCM framework, i.e., theory, context, characteristics, and methodology. There is a dearth of research that investigates the impact that innovation has on the ESG-CFP relationship, with the exception of a couple of studies (Coluccia *et al.*, 2020; Chouaibi, S., & Chouaibi, 2021). Finally, we propose a conceptual framework offering the future direction to the research scholars, to explore -How do *"innovation"* moderates the ESG-CFP relationship?

Theory

Our review indicates that researchers have used various sustainability theories to explain the ESG-CFP relationship like Stakeholders Theory, Stewardship Theory, Agency Theory, Legitimacy theory, and Slack Resource based theory. However, the above-mentioned theories do not capture the peculiarities of ESG-CFP relationship. Therefore, further collabourations across management, finance, accounting, marketing, sociology, psychology, philosophy, anthropology, economics and political science theories have the prospects to enlarge our understanding of the complicated trade-offs arising from undertaking ESG activities. For instance, merging portfolio theory and stakeholder theory can help in revealing the ideal level of diversification required across the ESG portfolios. Similarly, impression management theories from sociology and social psychology can be used with stakeholders' theory that can help in estimating the level of influence the strategic use of ESG/Sustainability reporting as a public relations vehicle can be on external stakeholder perceptions.

From the review of extant literature, we observe that the literature has obscured the inclusion of innovation in examining the ESG-CFP relationship. Research and development (R&D) investments and their effective implementation are usually considered critical for firms' success, as they can increase a company's uniqueness (Gobble, 2012). In particular, the investment of financial resources in R&D activities could result in innovations leading to new or updated organizational/ production processes and products able to responding better to all internal and external stakeholders' social and environmental concerns coupled with financial ones (Gallego Álvarez *et al.*, 2011; McWilliams & Siegel, 2000). Several innovation theories and frameworks, such as "The Three Horizons of Growth Model by McKinsey & Company" and "The Technology Adoption Lifecycle", can be applied to the study of the ESG-CFP connection. Given their usefulness in explaining the economic and psychological phenomena associated with disruptive technologies, these theories and models see extensive application in the marketing literature. Our findings suggest that the McKinsey & Company's Three Horizons of Growth Model and the Technology Adoption Lifecycle should be adopted by the academic community moving forward. Companies often experience stagnating growth as they age because their innovative spirit gives way to complacency. Maintaining a steady rate of growth over the course of a company's existence requires management attention to both the present and the future of the organisation. In order to evaluate future growth chances without ignoring current performance, businesses might use the three horizons approach. Business activities in Horizon one is the primary sources of revenue and profit for the corporation. In this case, maximising what's left of the value is the primary goal, so that better performance is the focus. The second horizon is made up of up-and-coming entrepreneurial initiatives that have the potential to yield large profits in the long run but may need a considerable initial financial outlay. Ideas for future profitable expansion can be found in horizon three, including things like pilot programmes, minority holdings in startups, and research projects. Business sustainability requires simultaneous management across the three time periods (McKinsey, 2009). The Technology Adoption Lifecycle provides a description of consumer behaviour in relation to the acceptance of a new product or service, and is frequently divided into innovators, early adopters, early majority, late majority, and laggards, all of whom can be useful in evaluating the ESG-CFP link (Gainsight, n.d.). Organizations can tailor their ESG efforts to the needs of their specific clientele.

Context

Our review indicates that a significant portion of the literature investigated ESG-CFP relationship in developed and politically stable countries (Aerts *et al.*, 2008; Harjoto and Jo, 2015; Richardson and Welker, 2001; Yadav *et al.*, 2016; Plumlee *et al.*, 2015), and very few studies focused on emerging markets in general (Akrout and Ben Othman, 2016; Malarvizhi and Matta, 2016; Siagian *et al.*, 2013; Aboud and Diab, 2018; Barako and Brown, 2008; De Villiers and Van Staden, 2006)[1]. The authors of the present work believe that emerging markets, with their idiosyncrasies in terms of cultural specificity and political volatility, merit special interest.

Characteristics

Research on ESG-CFP has gained traction in the recent past. Most of the prior research studies have considered ESG as an independent variable and CFP as the dependent variable to analyse the ESG-CFP relationship. The researchers examined how ESG activities affected firm financial performance under the presumption that causation could not go in the other direction. Due to the restricted generalizability caused by this incorrect assumption, academics should investigate the causal relationship between ESG and CFP, using CFP as the independent variable. Therefore, future study should focus on determining whether CFP is driven by ESG or ESG is driven by CFP. Furthermore, we believe that besides the above-mentioned independent and moderating variables, there are some other variables that demand attention in this research field. For example, except for a few studies (Coluccia *et al.*, 2020; Ruggiero & Cupertino, 2018; J. Chouaibi, 2020), there is scant literature exploring the impact of innovation on ESG-CFP relationship. Indeed, achieving and improving ESG performance requires firms to invest in R&D (Triguero *et al.*, 2018). Innovation represents the tool most companies use to initiate their sustainable change path, addressing earnings management, corporate social responsibility, accountability and transparency (Lombardi & Secundo, 2020), by adopting innovations that take into account the three dimensions of sustainability, i.e. ESG. This ultimately gives researchers more room to investigate the nature of this connection in the years to come. When a company starts reporting on larger, non-financial indicators, it quickly realises it needs to create objectives to manage them, and that this in turn requires it to drive change, or transformation, to achieve them. As ESG has become a standard requirement for all businesses, the question arises, "How can businesses and organisations differentiate themselves further through ESG?" The missing letter I, standing for innovation, holds the key. Innovation is the primary factor in advancing ESG and helping businesses realise their ESG objectives. In both the public and private sectors, the current level of attention paid to ESG would not have been possible without innovation (RSM US, n.d.). Technically, operationally, and executively, engineers are in a prime position to lead this innovation and assist their organisations, clients, and communities in making substantial progress towards adopting ESG standards. This agenda for innovation is not distinct from ongoing digital revolutions; rather, it will inform and build upon them, altering the context in which they occur. Senior leaders play a crucial role in driving this agenda (and their purpose). The degree to which a given business needs to adapt to its environment varies from one to the next. In the end, the agenda will include reporting, strategic, and business innovation initiatives, regardless of the initial impetus, be it an ambitious emissions target inspiring strategic reinvention, a deal to exit or restructure an unsustainable business, ambitious diversity, equity, and inclusion goals, or a supply chain overhaul.

Methodology

The widely used methodology in ESG-CFP research includes regression analysis, review papers and structure equation modelling. However, the other methods remain unexplored in the area of ESG-CFP study. Future research can also integrate mixed-method approaches, data collection approach and analytical tools, while studying the effects or relationship of antecedents on outcomes. Mixed method allows researchers to capitalize on the strength of both qualitative and quantitative approaches and help in addressing the problem with sufficient depth and breadth (Dawadi *et al.*, 2021; Malina *et al.*, 2011; Leech & Onwuegbuzie, 2010). We feel that a mixed-method approach will help to explain the underlying topic with adequate depth and breadth, as ESG-CFP is a relatively underexplored study area, particularly with regard to the factors affecting the ESG-CFP relationship. To better understand the elements that influence business managers' and investors' ESG plans, a qualitative technique will be used to conduct in-depth interviews. To further investigate the effect of the indicated components on the ESG-CFP link, a regression analysis can be conducted.

We conclude that "innovation's" moderating influence is an essential factor in analysing the ESG-CFP connection. Fig. 4.4 depicts these interconnections between several variables. Using the above-mentioned recommendations for future research, we have attempted to develop a conceptual framework for studying the link between ESG and CFP, one that takes into account the potential moderating effect of innovation. Corporations can use the proposed framework to integrate measures of both monetary and non-monetary corporate performance into their operational strategy and management practices.

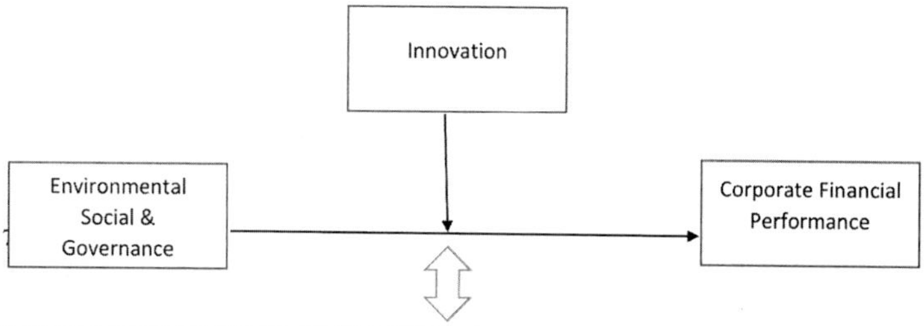

Stakeholders Theory	Agency Theory	The Three Horizons of Growth Model by McKinsey & Company
Legitimacy Theory	Trade off Theory	Technology Adoption Lifecycle

Fig. 4.4: Conceptual Framework.

Conclusion

In order to examine the ESG-CFP relationship, we conducted a systematic literature review that included 57 articles published over a period of nine years (2014-2022). A two-step methodology encompassing PRISMA guidelines and TCCM framework was being employed. This systematic review using TCCM analysis helped in identifying the most influential theories, contexts, characteristics and methodologies in the current ESG-CFP literature. The findings of the TCCM analysis demonstrate that ESG-CFP is an emerging research area where considerable number of publications have increased. TCCM analysis helps in identifying two major theories that are used in the ESG-CFP research stream that are, "Stakeholder theory" and "Legitimacy theory". Furthermore, developing nations like India and China have made a very little contribution in the area of ESG-CFP. As a result, it emphasises the need for researchers' scholars from emerging countries to make more noteworthy contributions to the core literature on ESG-CFP. Moreover, the review indicates that the majority of previous research has focused on analysing the influence of ESG activities on CFP, with the underlying premise being that causality cannot flow in the opposite direction. In future, more comprehensive studies need to be undertaken for an in-depth exploration of the impact of CFP on ESG, thus taking CFP as the independent variable. Given the complexities of the ESG-CFP association, it is vital for future scholars to assess the impact of various moderating or mediating variables that can have a substantial impact on ESG-CFP linkages—we recommend more research into sustainability-driven compensation policies, intangible resources and capabilities, stakeholder relations, firm characteristics, firm governance, and so on. Future research directions on each of the TCCM component is also provided that will aid researchers, academicians, and managers in gaining a detailed and complete picture of the ESG-CFP relationship. Furthermore, the study proposes a conceptual framework where "innovation" is highlighted as an important moderating variable to be considered while determining the ESG-CFP relationship. Given the fact that the number of publications has increased significantly since 2015, clearly this is an upcoming research area where we should expect to see improved and better-quality research in future. The study can serve to be informative and actionable to formulate new cutting-edge ESG-CFP strategies in future.

Implications

The study's findings are useful for academics, managers, and policymakers due to a dearth of research in the ESG-CFP field in developing nations.

Theoretical implications

From a theoretical standpoint, this work offers numerous insights. This is one of the earliest studies to employ TCCM analysis in its pursuit of ESG-CFP knowledge. Important theories, contexts, characteristics, and research techniques for ESG-CFP are also discussed and analysed in depth. The significance of "innovation" in the link between ESG and CFP is demonstrated by the study. This research can serve as a springboard for more investigations based on TCCM, illuminating avenues for future investigation in this dynamic and expanding field. Young scholars interested in ESG-CFP will also find it to be a valuable resource. The need of continuing to investigate the expanding ESG-CFP research topic has been highlighted in the TCCM analysis, results, and discussion sections.

Practical implications

For businesses, the evidence is helpful in establishing the criteria to identify important ESG-CFP issues that can support their strategic decisions. The insights can further assist managers in locating the key ESG-CFP indicators that are most suitable for transforming their firm into a more profitable and sustainable organisation. The results of the study would further push ESG Practitioners, Policymakers, and Regulators, and think tanks to rethink and prioritise as to which ESG-CFP areas are to be addressed first. They should develop such norms or codes for best ESG practices that would respond to the expanding need for good ESG structures. The accounting of environmental, social, and governance (ESG) impacts should be required by law so that impact performance may be monitored and compared in a manner analogous to that of financial performance. In order to make adoption of ESG standards more widespread, the government will need to take action in the form of legislation or regulation. As European and American regulators have started working on regulatory frameworks, there are some hopeful indicators that have been emerging so far. In conclusion, the findings of this study have relevance for all participants in the financial market. These participants include investors, asset managers, analysts, financial advisors, and consultants. The research will assist these individuals in better comprehending and evaluating ESG-CFP trends as well as the potential consequences of these trends. This won't be achievable if companies don't reveal enough information about these factors in their filings.

Social implications

Examining how various ESG-CFP dimensions influence the ESG-CFP decisions of businesses is a beneficial and enlightening endeavour for all community participants. Companies can use these findings to improve the quality of their financial reporting, the extent to which they disclose ESG information, and their ability to comply with ESG legislation. The research aims to shed light on the possible effects of ESG disclosure for firms, which in turn will help local, national, and global communities improve their social environments and mitigate the effects of climate change.

Limitations

There are several limitations to this study. We started by conducting a systematic literature review, which could have some subjective biases because different researchers have various cognitive structures, which could lead to outcomes that are inconsistent. More statistical techniques, such meta-analysis, can be used in the future to overcome this issue and help establish a more thorough understanding of the underlying study field. Second, for the purpose of the research, a total of only 57 papers were considered. In order to carry out a study that is both comprehensive and all-encompassing, subsequent scholars may choose to concentrate on a larger collection of papers. Thirdly, even though the author used a multitude of pertinent keyword combinations to select research articles from the Web of Science database, it is possible that the author missed some terms, thereby omitting some relevant publications. This is a possibility despite the fact that the author used a multitude of relevant keyword combinations. Lastly, errors in data extraction and miscalculations could have been caused by the author's inability to extract information and data from the selected papers in an accurate and appropriate manner, which could have led to the selection of papers that were not representative of the population being studied.

References

Aboud, A., & Diab, A. (2019). The financial and market consequences of environmental, social and governance ratings: The implications of recent political volatility in Egypt. *Sustainability Accounting, Management and Policy Journal, 10(3)*, 498-520. https://doi.org/10.1108/SAMPJ-06-2018-0167

Agarwal, N.D., & Kumar, V.V.R. (2020). Three decades of green advertising—a review of literature and bibliometric analysis. *Benchmarking: An International Journal, ahead-of-print.* https://doi.org/10.1108/bij-07-2020-0380

A legal framework for the integration of environmental, social and governance issues into institutional investment (2005). Freshfields Bruckhaus Deringer. https://www.unepfi.org/publications/investment-publications/a-legal-framework-for-the-integration-of-environmental-social-and-governance-issues-into-institutional-investment/

Almeyda, R., & Darmansya, A. (2019). The Influence of Environmental, Social, and Governance (ESG) Disclosure on Firm Financial Performance. *IPTEK*

Journal of Proceedings Series, 5, 278. https://doi.org/10.12962/j23546026.y2019i5.6340

Al-Shaer, H., & Zaman, M. (2017). CEO Compensation and Sustainability Reporting Assurance: Evidence from the UK. *Journal of Business Ethics, 1*, 233-252. https://doi.org/10.1007/s10551-017-3735-8

Araissi, M., Dah, M.A., & Jizi, M. (2016). Women on Boards, Sustainability Reporting and Firm Performance. *SSRN Electronic Journal*. https://doi.org/10.2139/ssrn.2990370

Bassen, A., Meyer, K., & Schlange, J. (2006). The Influence of Corporate Responsibility on the Cost of Capital. *SSRN Electronic Journal*. https://doi.org/10.2139/ssrn.984406

Battisti, E., Miglietta, N., Nirino, N., & Villasalero Diaz, M. (2019). Value creation, innovation practice, and competitive advantage. *European Journal of Innovation Management, 2*, 273-290. https://doi.org/10.1108/ejim-09-2018-0211

Battisti, E., Nirino, N., Leonidou, E., & Thrassou, A. (2022). Corporate venture capital and CSR performance: An extended resource based view's perspective. *Journal of Business Research*, 1058-1066. https://doi.org/10.1016/j.jbusres.2021.10.054

Baughn, C.C., (Dusty) Bodie, N.L., & McIntosh, J.C. (2007). Corporate social and environmental responsibility in Asian countries and other geographical regions. *Corporate Social Responsibility and Environmental Management, 4*, 189-205. https://doi.org/10.1002/csr.160

Behl, A., Kumari, P.S.R., Makhija, H., & Sharma, D. (2021). Exploring the relationship of ESG score and firm value using cross-legged panel analyses: case of the Indian energy sector. *Annals of Operations Research, 1*, 231-256. https://doi.org/10.1007/s10479-021-04189-8

Belyaeva, Z., Shams, S.M.R., Santoro, G., & Grandhi, B. (2020). Unpacking stakeholder relationship management in the public and private sectors: the comparative insights. *EuroMed Journal of Business, 3*, 269-281. https://doi.org/10.1108/emjb-06-2019-0085

Benlemlih, M., Shaukat, A., Qiu, Y., & Trojanowski, G. (2016). Environmental and Social Disclosures and Firm Risk. *Journal of Business Ethics, 3*, 613-626. https://doi.org/10.1007/s10551-016-3285-5

Berrone, P., & Gomez-Mejia, L.R. (2009). Environmental Performance and Executive Compensation: An Integrated Agency-Institutional Perspective. *Academy of Management Journal, 1*, 103-126. https://doi.org/10.5465/amj.2009.36461950

Broadstock, D.C., Chan, K., Cheng, L.T.W., & Wang, X. (2021). The role of ESG performance during times of financial crisis: Evidence from COVID-19 in China. *Finance Research Letters*, 101716. https://doi.org/10.1016/j.frl.2020.101716

Brogi, M., & Lagasio, V. (2019). Environmental, social, and governance and company profitability: Are financial intermediaries different? *Corporate Social Responsibility and Environmental Management, 26(3)*, 576-587. https://doi.org/10.1002/csr.1704

Buallay, A. (2019). Is sustainability reporting (ESG) associated with performance? Evidence from the European banking sector. *Management of Environmental Quality: An International Journal, 1*, 98-115. https://doi.org/10.1108/meq-12-2017-0149

Busch, T., Bauer, R., & Orlitzky, M. (2016). Sustainable Development and Financial Markets: Old Paths and New Avenues. *Business & Society, 55(3)*, 303-329. https://doi.org/10.1177/0007650315570701

Chams, N., García-Blandón, J., & Hassan, K. (2021). Role Reversal! Financial Performance as an Antecedent of ESG: The Moderating Effect of Total Quality Management. *Sustainability, 13*, 7026. https://doi.org/10.3390/su13137026

Chan, C.Y., Chou, D.W., & Lo, H.C. (2017). Do financial constraints matter when firms engage in CSR? *The North American Journal of Economics and Finance, 39*, 241-259. https://doi.org/10.1016/j.najef.2016.10.009

Chauhan, Y., & Kumar, S.B. (2018). Do investors value the non-financial disclosure in emerging markets? *Emerging Markets Review*, 32-46. https://doi.org/10.1016/j.ememar.2018.05.001

Chen, L., Yuan, T., Cebula, R.J., Shuangjin, W., & Foley, M. (2021). Fulfillment of ESG Responsibilities and Firm Performance: A Zero-Sum Game or Mutually Beneficial. *Sustainability, 13(19)*, 10954. https://doi.org/10.3390/su131910954

Cheng, B., Ioannou, I., & Serafeim, G. (2013). Corporate social responsibility and access to finance. *Strategic Management Journal, 1*, 1-23. https://doi.org/10.1002/smj.2131

Chouaibi, S., & Chouaibi, J. (2021). Social and ethical practices and firm value: the moderating effect of green innovation: evidence from international ESG data. *International Journal of Ethics and Systems, 3*, 442-465. https://doi.org/10.1108/ijoes-12-2020-0203

Claassen, D., & Ricci, C. (2015). CEO compensation structure and corporate social performance: Empirical evidence from Germany/CEO-Vergütungsstrukturen und Corporate Social Performance: Eine empirische Untersuchung deutscher Unternehmen. *Die Betriebswirtschaft, 75*(5), 327.

Coluccia, D., Dabiæ, M., Del Giudice, M., Fontana, S., & Solimene, S. (2020). R & amp; D innovation indicator and its effects on the market. An empirical assessment from a financial perspective. *Journal of Business Research*, 259-271. https://doi.org/10.1016/j.jbusres.2019.04.015

Combs, J.G., Crook, T.R., & Shook, C.L. (2005). The Dimensionality of Organizational Performance and its Implications for Strategic Management

Research. In *Research Methodology in Strategy and Management* (pp. 259-286). Emerald (MCB UP). http://dx.doi.org/10.1016/s1479-8387(05)02011-4

Cubas Díaz, M., & Martínez Sedano, M.Á. (2018). Measures for Sustainable Investment Decisions and Business Strategy—A Triple Bottom Line Approach. *Business Strategy and the Environment, 27(1)*, 16-38. https://doi.org/10.1002/bse.1980

Daszyńska-Zygadlo, K., Słoński, T., & Dziadkowiec, A. (2020). Corporate Social Performance and Financial Performance Relationship in Banks: Sub-Industry and Cross-Cultural Perspective. *Journal of Business Economics and Management, 2*, 424-444. https://doi.org/10.3846/jbem.2020.13892

Daugaard, D. (2019). Emerging new themes in environmental, social and governance investing: a systematic literature review. *Accounting & Finance, 2*, 1501-1530. https://doi.org/10.1111/acfi.12479

Dawadi, S., Shrestha, S., & Giri, R.A. (2021). Mixed-Methods Research: A Discussion on its Types, Challenges, and Criticisms. *Journal of Practical Studies in Education, 2*, 25-36. https://doi.org/10.46809/jpse.v2i2.20

Dobers, P., & Halme, M. (2009). Corporate social responsibility and developing countries. *Corporate Social Responsibility and Environmental Management, 5*, 237-249. https://doi.org/10.1002/csr.212

Dong, Y., Liang, C., & Wanyin, Z. (2022). Board diversity and firm performance: Impact of ESG activities in China. *Economic Research-Ekonomska Istraživanja*, 1-18. https://doi.org/10.1080/1331677X.2022.2090406

Drempetic, S., Klein, C., & Zwergel, B. (2019). The Influence of Firm Size on the ESG Score: Corporate Sustainability Ratings Under Review. *Journal of Business Ethics, 2*, 333-360. https://doi.org/10.1007/s10551-019-04164-1

Duque-Grisales, E., & Aguilera-Caracuel, J. (2019). Environmental, Social and Governance (ESG) Scores and Financial Performance of Multilatinas: Moderating Effects of Geographic International Diversification and Financial Slack. *Journal of Business Ethics, 2*, 315-334. https://doi.org/10.1007/s10551-019-04177-w

Duque-Grisales, E., & Aguilera-Caracuel, J. (2021). Environmental, Social and Governance (ESG) Scores and Financial Performance of Multilatinas: Moderating Effects of Geographic International Diversification and Financial Slack. *Journal of Business Ethics, 168(2)*, 315-334. https://doi.org/10.1007/s10551-019-04177-w

Eccles, R.G., Lee, L.E., & Stroehle, J.C. (2020). The Social Origins of ESG: An Analysis of Innovest and KLD. *Organization & Environment, 33(4)*, 575-596. https://doi.org/10.1177/1086026619888994

Eliwa, Y., Aboud, A., & Saleh, A. (2021). ESG practices and the cost of debt: Evidence from EU countries. *Critical Perspectives on Accounting, 79*, 102097. https://doi.org/10.1016/j.cpa.2019.102097

Enduring Ideas: The three horizons of growth | McKinsey. (2009, December 1). McKinsey & Company; McKinsey & Company. https://www.mckinsey.com/

capabilities/strategy-and-corporate-finance/our-insights/enduring-ideas-the-three-horizons-of-growth

Environmental, Social, and Governance Theory—Competitive Enterprise Institute. (n.d.). Competitive Enterprise Institute; https://www.facebook.com/CompetitiveEnterpriseInstitute. Retrieved September 12, 2022, from https://cei.org/studies/environmental-social-and-governance-theory/

Falagas, M.E., Manta, K.G., Betsi, G.I., & Pappas, G. (2006). Infection-related morbidity and mortality in patients with connective tissue diseases: a systematic review. *Clinical Rheumatology, 5*, 663-670. https://doi.org/10.1007/s10067-006-0441-9

Fama, E.F. (2020). Contract costs, stakeholder capitalism, and ESG. *European Financial Management, 2*, 189-195. https://doi.org/10.1111/eufm.12297

Fama, E.F., & Jensen, M.C. (1998). Separation of Ownership and Control. *SSRN Electronic Journal.* https://doi.org/10.2139/ssrn.94034

Freeman, R.E. (1999). Response: Divergent Stakeholder Theory. *The Academy of Management Review, 2*, 233. https://doi.org/10.2307/259078

Friede, G., Busch, T., & Bassen, A. (2015). ESG and financial performance: aggregated evidence from more than 2000 empirical studies. *Journal of Sustainable Finance & amp; Investment, 4*, 210-233. https://doi.org/10.1080/20430795.2015.1118917

Friedman, M. (1970). The social responsibility of business is to increase its profits. *New York Time Magazine*, 32-33, September 13.

Gallego Álvarez, I., Manuel Prado Lorenzo, J., & García Sánchez, I. (2011). Corporate social responsibility and innovation: a resourcebased theory. *Management Decision, 10*, 1709-1727. https://doi.org/10.1108/00251741111183843

Garcia-Blandon, J., Argilés-Bosch, J.M., & Ravenda, D. (2019). Exploring the Relationship Between Ceo Characteristics and Performance. *Journal of Business Economics and Management, 6*, 1064-1082. https://doi.org/10.3846/jbem.2019.10447

Garzón Jiménez, R., & Zorio-Grima, A. (2021). Sustainability engagement in Latin America firms and cost of equity. *Academia Revista Latinoamericana de Administración, 2*, 224-243. https://doi.org/10.1108/arla-05-2020-0117

Giannarakis, G., Konteos, G., & Sariannidis, N. (2014). Financial, governance and environmental determinants of corporate social responsible disclosure. *Management Decision, 52(10)*, 1928-1951. https://doi.org/10.1108/MD-05-2014-0296

Giese, G., Lee, L.E., Melas, D., Nagy, Z., & Nishikawa, L. (2019). Foundations of ESG Investing: How ESG Affects Equity Valuation, Risk, and Performance. *The Journal of Portfolio Management, 45(5)*, 69-83. https://doi.org/10.3905/jpm.2019.45.5.069

Gillan, S.L., Koch, A., & Starks, L.T. (2021). Firms and social responsibility: A review of ESG and CSR research in corporate finance. *Journal of Corporate Finance, 66*, 101889. https://doi.org/10.1016/j.jcorpfin.2021.101889

Girerd-Potin, I., Jimenez-Garces, S., & Louvet, P. (2012). Which Dimensions of Social Responsibility Concern Financial Investors? *SSRN Electronic Journal.* https://doi.org/10.2139/ssrn.2079525

Gobble, M. M. (2012). Innovation and Strategy. *Research-Technology Management, 3*, 63-67. https://doi.org/10.5437/08956308x5503005

Goswami, M., & Goswami, A.K. (2022). A comprehensive examination of psychological capital research using bibliometric, TCCM and content analysis. *Benchmarking: An International Journal.* https://doi.org/10.1108/bij-10-2021-0586

Hernandez, M. (2007). Promoting Stewardship Behaviour in Organizations: A Leadership Model. *Journal of Business Ethics, 1*, 121-128. https://doi.org/10.1007/s10551-007-9440-2

Hoepner, A.G.F., & McMillan, D.G. (2009). Research on "Responsible Investment": An Influential Literature Analysis Comprising a Rating, Characterisation, Categorisation and Investigation. *SSRN Electronic Journal.* https://doi.org/10.2139/ssrn.1454793

Huang, D.Z. (2022). An integrated theory of the firm approach to environmental, social and governance performance. *Accounting & Finance, 62(S1)*, 1567-1598. https://doi.org/10.1111/acfi.12832

Huang, D.Z.X. (2021). Environmental, social and governance (ESG) activity and firm performance: A review and consolidation. *Accounting & Finance, 61(1)*, 335-360. https://doi.org/10.1111/acfi.12569

Isaksson, L.E., & Woodside, A.G. (2016). Modeling firm heterogeneity in corporate social performance and financial performance. *Journal of Business Research, 69(9)*, 3285-3314. https://doi.org/10.1016/j.jbusres.2016.02.021

Jensen, M. (2001). Value Maximisation, Stakeholder Theory, and the Corporate Objective Function. *European Financial Management, 3*, 297-317. https://doi.org/10.1111/1468-036x.00158

Jitmaneeroj, B. (2016). Reform priorities for corporate sustainability: Environmental, social, governance, or economic performance? *Management Decision, 54(6)*, 1497-1521. https://doi.org/10.1108/MD-11-2015-0505

Kabir Hassan, M., Chiaramonte, L., Dreassi, A., Paltrinieri, A., & Piserà, S. (2021). The crossroads of ESG and religious screening on firm risk. *Research in International Business and Finance, 58*, 101500. https://doi.org/10.1016/j.ribaf.2021.101500

Ketter, W., Padmanabhan, B., Pant, G., & Raghu, T.S. (2020). Special Issue Editorial: Addressing Societal Challenges through Analytics: An ESG ICE Framework and Research Agenda. *Journal of the Association for Information Systems, 5*, 1115-1127. https://doi.org/10.17705/1jais.00631

Khemir, S. (2019). Perception of ESG criteria by mainstream investors: evidence from Tunisia. *International Journal of Emerging Markets, 5*, 752-768. https://doi.org/10.1108/ijoem-05-2017-0172

Kim, B., & Lee, S. (2020). The impact of material and immaterial sustainability on firm performance: The moderating role of franchising strategy. *Tourism Management, 77*, 103999. https://doi.org/10.1016/j.tourman.2019.103999

Kölbel, J.F., Busch, T., & Jancso, L.M. (2017). How Media Coverage of Corporate Social Irresponsibility Increases Financial Risk. *Strategic Management Journal, 11*, 2266-2284. https://doi.org/10.1002/smj.2647

Kullenberg, C., & Kasperowski, D. (2016). What Is Citizen Science?—A Scientometric Meta-Analysis. *PLOS ONE, 1*, e0147152. https://doi.org/10.1371/journal.pone.0147152

Lagasio, V., & Cucari, N. (2019). Corporate governance and environmental social governance disclosure: A meta-analytical review. *Corporate Social Responsibility and Environmental Management, 4*, 701-711. https://doi.org/10.1002/csr.1716

Leech, N.L., & Onwuegbuzie, A.J. (2010). Guidelines for Conducting and Reporting Mixed Research in the Field of Counseling and Beyond. *Journal of Counseling & amp; Development, 1*, 61-69. https://doi.org/10.1002/j.1556-6678.2010.tb00151.x

Li, T.T., Wang, K., Sueyoshi, T., & Wang, D.D. (2021). ESG: Research Progress and Future Prospects. *Sustainability, 13(21)*, 11663. https://doi.org/10.3390/su132111663

Limkriangkrai, M., Koh, S., & Durand, R.B. (2017). Environmental, Social, and Governance (ESG) Profiles, Stock Returns, and Financial Policy: Australian Evidence: ESG Profiles, Returns, and Financial Policy. *International Review of Finance, 17(3)*, 461-471. https://doi.org/10.1111/irfi.12101

Linnenluecke, M.K. (2022). Environmental, social and governance (ESG) performance in the context of multinational business research. *Multinational Business Review, 30(1)*, 1-16. https://doi.org/10.1108/MBR-11-2021-0148

Liu, Y., Kim, C.Y., Lee, E.H., & Yoo, J.W. (2022). Relationship between Sustainable Management Activities and Financial Performance: Mediating Effects of Non-Financial Performance and Moderating Effects of Institutional Environment. *Sustainability, 3*, 1168. https://doi.org/10.3390/su14031168

Lombardi, R., & Secundo, G. (2020). The digital transformation of corporate reporting—a systematic literature review and avenues for future research. *Meditari Accountancy Research, 5*, 1179-1208. https://doi.org/10.1108/medar-04-2020-0870

Ma, H.Y., & Park, S.J. (2021). Relationship between Corporate Sustainability Management and Sustainable Tax Strategies. *Sustainability, 13*, 7429. https://doi.org/10.3390/su13137429

Magon, R.B., Thomé, A.M.T., Ferrer, A.L.C., & Scavarda, L.F. (2018). Sustainability and performance in operations management research. *Journal of Cleaner Production*, 104-117. https://doi.org/10.1016/j.jclepro.2018.04.140

Mahadevan, K., & Joshi, S. (2021). A Bibliometric Analysis of Trends in Electronic Service Quality Research Over Two Decades. *International*

Journal of Integrated Supply Management, 1, 1. https://doi.org/10.1504/ijism.2021.10035820

Malina, M.A., Nørreklit, H.S.O., & Selto, F.H. (2011). Lessons learned: advantages and disadvantages of mixed method research. *Qualitative Research in Accounting & amp; Management, 1*, 59-71. https://doi.org/10.1108/11766091111124702

Martínez Ferrero, J., Lozano, M.B., & Vivas, M. (2020). The impact of board cultural diversity on a firm's commitment towards the sustainability issues of emerging countries: The mediating effect of a CSR committee. *Corporate Social Responsibility and Environmental Management, 2*, 675-685. https://doi.org/10.1002/csr.2080

Masulis, R.W., & Reza, S.W. (2014). Agency Problems of Corporate Philanthropy. *Review of Financial Studies, 2*, 592-636. https://doi.org/10.1093/rfs/hhu082

McWilliams, A., & Siegel, D. (2000). Corporate social responsibility and financial performance: correlation or misspecification? *Strategic Management Journal, 5*, 603-609. https://doi.org/10.1002/(sici)1097-0266(200005)21:5<603::aid-smj101>3.0.co;2-3

Melis, A., & Rombi, L. (2021). Country-, firm-, and director-level risk and responsibilities and independent director compensation. *Corporate Governance: An International Review, 29*(3), 222-251. https://doi.org/10.1111/corg.12357

Minutolo, M.C., Kristjanpoller, W.D., & Stakeley, J. (2019). Exploring environmental, social, and governance disclosure effects on the S&P 500 financial performance. *Business Strategy and the Environment, 28*(6), 1083-1095. https://doi.org/10.1002/bse.2303

Miralles Quirós, M.M., Miralles Quirós, J.L., & Redondo Hernández, J. (2019). The impact of environmental, social, and governance performance on stock prices: Evidence from the banking industry. *Corporate Social Responsibility and Environmental Management*, csr.1759. https://doi.org/10.1002/csr.1759

Moher, D. (2009). Preferred Reporting Items for Systematic Reviews and Meta-Analyses: The PRISMA Statement. *Annals of Internal Medicine, 4*, 264. https://doi.org/10.7326/0003-4819-151-4-200908180-00135

Nekhili, M., Boukadhaba, A., & Nagati, H. (2021). The ESG-financial performance relationship: Does the type of employee board representation matter? *Corporate Governance: An International Review, 29(2)*, 134-161. https://doi.org/10.1111/corg.12345

Nekhili, M., Boukadhaba, A., Nagati, H., & Chtioui, T. (2021). ESG performance and market value: The moderating role of employee board representation. *The International Journal of Human Resource Management, 32(14)*, 3061-3087. https://doi.org/10.1080/09585192.2019.1629989

Nguyen, T.T.D. (2020). The Relationship Between Board of Directors and Sustainability Reporting: An Empirical Study in German Large Listed Firms.

Acta Universitatis Agriculturae et Silviculturae Mendelianae Brunensis, 1, 211-218. https://doi.org/10.11118/actaun202068010211

Nirino, N., Santoro, G., Miglietta, N., & Quaglia, R. (2021). Corporate controversies and company's financial performance: Exploring the moderating role of ESG practices. *Technological Forecasting and Social Change, 162*, 120341. https://doi.org/10.1016/j.techfore.2020.120341

Oh, H.M., Park, S.B., & Ma, H.Y. (2020). Corporate Sustainability Management, Earnings Transparency, and Chaebols. *Sustainability, 10*, 4222. https://doi.org/10.3390/su12104222

Orlitzky, M., Schmidt, F.L., & Rynes, S.L. (2003). Corporate Social and Financial Performance: A Meta-Analysis. *Organization Studies, 3*, 403-441. https://doi.org/10.1177/0170840603024003910

Paul, J., & Criado, A.R. (2020). The art of writing literature review: What do we know and what do we need to know? *International Business Review, 4*, 101717. https://doi.org/10.1016/j.ibusrev.2020.101717

Paul, J., & Rosado-Serrano, A. (2019). Gradual Internationalization vs. Born-Global/International new venture models. *International Marketing Review, 6*, 830-858. https://doi.org/10.1108/imr-10-2018-0280

Paul, J., Merchant, A., Dwivedi, Y.K., & Rose, G. (2021). Writing an impactful review article: What do we know and what do we need to know? *Journal of Business Research*, 337-340. https://doi.org/10.1016/j.jbusres.2021.05.005

Pirtea, M.G., Noja, G.G., Cristea, M., & Panait, M. (2021). Interplay between environmental, social and governance coordinates and the financial performance of agricultural companies. *Agricultural Economics (Zemědělská Ekonomika), 67* (No. 12), 479-490. https://doi.org/10.17221/286/2021-AGRICECON

Profitlich, M., Bouzzine, Y.D., & Lueg, R. (2021). The Relationship between CFO Compensation and Corporate Sustainability: An Empirical Examination of German Listed Firms. *Sustainability, 21*, 12299. https://doi.org/10.3390/su132112299

Revelli, C., & Viviani, J.L. (2014). Financial performance of socially responsible investing (SRI): what have we learned? A meta-analysis. *Business Ethics: A European Review, 2*, 158-185. https://doi.org/10.1111/beer.12076

Rey-Martí, A., Ribeiro-Soriano, D., & Palacios-Marqués, D. (2016). A bibliometric analysis of social entrepreneurship. *Journal of Business Research, 5*, 1651-1655. https://doi.org/10.1016/j.jbusres.2015.10.033

Ruggiero, P., & Cupertino, S. (2018). CSR Strategic Approach, Financial Resources and Corporate Social Performance: The Mediating Effect of Innovation. *Sustainability, 10*, 3611. https://doi.org/10.3390/su10103611

Saygili, E., Arslan, S., & Birkan, A.O. (2022). ESG practices and corporate financial performance: Evidence from Borsa Istanbul. *Borsa Istanbul Review, 22(3)*, 525-533. https://doi.org/10.1016/j.bir.2021.07.001

Scherer, A.G., & Palazzo, G. (2007). Towards a political conception of corporate responsibility: Business and society seen from a Habermasian perspective. *Academy of Management Review, 4*, 1096-1120. https://doi.org/10.5465/amr.2007.26585837

Scherer, A.G., & Palazzo, G. (2011). The New Political Role of Business in a Globalized World: A Review of a New Perspective on CSR and its Implications for the Firm, Governance, and Democracy. *Journal of Management Studies, 4*, 899-931. https://doi.org/10.1111/j.1467-6486.2010.00950.x

Scott, W. R. (2005). Institutional theory: Contributing to a theoretical research programme. *Great minds in management: The process of theory development, 37*(2), 460-484.

Sepúlveda-Alzate, Y.M., García-Benau, M.A., & Gómez-Villegas, M. (2021). Materiality assessment: the case of Latin American listed companies. *Sustainability Accounting, Management and Policy Journal, 1*, 88-113. https://doi.org/10.1108/sampj-10-2020-0358

Shahbaz, M., Karaman, A.S., Kilic, M., & Uyar, A. (2020). Board attributes, CSR engagement, and corporate performance: What is the nexus in the energy sector? *Energy Policy, 143*, 111582. https://doi.org/10.1016/j.enpol.2020.111582

Shahrokhi, M., Parhizgari, A.M., Hashemijoo, M., Okafor, C.E., Nishikawa, Y., & Dastan, A. (2022). Corporate governance and stakeholder capitalism. *Managerial Finance, 8*, 1123-1136. https://doi.org/10.1108/mf-01-2022-0056

Shakil, M.H., Tasnia, M., & Mostafiz, M.I. (2021). Board gender diversity and environmental, social and governance performance of US banks: Moderating role of environmental, social and corporate governance controversies. *International Journal of Bank Marketing, 39*(4), 661-677. https://doi.org/10.1108/IJBM-04-2020-0210

Shamseer, L., Moher, D., Clarke, M., Ghersi, D., Liberati, A., Petticrew, M., Shekelle, P., & Stewart, L. A. (2015). Preferred reporting items for systematic review and meta-analysis protocols (PRISMA-P) 2015: elabouration and explanation. *BMJ, jan02 1*, g7647-g7647. https://doi.org/10.1136/bmj.g7647

Sharma, D., Taggar, R., Bindra, S., & Dhir, S. (2020). A systematic review of responsiveness to develop future research agenda: a TCCM and bibliometric analysis. *Benchmarking: An International Journal, 9*, 2649-2677. https://doi.org/10.1108/bij-12-2019-0539

Singh, S., Akbani, I., & Dhir, S. (2020). Service innovation implementation: a systematic review and research agenda. *The Service Industries Journal, 7-8*, 491-517. https://doi.org/10.1080/02642069.2020.1731477

Snyder, H. (2019). Literature review as a research methodology: An overview and guidelines. *Journal of Business Research*, 333-339. https://doi.org/10.1016/j.jbusres.2019.07.039

Srivastava, S., Singh, S., & Dhir, S. (2020). Culture and International business research: A review and research agenda. *International Business Review, 4,* 101709. https://doi.org/10.1016/j.ibusrev.2020.101709

Suchman, M.C. (1995). Managing Legitimacy: Strategic and Institutional Approaches. *The Academy of Management Review, 3,* 571. https://doi.org/10.2307/258788

Tavares, M. da C. da C., & Dias, A.P. (2018). Theoretical Perspectives on Sustainability Reporting: A Literature Review. In *Accounting from a Cross-Cultural Perspective.* InTech. http://dx.doi.org/10.5772/intechopen.76951

Technology Adoption Lifecycle | Gainsight. (n.d.). Gainsight Software; https://www.facebook.com/gainsight. Retrieved October 18, 2022, from https://www.gainsight.com/glossary/what-is-the-technology-adoption-lifecycle/#:~:text=What%20is%20the%20technology%20adoption,majority%2C%20late%20majority%20and%20laggards.

Terzani, S., & Turzo, T. (2020). Religious social norms and corporate sustainability: The effect of religiosity on environmental, social, and governance disclosure. *Corporate Social Responsibility and Environmental Management, 1,* 485-496. https://doi.org/10.1002/csr.2063

The importance of innovation in ESG. (n.d.). RSM US—Audit, Tax, Consulting Services for the Middle Market. Retrieved September 9, 2022, from https://rsmus.com/insights/economics/the-importance-of-innovation-in-esg.html#:~:text=Innovation%20drives%20ESG%20progress%20and,both%20public%20and%20private%20domains.

Tilba, A. (2022). Appearance or substance of Stewardship and ESG reporting? The challenges of translating 'commitment' into tangible outcomes. *Sustainability Accounting, Management and Policy Journal.* https://doi.org/10.1108/SAMPJ-03-2021-0091

Tranfield, D., Denyer, D., & Smart, P. (2003). Towards a Methodology for Developing Evidence-Informed Management Knowledge by Means of Systematic Review. *British Journal of Management, 3,* 207-222. https://doi.org/10.1111/1467-8551.00375

Uyar, A., Kilic, M., Koseoglu, M.A., Kuzey, C., & Karaman, A.S. (2020). The link among board characteristics, corporate social responsibility performance, and financial performance: Evidence from the hospitality and tourism industry. *Tourism Management Perspectives, 35,* 100714. https://doi.org/10.1016/j.tmp.2020.100714

van Duuren, E., Plantinga, A., & Scholtens, B. (2015). ESG Integration and the Investment Management Process: Fundamental Investing Reinvented. *Journal of Business Ethics, 3,* 525-533. https://doi.org/10.1007/s10551-015-2610-8

Vásquez-Carbonell, M. (2022). A Systematic Literature Review of Virtual Reality in Engineering Education. *International Journal of Virtual and Personal Learning Environments, 1,* 1-18. https://doi.org/10.4018/ijvple.307021

Velte, P. (2016). Women on management board and ESG performance. *Journal of Global Responsibility, 1*, 98-109. https://doi.org/10.1108/jgr-01-2016-0001

Waddock, S.A., & Graves, S.B. (1997). The corporate social performance-financial performance link. *Strategic management journal, 18*(4), 303-319.

Xie, J., Nozawa, W., Yagi, M., Fujii, H., & Managi, S. (2019). Do environmental, social, and governance activities improve corporate financial performance? *Business Strategy and the Environment, 28(2)*, 286-300. https://doi.org/10.1002/bse.2224

Yoon, B., Lee, J.H., & Cho, J.H. (2021). The Effect of ESG Performance on Tax Avoidance—Evidence from Korea. *Sustainability, 12*, 6729. https://doi.org/10.3390/su13126729

Zhou, G., Liu, L., & Luo, S. (2022). Sustainable development, ESG performance and company market value: Mediating effect of financial performance. *Business Strategy and the Environment*, bse.3089. https://doi.org/10.1002/bse.3089

5

Disaster Management and "Good Governance"

Concerns and Strategies

Santosh Kumar

Introduction

Disaster are sudden, catastrophic, and unfortunate events that causes human and financial damages, destruction, and devastation. Disasters also impede ongoing and impending development projects, and the impacts—outputs and outcomes—varies from topographies to topographies. Major reasons could be due to diversities and differences in the climatic and geo-spatial conditionalities which leads to the difference in the degrees of vulnerabilities caused to the physical environment and to the human resources. Countless incidents which take place in nature are beyond human control. Averting these and foreseeing their occurrence at some of the geographical locations are beyond science explanation too. As per the definition given by National Disaster Management Institute of India (NDMI), disaster is an event or series of events, which gives rise to casualties and damage or loss of properties, infrastructure, environment, essential services or means of livelihood on such a scale which is beyond the normal capacity of the affected community to cope with. Disaster is also sometimes described as a "catastrophic situation in which the normal pattern of life or ecosystem has been disrupted and extraordinary emergency interventions are required to save and preserve lives and or the environment".

The term disaster owes its origin to the French word "*Desastre*" which is a combination of two words 'des' or bad and 'aster' or star (Singh: 2008). Thus, the term refers to 'Bad or Evil star'. The United Nations defined Disasters as "A serious disruption of the functioning of a community or a society causing widespread human, material, economic and environmental losses which exceed the ability of the affected community/society to cope using its own resources". Disasters have constantly been there and human beings have co-existed with them at the same point of time though they have tried to overcome the situation but frequently these extreme events either natural or man-induced have exceeded the endurable scale causing massive damage to the human life, property and natural environment within or beyond certain time limits, paralyzing the daily life. The Indian subcontinent is massively susceptible to cyclones, droughts, earthquakes, and floods. Avalanches, forest fire and landslides these are very frequent in Himalayan region of the country, almost 90 per cent of the landmass of the country is prone to disaster. The disasters directly affect economies, agriculture, food security, water, sanitation, the environment, and health conditions every year all around the world. And therefore, it is has become one of the solitary major concerns for most of the developing and underdeveloped nations. Different hazards because of the varying levels of physical damage caused to infrastructure and agriculture with their direct sometimes indirect implications has led to the development of disaster management because disasters result not only in loss of shelter but also create adversities, lack of food availability, temporary loss of source of income and interrupt with socio-economic activities, such instabilities have their psychological and social magnitudes which are difficult to replace, nevertheless some of the losses may be redeemable and compensated by developing a systematic disaster management.

Disaster Management involves a continuous and integrated process of planning, organising, coordinating, and implementing measures which are necessary or expedient for:

- Prevention of danger or threat of any disaster.
- Mitigation or reduction of risk of any disaster or its severity or consequences.

- Capacity building research and knowledge management.
- Preparedness to deal with any disaster.
- Prompt response to any threatening disaster situation or disaster.
- Assessing the severity or magnitude of effects of any disaster.
- Evacuation, rescue and relief.
- Rehabilitation and reconstruction (DMA: 2005).

In 2005, the 'Disaster Management Act (DMA)' was passed by the Government of India for the "efficient management of disasters and other matters connected to it." This Act proposed the formation of the National Disaster Management Authority (NDMA) which will be headed by the Prime Minister, it has the charge for laying down policies, plans and strategies for DM (Disaster Management) and synchronizing their enforcement and enactment for guaranteeing timely and effective response to disasters. These plans will support the Central Ministries, Departments and States to formulate their respective disaster management plans. It will approve the National Disaster Management Plans of the Central Ministries/Departments. The National Executive Committee (NEC) is the executive committee of the NDMA, and is delegated to assist the NDMA in performing its duties and also ensure compliance of the directions issued by the Central Government. SDMAs (State Disaster Management Authorities) led by the Chief Ministers of the states, will lay down guidelines and plans for DM in the State. It will, inter alia approve the State Plan in accordance with the guidelines laid down by the NDMA, and the District Disaster Management Authorities (DDMAs) headed by the District Magistrates or District Collector, DDMA will act as the planning, coordinating and implementing body for DM at the District level and take all essential actions for the tenacities of DM, likewise local authorities would include Panchayati Raj Institutions (PRIs), Municipalities, District and Cantonment Institutional and Legal Arrangements Boards, and Town Planning Authorities which control and manage civic services. The structure of DM will guarantee capacity building of their officers and employees for managing disasters in country, and at the similar time will give procedures for carrying out relief, rehabilitation and reconstruction activities in the affected areas and will prepare DM Plans in harmoniousness with the guidelines of the NDMA, SDMAs and DDMAs. Specific institutional development in the form of National Institute of Disaster Management has assisted to forefront and approve a holistic and cohesive approach to DM. There is a shift from the relief-centric response to a 'proactive prevention', 'mitigation' and 'preparedness-driven approach' for safeguarding developmental advances and to minimize loss of life and property.

Significance of Governance in Disaster Management

The subsequent step after disaster management, to make it more effective is good governance its implementation at every stage can lead to desirable results of DM. Governance, as defined by UNDP, is the exercise of political, economic and administrative authority in the management of a country's affairs at all levels. It comprises mechanisms, processes and institutions through which citizens and groups articulate their interests, exercise their legal rights, meet their obligations and mediate their differences. Governance encompasses, but also transcends, government. It encompasses all relevant groups, including the private sector and civil society organizations. "There is now an international acknowledgement of the fact that efforts to reduce disaster risks must be systematically integrated into policies, plans and programmes for sustainable development and poverty reduction... Sustainable development, poverty reduction, good governance and disaster risk reduction are mutually supportive objectives and in order to meet the challenges ahead, accelerated efforts must be made" (Hyogo Framework for Action 2005-2015).

Disaster governance is considered as a synchronized system in which collabourative efforts of several organizations are brought under one umbrella to resolve the issue that outspread beyond the horizon of any single organization (Ansell, C.; Gash, A.: 2007). A commonly accepted view of the concept of collabourative governance is that it refers to "the processes and structures of public policy decision making and management that engage people constructively across the boundaries of public agencies, levels of government, and/or the public, private and civic spheres in order to carry out a public purpose that could not otherwise be accomplished" (Emerson *et al.*, 2012).

The disaster governance, more specifically, comprises of the interconnected factions of rules, administrative, legislative and executive actors, and practices spreading across the pre-disaster, trans-disaster, and post-disaster periods that are intended to diminish the impact and fatalities related with the catastrophes arising from natural or man-made causes for the disasters. Good Governance includes the various rules and regulations at multiple levels, informal practices, consensus-based ideals and agendas, and various other mechanism that reassure cooperative actions, such as dissemination of greatest practices which have given best of the results through policy implementations with the synchronization of various governmental institutes and non-profit making organizations, these also includes various transnational and global organizations, technical and specialized institutes, coalitions of these organizations connects scientific and policy-making bodies, and various social movement which has taken place across the globe for disaster risk reduction.

The governance plays a very important role in various disaster phases, disaster susceptibilities can be reduced through pre-disaster arrangements, for e.g., risks and susceptibility assessments; land-use guidelines; building code development, implementation, and execution; cautioning systems; and education and training programmes. When catastrophes occur, adverse effects can be abridged to certain extent through suitable disaster response measures, e.g., lifesaving and the provision of emergency food and shelter, and through providing effective decision support to emergency responders. Post disaster measures include short-and longer-term recovery programmes, as well as the formulation and implementation during disaster recovery of interventions designed to reduce future disaster losses and promote sustainability. Governance arrangements and key actor participation typically vary across these disaster phases, adding to the complexity of governance challenges. Risk-recovering initiatives, such as insurance and reinsurance, are few of the important components for disaster governance. Worldwide, societies differ significantly in the extent to which potential disaster losses are covered by insurance and in the insurance arrangements for different types of hazards.

Disaster governance can be added advantage to comprehend institutional measures concentrating on the management of natural or manmade hazards or potential threats, which seek to decrease vulnerabilities and exposures during pre-disaster times, and provisions related to mitigation and rehabilitation when once the disaster has taken place and managing the consequences of disastrous events. As said by Burton and others, governance infrastructures can concentrate on various combinations of adjustments to hazards and disasters that include avoiding hazardous areas restricting activities (e.g., construction and settlement) within exposed areas; modifying the physical and built environment to attenuate disaster impacts; preplanning and training to build response capacity; developing disaster warning systems when feasible to protect at-risk populations; responding when events occur to protect life safety and property and cope with the social disruption caused by disasters; and providing various types of assistance to societies, communities, households, and other entities that are affected by disasters (Burton *et al.*, 1993).

International Strategies for Disaster Governance and Risk Reduction

The very first global breakthrough for making disaster management part of development procedure and policy making appeared in the form of International Decade for Natural Disaster Reduction (IDNDR), decade of 1990s was designated for the same. The main aim of the action was to reduce the massive loss of the life and assets along with other social, economic, and infrastructural losses caused because of the reoccurrence of the disaster. In order to achieve these goals, an international strategy was evolved to designate the responsibilities to the important role players for the effective and efficient management of the disaster management along with coordination from government of the nations and UN.

Important goals of IDNDR were:

- To improve the capacity of each country to mitigate the effects of natural disaster expeditiously and effectively.
- To devise appropriate guidelines and strategies for applying existing scientific and technical knowledge, considering the cultural, economic diversity among nations.
- To foster scientific and engineering endeavors aimed at closing

critical gaps in knowledge in order to reduce the loss of life and property.

- Develop measures for the assessment, prediction, prevention, and mitigation of natural disasters through programmes of technical assistance and technology transfer, demonstration projects, and education and training, tailored to specific disasters and locations, and to evaluate the effectiveness of those programmes (UN: 1987).

The IDNDR was implemented with much of the enthusiasm and coordinated way by the government of various nations and UN agencies. All the nations tried to develop an integrated framework for the disaster management as a part of their development plan. However, in spite of the passion and understanding the importance of the IDNDR, most of the nations faced economic and logistic challenges to implement the plan in the ground reality and therefore the IDNDR was not of great success but still it managed to make people understand that the disasters are not just acts of God but it can be managed in more efficient and effective manner with development of science and technology and national and international cooperation and efforts. IDNDR played an important role in letting countries erecting daunting system for disaster management. For instance, in India, by the end of IDNDR, a High-Powered Committee (HPC) was set up in (1999) to review the issues related to disaster. In fact, the present Disaster Management Act, 2005 of the country owes it origin to the HPC report. Despite of lack of knowledge, funds, and technological development, all the countries tried to develop some sort of disaster management system in compliance with IDNDR which played a foundational role for the further upcoming development in the area.

Over the years, Worldwide determination for disaster management has been managed by the events of the decadal conferences organized mainly under the patronages of UN in partnership with government and other international organizations. The standard practice to upheld the good governance in the disaster management and disaster risk reduction is to include voluntary organizations, independent researchers, community leaders, local level activist as stakeholders for the same. Also, assessment of the previous conference set targets and reviewing of the policies at regular interval, along with suggestions for the best strategies are welcomed so that set standards of disaster risk reduction can be achieved. This has helped to achieve dynamic reinventions of ideas and practice of disaster management over the period on time.

The Yokohama Strategy and Plan of Action for a Safer World was pioneer in this area which was adopted in the year 1994 following the United Nations World Conference on Natural Disaster Reduction, held in Yokohama, Japan. It is the initial document discussing the strategies at the transnational level for research, training and preparation for disaster, prevention and mitigation of disaster impact. The Yokohama Strategy was the outcome of the International Decade for Natural Disaster Reduction (1990-2000) and, to be précised, it was the brain child of the World Conference on Natural Disaster Reduction held in 1994. These two global proceedings have recognized the importance of the community participation in disaster risk reduction which further leads to good governance in various aspects, which is very much evident in the following paragraph, extracted from the Yokohama Strategy (IDNDR, 1994, p. 4):

> *"Active participation should be encouraged in order to gain greater insight into the individual and collective perception of development and risk, and to have a clear understanding of the cultural and organizational characteristics of each society as well as of its behaviour and interactions with the physical and natural environment. This knowledge is of the utmost importance to determine those things which favor and hinder prevention and mitigation or encourage or limit the preservation of the environment for the development of future generations, and in order to find effective and efficient means to reduce the impact of disasters".*

Yokohama Strategy offers a set of ideologies based on which disaster risk reduction strategies should be planned, rendering to the international world of the mid-1990s. It advocates development of the global culture for the involvement of local actors in risk management practice, and developing a community embracing capacity building, self-sufficiency by allocating adequate resources and valuing community experience for disaster risk reduction and ensuring that the plans are in safe hands. It especially emphasized on improving survival techniques so that the community has a mechanism which not only help them to cope up with the disaster but also helps in recovering from disasters impacts. It has also highlighted the importance of identifying and connecting the centers for the research in the particular area in order to enhance the prevention, reduction and mitigation activities in a more scientific manner, media has to play a more constructive role by updating vulnerable community for disaster reduction. Disaster prevention, preparedness can be done only by the active participation from the community the Yokoyama strategy believed in this philosophy. The strategy emphasized that in the second half of the decade community-based approach needs to be adopted so that the vulnerable or marginalized sections can be benefitted by improved risk monitoring and better communication of forecasts and warnings. It has also highlighted the fact how it can be achieved by encouraging mobilization of community resources, political commitment by legislation and policy-making on and for risk reduction and prevention programmes, deliberation and authority to the local level government officials for safety measurements and strengthening the institutional capacity, considering support of the NGOs for people's involvement developing disaster resistance infrastructure last but not the least international communities should support should provide assistance to the developing nations to establish measure and techniques for disaster prevention and reduction withing the prevailing resources and in alignment to the sub-regional, regional and national policies. To enable an easy and fast recovery process, this approach treasured the knowledge and experience in managing emergencies that exists at the local level among at-risk communities. The following decade of 2000s signifies a change in the way disaster risk reduction is professed, moving its major focus from coping capacities and relief interferences to an increased consideration brought to risk preparedness and prevention by the better governance method where people's involvement was given major consideration (Baudoin & Wolde Georgis, 2015).

Apart from this Yokohama Strategy has also emphasized upon activities at regional, sub-regional levels and at international level particularly through bilateral and multilateral co-operations. This will help to accumulate and circulate the information regarding disaster management to the various developing nations so that they can take it as the instance and reduce the impact of the disaster, this will also help in creating training programmes and exchange of the technical knowledge and understanding for the human resource development, mutual assistance and joint agreement programmes can be developed for the same. It has also suggested for the extra budgetary resources to be provided for the implementation of the strategy they have encouraged the voluntary contributions from national, international organizations, private organizations and government should be encouraged to prioritize the importance of disaster management. Establishment and development of the early warning system as a priority for the sub-regional, regional, and national level for more effective dissemination of warnings and lastly holding a review conference on the natural disaster reduction at the end of the decade in order to map the activities which must be taken up in the 21st century for the disaster reduction programme. Dissemination of information, transparency and taking feedback for the assessment of the work at the various level are the few of the indicators which reflect good governance approach in the Yokohama strategy.

The second conference on disaster risk reduction has gained popularity with the World Conference for Disaster Reduction held in Kobe, Hyogo, Japan in January 2005. The conference inadvertently was held aftermath of the 2004 tsunami in the Indian Ocean, which has affected the lives and livelihood of millions of people and raised public awareness regarding natural disasters, their hazards, and their grave impact not only on the humans but also on the environment. The result of the Hyogo Framework for Action 2005-2015 (HFA), is perhaps the utmost significant international pronouncement propagating the concept of disaster risk reduction. The first decade of the twentieth century was shifting its concentration from disaster to increased focus on risk preparedness in which governance had the major role to play. This change in the perspective to prioritize governance can be seen both in academics (Holloway, 2003) and major organizations working in the field of disaster management and among major organizations working in the field of disaster risk reduction as well (UNISDR: 2012; USAID: 2012). With end of International

Decade for Natural Disaster Reduction (IDNDR) in the year 1999, various follow-up approaches have originated which has led to the formation of the International Strategy for Disaster Reduction (ISDR) in December 1999, which serves as secretariat for the International Strategy for Disaster Reduction (ISDR) system and was adopted by the United Nations Member States in 2000. The primary objective of the ISDR strategic framework is to ensure "the implementation of the International Strategy for Disaster Reduction" through the advancement of combined efforts for international collabouration and good governance initiative to bring everyone under one umbrella for reduced risk susceptibility through early warning system (Olowu, 2010). The Hyogo framework for action was adopted as part of ISDR, it was first plan of its type which has not only talked about the disaster reduction but has also deliberated exhaustive progressions needed for the reduction in disaster risks in various sectors and of different scales across the globe.

The Hyogo frame for Action (HFA) reflects a stronger emphasis on risk preparedness and prevention, other than on response and recovery which was emphasized during the earlier decades of disaster planning. HFA signifies five priorities for action, and suggests importance for community involvement. These are:

(a) Ensure that disaster risk reduction is a national and a local priority with a strong institutional basis for implementation: for this purpose, it proposed that conception and establishment of nationwide unified disaster risk reduction mechanisms, so that responsibilities can be designated from the national levels to the local levels to enable smooth functioning and coordination across sectors. Development of the policies should be such so that they integrate advancement policies, mechanisms that encourage acquiescence and incentives for undertaking risk reduction and mitigation activities which should be done at all levels of government, including poverty reduction approaches. Identifying the importance and peculiarity of local risk patterns and tendencies, and decentralizing authority, responsibilities, and resources for disaster risk reduction to such areas, to promote community participation in disaster risk reduction through the adoption of specific policies, the promotion of networking, the strategic management of volunteer human resources.

(b) Identify, assess, and monitor disaster risks and enhance early warning: Government at all levels must develop, update and disseminate information which must include risk maps, record on disaster occurrence, statistical evidence related to impacts and losses, on a regular interval this will enable decision-makers to assess the impact of disasters on social, economic and environmental conditions and plan accordingly. Develop early warning systems that are people centred, systems whose warnings are timely and understandable to those at risk, which take into account the demographic, gender, cultural and livelihood characteristics of the target audiences, including guidance on how to act upon warnings, and that support effective operations by disaster managers and other decision makers.

(c) Use knowledge, innovation, and education to build a culture of safety and resilience at all levels: Providing easily comprehensible information on disaster risks and protection options, especially to citizens in high-risk areas, to encourage and enable people to take action to reduce risks and build resilience. The information should incorporate relevant traditional and indigenous knowledge and culture heritage and be tailored to different target audiences, considering cultural and social factors. Inclusion of disaster risk reduction knowledge in relevant segments of school curriculum at all levels and the use of other formal and informal channels to reach youth and children with information. Promotion of community-based training initiatives which must include women and vulnerable sections to considering the role of volunteers for the promotion of gender and cultural sensitivity and to enhance local capacities to mitigate and cope with disasters.

(d) Reduce the underlying risk factors: Disaster risks related to changing social, economic, environmental conditions and land use, and the impact of hazards associated with geological events, weather, water, climate variability and climate change, are addressed in sector development planning and programmes as well as in post-disaster situations. Promote food security as an important factor in ensuring the resilience of communities to hazards, particularly in areas prone to drought, flood, cyclones, and other hazards that can weaken agriculture-based livelihoods. Protect and strengthen critical public facilities and physical infrastructure, particularly schools, clinics, hospitals, water and power plants, communications and transport lifelines, disaster warning and management centres, and culturally important lands and structures through proper design, retrofitting and re-building, in order to render them adequately resilient to hazards.

(e) Strengthen disaster preparedness for effective response at all levels: At times of disaster, impacts and losses can be substantially reduced if authorities, individuals, and communities in hazard-prone areas are well prepared and ready to act and are equipped with the knowledge and capacities for effective disaster management (UNISDR: 2005).

Hyogo framework, has emphasized on native knowledge and considered cultural tradition as one of the key indicators in order to develop information appropriate for "target" audiences (UNISDR, 2005: p. 9) HFA did not talk about partnership and collabouration which was one of the important aspects of Yokohama Strategy, but it has emphasized one how to the best of the abilities we can integrate local knowledge to successful the programme of external experts and facilitate DRR execution within certain groups. It has also highlighted the importance of "inclusion of gender and marginalised section perspective" which was further reviewed in mid-tern review report of HFA. HFA as one of the drives to promote a greater participating approach in DRR and increased collabouration among local governments and communities would help support DRR planning at larger scale (Mercer *et al.*, 2008).

The Third World conference on Disaster Risk Reduction was Sendai Framework which has emerged out of inferences from the prior two conferences. In contrast to the previous frameworks, it was presented with 15 years of time line for DRR across the globe. Sendai has specifically conferred the accountability of DRR on national government with active and enthusiastic participation from regional and local government. It has also emphasized the significant role of communities in enactment of the action drawn in the framework at the local level. The Sendai framework is the foundational document in the present setup providing the inclusive and integrated framework for DRR with the fine strategy for carrying necessary changes in the setting of disaster management practices across the world. Sendai Framework for Disaster Risk Reduction (SFDRR) priorities for the implementation of DRR Program:

Understanding disaster risk: Ensure the use of traditional, indigenous and local knowledge and practices, as appropriate, to complement scientific knowledge in disaster risk assessment and the development and implementation of policies, strategies, plans and programmes of specific sectors, with a cross-sectoral approach, which should be tailored to localities and to the context (UNISDR: Activity I, p. 11) Enhance collabouration among people at the local level to disseminate disaster risk information through the involvement of community-based organizations and non-governmental organizations (UNISDR: Activity O, p. 11).

Strengthening disaster risk governance to manage disaster risk: Assign, as appropriate, clear roles and tasks to community representatives within disaster risk management institutions and processes and decision-making through relevant legal frameworks. Undertake comprehensive public and community consultations during the development of such laws and regulations to support their implementation (UNISDR: Activity F, p. 13). Empower local authorities, as appropriate, through regulatory and financial means to work and coordinate with civil society, communities and indigenous peoples and migrants in disaster risk management at the local level (UNISDR: Activity H, p. 14).

Investing in disaster risk reduction for resilience: Public and private investment in disaster risk prevention and reduction through structural and non-structural measures are essential to enhance the economic, social, health and cultural resilience of persons, communities, countries, and their assets, as well as the environment. These can be drivers of innovation, growth, and job creation. Such measures are cost-effective and instrumental to save lives, prevent and reduce losses and ensure effective recovery and rehabilitation. (UNISDR: Activity J, p. 17).

Enhancing disaster preparedness for effective response, and to "Build Back Better" in recovery, rehabilitation and reconstruction: The steady growth of disaster risk, including the increase of people and assets exposure, combined with the lessons learned from past disasters, indicates the need to further strengthen disaster preparedness for response, take action in anticipation of events, integrate disaster risk reduction in response preparedness and ensure that capacities are in place for effective response and recovery at all levels. Empowering women and persons with disabilities to publicly lead and promote gender equitable and universally accessible response, recovery, rehabilitation, and reconstruction approaches is key. Disasters have demonstrated that the recovery, rehabilitation, and reconstruction phase, which needs to be prepared ahead of a disaster, is a critical opportunity to "Build Back Better", including through integrating disaster risk reduction into development measures, making nations and communities resilient to disasters (UNISDR: Activity K, p. 18).

Sendai Framework (SF) has set the tangible and quantifiable targets on the uniform basis to be accepted by countries across the globe and most importantly these targets are to be achieved within the specifies time period.

1. Considerably reduction in global disaster mortality rate by 2030, targeting to lower the average per 1,00,000 global mortality rates in the decade 2020-2030 compared to the period of 2005-2015.
2. Considerably reduction in the number of people affected globally by 2030, targeting to lower the average per 1,00,000 global mortality rates in the decade 2020-2030 compared to the period of 2005-2015.
3. Substantially reducing the direct economic loss because of the disaster in relation to global gross domestic product.
4. Substantially reducing critical infrastructure damage and commotion of basic services, like education and health, developing their resilience by 2030.
5. Increase in the number of countries with national and local DRR policies by 2030.

6. Increase in sustainable international cooperation to the developing nations, so that they can comply with their national actions for DRR as per present Sendai framework 2030.
7. Significant increase in the easy access and availability to early warning system and disaster risk information and assessment to the people by 2030 (UNISDR: 2015).

Sendai framework has tried to bring all the countries under one umbrella so that the considerable changes can be seen in the life of the people across the globe and none of the country is left behind when the disaster management is talked about.

Case Study of Disaster Governance

In continuation to the above conferences for the disaster risk reduction let us study how far India has adopted them and tried to implement them as per the Disaster Management Act, 2005. Orissa, situated in the eastern part of the country along the coastline of Bay of Bengal, is natural disaster prone, vulnerable, and susceptible, and has often witnessed the cyclones, floods and therefore it is often referred to the disaster capital of the country. Yet in August 2020, its two coastal villages Venkatraipur in Ganjam district and Noliasahi in Jagatsingpur district which earned the recognition of being 'Tsunami Ready' from the UNESCO-Intergovernmental Oceanographic Commission, making India the first country in the Indian Ocean Region to establish such high levels of disaster preparedness at the community level (Hindu: 2020).

Odisha has recently been in news for setting an example the way it has managed to cope up with the natural disaster that has stuck its coast. Community based disaster management is the very core of its disaster management and risk reduction approach and they have highlighted this aspect is also one of the central themes in State disaster management plan (OSDMA: 2017). This is because in any type of disaster community is the first in the line to face the heat and to respond to the situation at the same point of time. Also, government can easily employ the indigenous knowledge of the local community for disaster risk reduction as highlighted in the Hyogo and Sendai Framework of Action as one of the aspects of good governance where people's participation is given highest importance for the citizen-oriented government. Odisha's way of disaster management has not only setup an example for other states in the country but also has earned global appreciation for itself which needs to be identified.

Community preparedness is not only limited to the people's participation in the disaster management activities but empowering them with efficient training from governmental and non-governmental agencies and active cooperation from community members with the local and national disaster management authorities. Lessons from the past are also kept in mind while preparing prevention and response activities, lives of more than 10,000 peoples have been lost in the Super Cyclone witnessed by Odisha in the year 1999 and therefore as a lesson from this ill-fated experience state has felt the need to build a multipurpose cyclone shelter along its 480 km long coastline, the shelter had been equipped with all the basic services which are required during the emergencies such as: community kitchens, life-saving equipment, announcement vehicles so that evacuees do not get scattered at different locations but can within their communities (Manorama: 2019).

Based on the early tsunami experience where seawater has exceeded up to 1.5 kms in the mainland government has identified 328 tsunami prone villages and took various measure to enhance their disaster preparedness. The two villages Venkatraipur in Ganjam district and Noliasahi in Jagatsingpur district has been declared 'Tsunami Ready' under Indian Ocean Tsunami Ready Programme of IOC-UNESCO based on the community performance (Indian Express: 2019). The preparedness of the village communities was examined by the officials, they were displayed with wide range of activities they have taken up which ranged from having community tsunami risk reduction plans, to designating tsunami hazard zones, having easily understandable evacuation maps, an annually conducted tsunami community exercise, and a reliable means to receive official tsunami alerts round the clock (Hindu: 2020).

In the recent disaster of Amphan in the state it has proven its efficiency in implementing the evacuation operations through the community outreach programme. It was one of the strongest cyclone recorded in the Bay of Bengal in which around 2,00,000 people were evacuated immediately after alerts were issued by the Indian Meteorological Department and refurbishment works were also undertaken on priority basis so that by the time the cyclone steered away from Odisha towards West Bengal more than 85 per cent of the power restoration work was already done (India Today: 2020). Later when the central steering committee visited Odisha post Amphan they stated in their report that community involvement is one of the best practices adopted by Odisha government in disaster management.

Odisha government has already set a preceding example in super cyclone Fani in 2019, where they have targeted for 'zero causality' and carried out history's biggest evacuation operation in which evacuees were accommodated in over 4000 shelters in which 800 are especially designed to survive cyclones (Business Standard: 2019). Another such success story of Odisha is Cyclone Phailin which struck in 2013 in which approximatively 1 million people were evacuated. Post Phailin, the UN had recognised Odisha's preparedness as a 'global success story' and made plans to use it as a model for other cities (TOI: 2013). As the World Bank puts it, "Odisha has a good community outreach system through which people can be contacted on time. There is a network of 450 cyclone shelters and each shelter has a maintenance committee trained in rescue and relief activities. Through a network of these shelters and committees, the state has involved the entire community making it easy to disseminate warnings and evacuate people" (World Bank Report: 2019). Odisha as a case study will always set an example to rest of the world that how important community involvement and disaster safe infrastructure is for the zero causality and minimum social and economic loss.

Conclusion

Afore stated discussions lead us to conclude that the three international frameworks indicate towards major development for disaster risk reduction in which the priority has been given to partnerships and involvement of relevant local stakeholders and communities are widely recognized as an important constituent for the successful development and DRR plans and approaches. The three frameworks treated local communities as esteemed partners with their indigenous expertise who can provide the custom-made solutions for the disaster risk, the case study of Odisha can be the best example to prove the fact that how important it is for the community to participate along with other stakeholders. Alignment of national disaster management policy with the three international framework is important as these serve as guidelines to direct the flow of funding and the implementation of projects in a specific field and it would help to develop the international policies and agendas for disaster risk reduction.

The author has sought to highlight the aspects of good governance can only be implemented if the various guidelines given by the international framework is taken into consideration, for example scientific development, dissemination of disaster data and analysis report for the disaster related risk and damage, early warning signs and many more. The social economic loss and lives of people can only be saved when they are well informed about the upcoming unfortunate event. Increase in finance flows at the local scale, and, overall, improve the bottom-up participatory process within international DRR frameworks are few of the important aspects which needs to be considered by all the nations. With the change in the climatic conditions, it becomes more pivotal that the disaster risk reduction policies are aligned with sustainable development goals of UN so that a safer place for the next generation can be passed on.

References

Ansell, C., Gash, A. (2007). Collabourative governance in theory and practice. *J. Pub. Admin. Res. Theory*, 18: 543-71.

Baudoin, M., A.T., Wolde, Georgis (2015). Disaster risk reduction efforts in the Greater Horn of Africa. *International Journal of Disaster Risk Science 6*(1): 49-61.

Burton, I.R., Kates, R.W., White, G.F. (1993). *The Environment as Hazard.* New York: Oxford University Press. 2nd ed.

Cyclone Fani: Odisha teaches the world how to prepare for disasters | Business Standard News (business-standard.com)

Disaster of Management Act 2005, Gazette of India, 2005, GOI.https://www.ndma.gov.in/sites/default/files/PDF/DM_act2005.pdf

Emerson, K, Nabatchi, T., Balogh, S. (2012). An integrative framework for collabourative governance. *Public Adm. Res. Theory, 22*(1):1-29.

Holloway, A. 2003. Disaster risk reduction in Southern Africa. *African Security Review, 12*(1): 29-38.

How Odisha dealt with Cyclone Amphan while battling Covid-19 pandemic -India News (indiatoday.in)

https://gfmc.online/programmes/un/idndr/idndr2.html

https://indianexpress.com/article/india/unesco-recognises-two-odisha-villages-as-tsunami-ready-6543017/

https://sendaiframework-mtr.undrr.org/

https://timesofindia.indiatimes.com/city/bhubaneswar/UN-praise-for-Odisha-disaster-management/articleshow/24220989.cms

https://www.humanitarianlibrary.org/sites/default/files/2019/05/Government%20of%20Odisha%20State%20Disaster%20Management%20Plan%20June%202017.pdf

https://www.onmanorama.com/news/india/2019/05/10/how-lessons-from-1999-prepared-odisha-to-face-cyclone-fani.html

https://www.orfonline.org/expert-speak/following-the-odisha-example-for-developing-community-based-disaster-management-in-india/

https://www.preventionweb.net/files/resolutions/N1516716.pdf

https://www.thehindu.com/news/cities/Hyderabad/two-odisha-villages-become-tsunami-ready-get-unesco-ioc-recognition/article32299720.ece

https://www.unisdr.org/files/58158_unisdr2017annualreport.pdf

IDNDR (International Decade for Natural Disaster Reduction). 1994. Yokohama strategy and plan of action for a safer world: Guidelines for natural disaster prevention, preparedness and mitigation. http://www.unisdr.org/files/8241_doc6841conte nido1.pdf

Mercer, J., I. Kelman, K. Lloyd, and S. Suchet-Pearson (2008). Reflections on use of participatory research for disaster risk reduction. *Area, 40*(2): 172-183.

Olowu, D. 2010. The Hyogo Framework for Action and its implications for disaster management and reduction in Africa. Ja'mba': *Journal of Disaster Risk Studies, 3*(1): 303-320.

Singh, B.K. (2008). *Handbook of Disaster Management*, Rajat Publication, New Delhi.

UN: 1987, International Decade for Natural Disaster Reduction https://gfmc.online/programmes/un/idndr/idndr2.html

UNISDR (United Nations International Strategy for Disaster Reduction). 2005. Hyogo framework for action 2005-2015: Building the resilience of nations and communities to disasters. Geneva: UNISDR.

UNISDR (United Nations International Strategy for Disaster Reduction). 2005. Hyogo framework for action 2005-2015: Building the resilience of nations and communities to disasters. Geneva: UNISDR https://www.unisdr.org/2005/wcdr/intergover/official-doc/L-docs/Hyogo-framework-for-action-english.pdf

UNISDR (United Nations International Strategy for Disaster Reduction). 2015. Sendai framework for disaster risk reduction 2015-2030. Geneva: UNISDR.

https://www.preventionweb.net/publication/sendai-framework-disaster-risk-reduction-2015-2030

UNISDR Yokohama strategy and plan of action for a safer world: Guidelines for natural disaster prevention, preparedness, and mitigation.1994. 8241_doc6841contenido1.pdf (unisdr.org)

6

Environment and Society—A Theoretical Overview

Special Reference to Eco-Marxism

Binu, K.

Introduction

Environmental sociology deals with social, cultural and ecological areas of environment. This area of research is very useful for the developments of environmental policies for the equitable distribution of resources of a nation. It also helps to cultivate environmental awareness and to solve environmental problems and to discuss the relationship between society and environment with sociological outlook. Environmental sociology expands our knowledge of our natural ecosystem and also warm us the hidden and manifested form of environmental crises. Environmental sociology is a sub-discipline within the field of sociology that studies the interactions between the physical environment, social organization, and social behaviour. An environmental sociologist typically places special emphasis on studying the social factors that cause environmental problems and provides efforts to solve the problems. Environmental sociology is a cross-disciplinary research area. It covers subjects from organic farming, nature management and transport through technological development on a more general level, and deals with themes such as environmental policy, democracy, planning, and communication of individual with nature in everyday life. It is a fast growing discipline generally focuses on:

(1) Peoples roles in environmental problems and how these can be dealt with,
(2) Human understanding of and practice in relation to nature and environment,
(3) Social changes and their underlying driving forces and its repercussions,
(4) Structural conditions, barriers and opportunities in relation to environment and nature,
(5) Different solution strategies, forms of organization and methods.

There is growing and mutually influencing interrelatiohips between the environment and social life from life immemorial. The outlook of human beings about the natural habitat was different from periods to periods, different civilizations have formed different perspectives and works about the degree and interrelationships between society and environment. This chapter is primarily assessing the various theoretical backgrounds related to the environment and society. The study is also highlighting the views of different theorists in the realm of society and environment from biological determinism to theories of modern period and especially the works of Marx and neo-Marxian thinkers.

Biological determinism is the interpretation of humans and human life from a biological point of view. This theory says that the development of human beings is directly or indirectly determined by the circumstances in which he lives. This sociological interpretation by Spencer (1) stress that the personality and biological features of human behaviour are the product of the social cultural environment in which an individual lives. The socio-cultural environment makes the existence and the vitality of human life. These theories suggest that biological makeup of man is directly or indirectly related to the environment in which an organism survive and strive of its existence. Sociologists and anthropologists opined that a charge of biological factors may be the result of adaption and enculturation. The main proponents of this theory Herbert Spencer stress that society is in the from of consensus equilibrium. Changes in the equilibrium of society are the primary reason for social change. When social equilibrium collapses it directly or indirectly influences the structure and functions of the society, in that way biological determinism says that the persistent envoirmental crises due to disequilibrium of the society.

Social Darwinism and Environmental Sociology

Social Darwinism is an ideology of sociology that seeks to apply biological concepts of Darwinism or of evolutionary theory to social sciences, often with the assumption that conflict between groups in society leads to social progress as superior groups and inferior ones. The name *Social Darwinism* is a modern name given to the various theories of society that emerged in England and the United States in the 1870s, which, it is alleged, sought to apply biological concepts to sociology and politics. The main discourse of Social Darwinism to sociology was done by Herbert Spencer the distinguished biologist. His concept of organic analogy is the best suitable example to define the interrelationships between the society and organism. He equated the society with an organism and corresponds the ideology of social evolution with respect to biological evolution. For him, change is continuous process of simple complex stages homogeneity to heterogeneity. For them society is in the state of perpetual equilibrium striving for better and complex life.

From primitives to savagery and to modern men the sequential pattern of change and progress can be seen in human social life. *Social Darwinism* gained widespread currency when used in 1944 to oppose these earlier concepts. Social Darwinism is generally understood to use the concepts of struggle for existence and survival of the fittest and struggle for existence to justify social policies which make no distinction between those able to support themselves and those unable to support them. Many such views stress competition between individuals in laissez-faire capitalism but the ideology has also motivated ideas of eugenics and struggle between national or racial groups. Some even extended this philosophy into a microeconomic issue, claiming that social welfare programmes that helped the poor and disadvantaged were contrary to nature itself. In nature, the strong survive and those best suited to survival will outlive the weak. According to Social

Darwinism, those with strength (economic, physical, technological) flourish, and those without are destined for extinction. It is important to note that Darwin did not extend his theories to a social or economic level, nor are any credible evolutionists subscribing to the theories of Social Darwinism. Herbert Spencer's philosophy is only loosely based on the premises of Darwin's work. According to evolutionary theory, nature is a "kill-or-be-killed" system.

Resources Mobilization and Relative Deprivation in Ecological Movement

Resources mobilization theory asserts that the main reason for environmental activities and movements are one or other forms of the resources attainments and its mobilization for the accomplishment of certain goals. This theory says that in all environmental protection movements, the human resources-based struggle is mobilized against degradation and its depletion. The relative deprivation theory says that the inherent deprivation of some particular sections or the separation of some sections from the mainstream society is the main reason for the existing crisis in the interaction between human beings and environments. The environmental problem and issues are collective deliberate or spontaneous attempt of person, or category of person to resist or to promote change in any direction to bring anticipated changes in the society. Every environmental exploitative action has been influencing the natural balance or the perpetual source of equilibrium in society. It may have economical, social or political intervention but the ultimate goal of any environmental movement is to create balance in natural equilibrium and also protection of life.

The environmental movement is an international movement, represented by a range of organizations and stakeholders from the large to grassroots, and varies from country to country. Due to its large membership, varying and strong beliefs, and speculative nature, the environmental movement is not always united in its goals. At its broadest, the movement includes private citizens, professionals, religious devotees, politicians, scientists, non-profit organizations, and individual advocates. Environmental and ecological movements are the best examples of the collective actions of several social groups. Protection and recognition of constitutional and democratic rights.

These movements are primarily focused on the upliftment of most disadvantaged sections like tribes and ecologically alienated people to mobilize their natural resources for livelihood and to attain the process of equitable distribution of resources. This movement is also agitation for the right of indigenous people to preserve their culture, protection of the environment, and maintenance of ecological balance are significant concerns of these movements, as they affect human life to a great extent. Economic justice sought by these movements does not mean mere distribution of resources but encompasses a larger vision like enhancement in the quality of life through the recognition of people's rights over their natural resources, their right to live with dignity, and their participation in the decision and development. These movements focus not only on basic survival issues but also on larger ecological concerns. These are different from earlier social movements and there is a need to understand them in terms of their nature and strategies. It may be mentioned here that scholars have tried to understand and analyze these movements in diverse ways. In general, these movements are grouped under tribal and peasant movements and as well under New Social movements

Eco-Marxism and Environmental Crisis

Eco-Marxism can be defined as the interpretation of ecological parameters with economic basis of the society. This modern concept assesses that the present problems and crises in environments are primarily due to the overexploitation of natural resources for human development. Ecology is only becoming one of the pivotal factors in their economic development by usage or over-usage of the natural ecosystem, Capitalism and corresponding developments in society led to the optimum utilization of resources for maximizing capital with the help of minimum resources. Nature and its supporting components become of the resources for capitalism, such a utilitarian usage of nature resulted in the exportation of motherland. According to Marx, this led to humans beings increasingly isolated from the lands that they had known so well, and was a contributing factor to a lesser understanding of the earth, its natural systems, and what is required to sustain them. Marx believed that, above all else, labour is what set human beings apart from the rest of the animal kingdom, and defined us as a species. Labour is the unique identification of human beings from the rest of the species. With the creation of tools and machines, it became possible for the ruling class to live off the labour of others, "but in the process, the producers lost control of their lab, and of the products they produced. In all cases, it meant the complete alienation of humans from nature." The ruling class was technologically competent to control the will and wishes of the ruled. They tried to impose intellectual as well as material domination over the disadvantaged section of society. The alienation of the working class and peasants by the bourgeoisie can be described as the essential element of private property and had existed in feudal landed property, which was the root of private property and the procession of private land for agriculture. In such circumstances, the concept of public property emerged in the world. In feudal landownership, we already find the domination of the earth as an alien power over man. Already the land appears as the inorganic body of its lord, who is its master and who uses it to dominate the peasantry. But it is the bourgeois society that brings this domination of the earth (and through the domination of the earth, domination of humanity) to perfection.

Such a class of people was remarkable for the differentiation of power and the domination in social economic and can political scenarios of the society. Furthermore, in the first volume of *Capital*, Marx identifies the loss of soil fertility as being directly related to the capitalist system: "All progress in increasing the fertility of the soil for a given time is a progress towards ruining the more long-lasting sources of that fertility. Capitalist production therefore only develops the technique and the degree of combination of the social process of production by simultaneously undermining the original sources of all wealth — the soil and the worker." The isolation/alienation of humans from the rest of nature is one of the primary causes of the earth's environmental woes, leading to increased exploitation and abuse of the land. Eco-Marxists assert that in modern society the internal and external balances of nature is disturbed by the involvement of utilitarianism and profit motives of human beings. Or all the crises of modern society have deep relationships with one or other forms of capitalism and profit motives, the capitalist is using their power for their personal purposes and development. For eco-Marxists, there is also the failure to recognize the earth as an environment that can be seriously and irreparably harmed by human actions. This is one of the primary criticisms of modern agricultural methods.

According to many eco-Marxists, another fundamental flaw of the capitalist system is the process of "under-production", which means that capitalists treat nature as if it were a free commodity. There is a tendency inherent to capitalism to "undervalue, and thus, under-produce the conditions of production." Or the separation of people from the process of production also signifies that capitalism is constantly separating people from their natural habitats and ecosystems. Baudrillard pointed that capitalism is separating people from the harsh realities of life and converting the natural conditions of the people into synthetic or artificial ecosystems. Moreover, according to some economists, "under capitalist system men change their own nature as they progressively deprive nature of its externality, as they mediate nature through themselves, and as they make nature itself work for them and their own purposes. Basically, this means that the capitalist system does not take into account the true costs of environmental degradation, resource depletion, etc. into the costs associated with the product, and views nature as a commodity that is here for humans to exploit. This can lead to many environmental catastrophes, such as clear-cutting the rainforest, and the overexploitation of the ocean's marine life.

Eco-Marxism is an anthropocentric view that sharply criticizes western capitalism; eco-Marxists claim that a capitalist system negatively influences the relation of humans and nature, and that "democratic and capitalist economies are mutually exclusive from the protection of nature." In the mind of Marx, the only way to solve the problem of environmental degradation, and the dreadful conditions of the worker, was through liberation from the capitalist system; Marx's notion of human emancipation was linked to his vision of overcoming humanities isolation from nature through the development of a socialist society. "For humanity to progress beyond alienation, it is necessary 'to govern the human metabolism with nature in a rational way', a goal only obtainable with the elimination of capitalism." Eco-Marxists (*ibid*) expanded that western capitalism is completely depending on nature and natural resources for the optimization of their capital and popularizing the view that they are the true proponents if the environmental protection and safeguards. The neo-Marxist Althusser says that conditions of alienation defined by Karl Marx have been redefined today because the capitalist is making new particles and agendas to impose the principles of capitalism to the masses, they are creating the conditions of alienation by making a technocratic consciousness that human beings are equal in all spheres of social life. In modern capitalism blocks, the cognitive capacity of human beings and their natural ability of cognitive power and induces artificial intelligence and thinking power.

Modern trends in Environmental-Sociological Theory

Core notions of environmental sociology came in the late 1970s and early 1980s and were strongly influenced by trends in environmental mobilization and ecological movements. The first major influence was the explosion of attention to global warming and global environmental change from 1988 onwards. Dunlap and Catton (1994) have demonstrated that public attention to global change facilitated growth in environmental sociology. Another dissemination of scientific information about global change served to shore up the confidence and resolve of many environmental sociologists that their theories can and should give priority to the material-ecological substratum of social structure and social life.

Cultural, structural and materialistic interpretations of environmental sociology was emerged recently in the world. Marxism and socialism have contributed to the decreased persuasiveness of some of the more materialist components of sociology such as neo-Marxism and political economy. At the same time, the contribution generated by cultural studies, constructivism, feminism, post-modernism, semiotics, and so on in academia at large has spilled over into sociology. This has led to rapid growth of cultural sociology, growing influence of micro sociological perspectives, and a reduced stature of structural theories.

Ecological modernization characterized by mechanization and modern technology resulted new researches and understanding in the area of environmental sociology. In modern era, the new epistemological quest resulted new areas of studies to identify the interrelationships between society and environmentalists. It is very evident that recent postulates postures of environmental sociology have essentially defined the core of environmental sociology in the form of neo-materialism, structuralism, and realism etc. in the background of environments and human interaction. Dunlap and Catton (1994) and Murphy (1994), explained the cultural-constructivist invasion of environment in the industries nation. Each has argued that cultural-environmental sociology is essentially incompatible with a sociology that is able to recognize the material and biophysical substructure of nation-states and global society.

Environmental sociology over the past half decade or so has become more specialized and, to some degree, balkanized. Also, because some of the most influential theories are essentially metatheories, and do not readily lend themselves to test and falsification; there has been some trend to embracing more middle range theories (e.g., Freudenburg and Gramling, 1994a, 1994b). Other scholars, particularly those whose interests lie in resource extraction processes such as agriculture, mining, and timber, have found themselves more at home with theoretical views that come without presuppositions as to the singularity of environmental quality and degradation (see, e.g., Bunker 1992; Freudenburg *et al.* 1995).

Thus, environmental sociology in the 1990s has a dual character. On one hand, it remains strongly influenced by several viewpoints of realist-materialist discussions and debate, that place major emphasis on revealing the material-ecological substructures of modern societies. At the same time, environmental sociology is now a less consensual and more contested area of scholarship than it was a decade ago. In large part this has been due to the cultural turn of environmental sociology and the challenge that cultural-environmental sociology has presented to the materialist core of the subdiscipline.

Environmental sociology faces a major challenge to strife over the role that social constructionist and cultural sociology and other fields. The intense debates and discussions that now crop up in the literature and, more commonly, take place in annual meeting hallways and classrooms are providing the raw material for advance in the field. Envionmetal sociology deveopleed to create new epistemological outlook to understand nature and natural resourses.

Conclusion

Environmental sociology as a systematic interpretation of environmental principles has made remarkable contributions in the study of environments and human interactions. As a fast growing branch of sociology, it has gained the attention of national and international environmentalists, academicians and scholars. As a discourse and discipline, it systematically explains the causes or factors that influence the ecological balance of the society. There are different theoretical formulations explaining the interrelationships between human beings and its nature. The traditional perspective like the biological determinism explains that society and organism have number of similar characteristics and in both the developmental patterns are from simple to complex. Ranging from homogeneity to heterogeneity or instability to stability, the Social Darwinism cites that the existence of society is from the maintenance of societal equilibrium by loose and gain process. Existential dualism as branch of sociology explains that society and environments are two sides of the same coin. Marxism is intrinsically "exemptionalist" and uneconomical are among the major focal points of debate. These debates as currently undertaken in which there is less focus on the specific issues at stake than on the ostensible superiority or inferiority of one or another theoretical systems or "paradigms" are not likely to be fruitful. Typically, there is little to choose between the core arguments of each. Eco-Marxism as the central concern of this chapter highlights that the inherent social division in the society on the basis of the possession of wealth and material are the fundamental reason of environmental crisis and issues. Overexploitation of the nature and material refocuses for economic and developmental purposes resulted in the alienation of people from the harsh realities of life. For Marx, the only solution to the problem of environmental crises is the liberation of capitalism and formation of a classless egalitarian society.

References

Avineri, Shlomo (ed.) (1977). *Varieties of Marxism.* The Hague, Netherlands: Martinus Nijhoff.

Bannister R. William Graham (1973). Sumner's Social Darwinism: reconsideration. *History of Political Economy, 4,* 89-109.

Benton, T. (1989). "Marxism and natural limits: An ecological critique and reconstruction". *New Left Review, 178,* 51-86.

Buttel, Frederic (1996). "Environmental and Resource Sociology: Theoretical issues and Opportunities for Synthesis." In *Rural Sociology,* Vol. *61*(1), pp. 56-75.

Ecological modernization as social theory.

F.H. Buttel, Department of Rural Sociology, University of Wisconsin, Madison, 1450 Linden Drive, Madison, WI 53706, USA.

Foster, J.B. (2000). *Marx's Ecology: Materialism and Nature.* New York: Monthly Review Press.

Foster, James B. (2000). *Marx's Ecology.* New York: Monthly Review Press.

Francis Fox *et al.* (1991). "Collective protest a critique of resource mobilization theory". *International Journal of Culture Politics and Society,* Vol. 4, No. 4,

Giddens, Anthony (1971). *Capitalism and Modern Social Theory.* United Kingdom: Cambridge University Press.

Grundmann, R. (1991). *Marxism and ecology.* Oxford: Oxford University Press.

Han, L. (2001). *Ecology and Marx—The Unification of Naturalism and Humanism.* Japan: Jichousha Preview.

Jean Baudrillad (1991). *Science Fiction Studies,* Part 3.

Marx, Karl and Engels, Frederick (1894). *Capital, Volume 3.* Edited and translated by Frederick Engels. New York: International Publishers.

Marx, Karl (1887). *Capital, Volume 1.* Trans. Samuel Moore & Edward Aveling. Moscow: Progress Publishers.

Marxism and Humanism' first appeared in the *Cahiers de l'I.S.E.A.,* June 1964.

Riley E. Dunlap and William R. Catton, Jr (1979). *Annual Review of Sociology,* Vol. 5, pp. 243-273.

Spencer Herbert (1891). *Essays: Scientific, Political, and Speculative.* London: Williams and Norgate

Spencer, Herbert (1882). *Principles of Sociology.* London: Williams and Norgate.

7

Climate Crisis and Water Scarcity

Can Sustainable Practices Save India's Rice Exports?

Swati Pathak, Hitesh Solanki and *Shefali Dani*

Introduction

Climate change is witnessed by whole universe in terms of increasing surface temperature, anomalies in quantity of rainfall, number of heat and cold days, rise in sea level, melting glaciers and extreme events like, droughts and floods. Effects of climate change, its implication, adaptation, and mitigation are divergent within states and across countries based on climatic zone and its socio-political-economic situation. However, agriculture and hydrological sectors are badly challenged by climate impacts. Therefore, water stressed agro-based country like India where livelihood of 70% population depends on agriculture is facing a huge threat in terms of sustainable crop production especially water guzzler crops, judicial water management and food security.

Rice is a main staple food for more than half of India's population and is considered as primary crop in terms of food security. Climate pattern, soil quality, food habit, lucrative price, and huge international rice demand support intensive rice production and together form a comparative advantage for India to encourage large scale of export of rice to rest of the world. However, India is the second largest rice producer after China and largest exporter of rice (FAO, 2019), followed by USA, Thailand, and Vietnam. However, productivity of rice (2.5 tonne/ha) in India is much below global average 3.1 tonne/ha (Despande, 17). Water guzzler rice needs a great amount of water about 3000-5000 lit to grow1 kg of rice consumes one third of total water needed for agriculture in India (Sharma *et al.*, 2018). Major rice producing states in India are expected to experience acute water scarcity in future years and identified globally as acute water hotspots (Sharma *et al.*, 2018) have gained lots of attention from agriculturists and economists in terms of sustainable production and export of highly irrigated water intensive rice. Therefore, sustainability of rice production and export of rice at larger scale in India for coming years is in question.

There is a strong relationship between climate change on agriculture. Existing studies have established the direct impact of climate change on trade infrastructure and transport systems due to extreme events like storm, drought, flood, sea level surges and sea storm (Goyol and Pathirage, 2017; Asariotis *et al.*, 2018; Nemry and Demirel, H., 2012). But indirect impact of climate change on comparative advantage of a country's trade through supply or availability of factors of production such as water, crops is less in quantity (Dellink, 2017). Studies on exploring relation between impact of climate change and water intensive agricultural trade are scanty in India. Our study is an attempt to light on the linkage between climate, water availability and usage of water for producing exportable rice and get an in-depth understanding on future sustainability of export of rice within constraints of climate change and water stress in India.

The chapter is organized as follows. Section 2 demonstrates the background of the study. Section 3 presents data sources, hypothesis, and methodology. Section 4 summarizes the findings and includes detailed discussion on results. Section 5 concludes the chapter with listing down the limitations and probable policies of the study.

Background

Climate Change

"Climate change" refers to change in global average temperature and global average rainfall for an extended period of time.

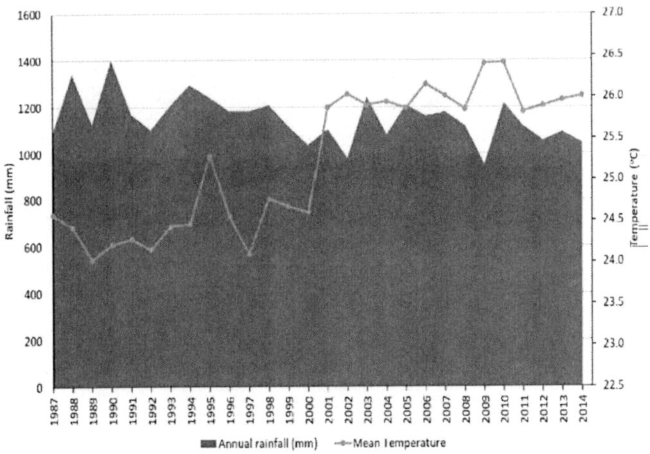

Fig. 7.1a: Pattern of annual rainfall and average temperature in India.
Source: MoSPI (2018), IMD (2018).

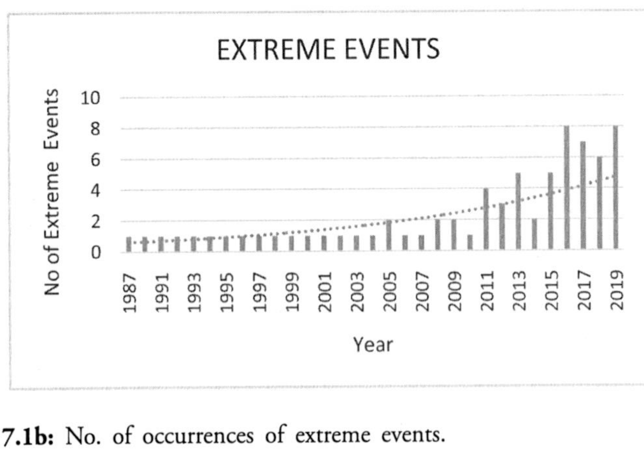

Fig. 7.1b: No. of occurrences of extreme events.
Source: EM-DAT, NDMA, author's estimation.

Global warming showed 1°C above pre-industrial levels in 2017 with a rate of 2°C by each decade will expect to reach of 1.5 °C around 2040 (IPCC, 2018). Past thirty years showed a decreasing and uneven trend of precipitation, rising average temperature and increasing number of extreme events especially floods and droughts (Fig. 7.1). In 1990, annual rainfall was estimated around 1400 mm dropped to 1150 in 2014-15 whereas temperature sored in all past years.

According to the International Disaster Data base, rates have been surged at higher level in different parts of India; more prominently in Assam, Kerala, West Bengal compared to last decade. Published data by Central Water Commission (CWC) in 2019 revealed that various rivers cross their high flood level in various states in India like Bihar, Kerala, Orissa due to huge rainfall for certain period but at the same time many states experience lower rainfall (Kapil, 2019).

Water Situation in India

Average temperature rise caused huge water stress. Various studies show that climate change would cause a sheer number of variations in precipitation, surface water availability and resulting water stress, increase in salinity in groundwater resource (Postel, *et al.*, 1996; Oki Kanae, 2006, Pfister, *et al.*, 2009; Alcamo, *et al.*, 2016). Figure 7.2 (a), (b), (c) and (d) portray present and projected per capita water availability, water demand for irrigation vs. water availability, sector-wise water demand trend and share of different irrigation types. Results represent an alarming situation, where on one hand, falling per capita availability of water, stagnant rate of water availability with high growth rate of water demand for irrigated agriculture lower the gap between water supply and demand and is expected the latter would outweigh the former in future years making India acute water stressed country if the necessary water related measures are not taken immediately. On the other hand, agricultural irrigation sector managed to be the highest water consuming sector in past, present and in next three decades where groundwater irrigation is being practiced more compared to surface water irrigation. About 60% of irrigated area is now covered under groundwater irrigated putting extra burden on water withdrawals for different river basins and cause depletion of groundwater level (Amrasinghe *et al.*, 2008). This causes monetary burden on farmers in terms of irrigation cost and higher fuel consumption.

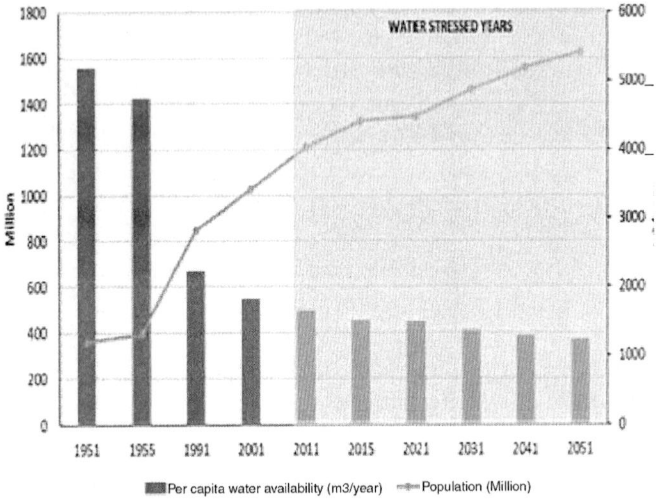

Fig. 7.2a: Per-Capita water availability and Population.
Source: CWC, 2018, authors' estimation.

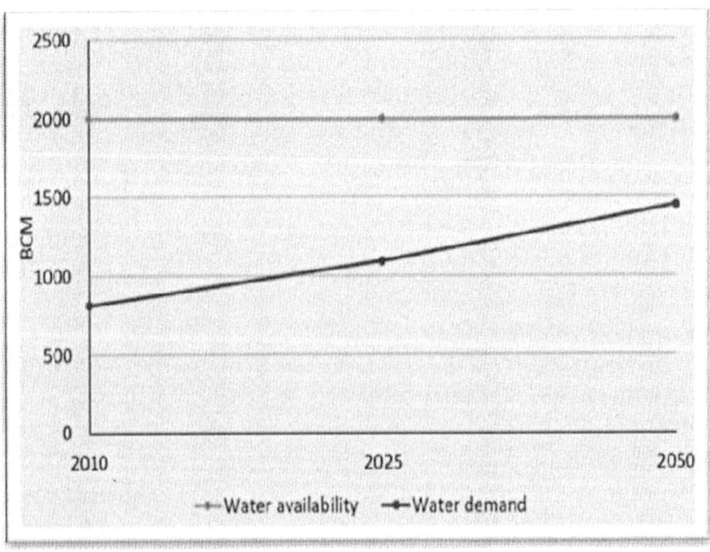

Fig. 7.2b: Water Availability vs. Water Demand.
Source: CWC, 2002, authors' estimation.

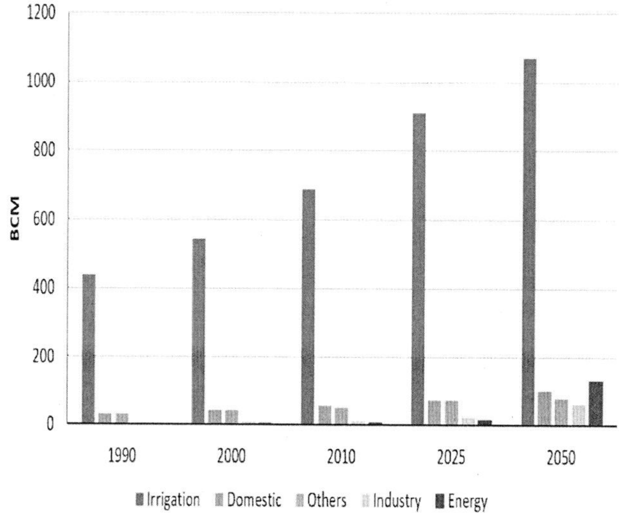

Fig. 7.2c: Water Demand by Sectors.
Source: MoSPI, 2002.

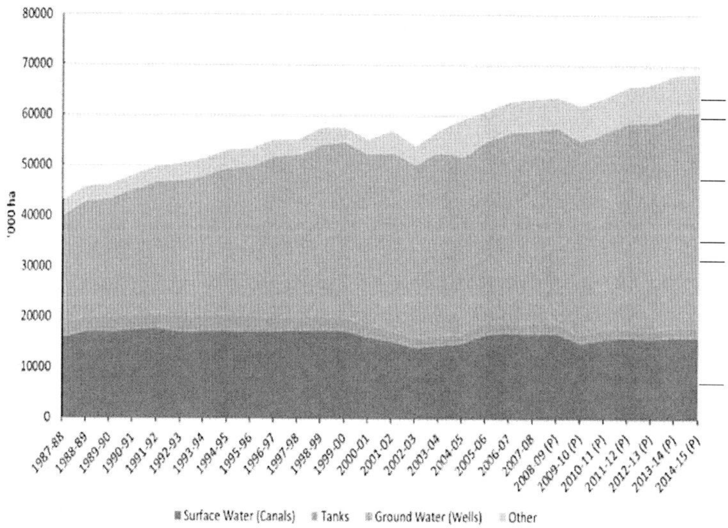

Fig. 7.2d: Different modes of irrigation.
Source: MoA, 2019.

Poor water management, inadequate water storage, lack of awareness, loosely pricing water and isolates water policies are the causes of growing scarcity of waterbody in India. Indian Think tank, Niti Ayog (2018) revealed in his report, that by 2030 India's water demand will be doubled compared to water availability and pose serious threat to livelihood of millions of people. At present, 600 million people in India are facing acute water shortage and about 2,00,000 people lose their lives on account of dearth of this resource (Ayog, 2018). This also indicated that 6% GDP will fall due to this water crisis.

Interdependence between Climate Change, Water Availability, and water usage for exportable rice

Post Green revolution, high yielding variety seeds, improved technology, advanced agricultural know-how, improved fertilizers and pesticides made India strongest competitor globally in agricultural trade market specifically for water intensive rice. However, rise in per capita income and change in taste for non-cereal crops and meat items kept production of rice slightly low in previous years, presently India contribute 29% to world rice market. On account of that, water consumption for producing exportable rice has been increased by leaps and bound over the years compared to rate of increase in water availability. Water recharge rate was high till the year 2011, beyond this recorded a nearly constant rate whereas, water for export showed a steep rise over the past years (Fig. 7.3).

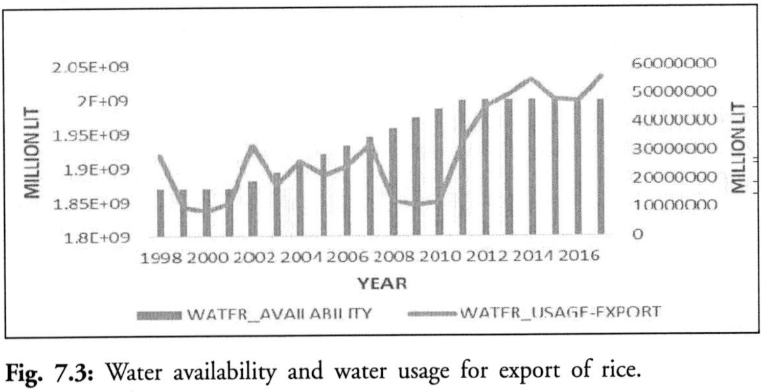

Fig. 7.3: Water availability and water usage for export of rice.

Source: CWC, (2018), authors' estimation.

Water availability in any country depends on amount of precipitation, availability of surface water (rivers, ponds, tanks etc.) and groundwater. The need of water for irrigation is met from two sources, surface water and groundwater. Due to unpredicted and inconsistent rainfall in India, rice production largely depends on irrigation. Climate change would impact on surface water and groundwater both altering precipitation level (Roson and Sartori, 2010). A total of 17% of world crop land is irrigated and it is expected to increase in future because of limited opportunities to expand rainfed crop production (Postel *et al.*., 1996). The rising temperature may increase precipitation and river discharges by glacier melting, thus cause higher water availability and lower water stress (Oki and Kanae, 2006). But at the same time other studies argued that the increase in water availability will be short run phenomenon but in long run water availability will fall considerably based on amount through low groundwater recharge (IPCC, 2008).

Altered precipitation amount, change in temperature and sudden calamities such as flood, drought etc. have impact on agricultural comparative advantages of a nation as well hence change flows of trade in agricultural goods (Nelson, 2009). A declining trade position in terms of increase in import of cereals due to rising water scarcity and lower yield had been found in Pakistan (Zhu, *et al.*, 2014). Mediterranean countries are expected to increase their water intensive imports to secure its water body from anticipated adverse impact of climate change (Hoekstra, 2010). Effects of climate change on agricultural productivity and virtual water trade in Mediterranean countries showed that climate change related water stress have differential impact on crops based on their type and modes of irrigation (Roson, 2010). A world bank report estimated imports on food grains by India will be doubled in year 2050 due to climate change (Gandhi, 2017) and is going to face huge amount of loss in terms of GDP due to fallout of extreme events (Mohan, 2017). India was a 'net importer' of virtual water until around the 1980s, but with the increase in grain exports, India has now become a net exporter of virtual water—about 1% of total available water every year (Singh, 2016). India uses domestic water resources more for export products than any other country does (Mudur, 12). On the other hand, extreme events such as untimely, uneven monsoon rainfall result in drought or flood also has adverse impact on yield of *khariff* rice crops in India (Auffhammer, *et al.*, 2012). More than 97% of farmers in Bangladesh believed that the rainfall is reduced and lower the rice production in Bangladesh (Maya, *et al.*, 2019). Despite of this fact, India uses almost twice the amount of water to grow crops as compared to China and United States (Qazi, 2017). Given the adverse impact of climatic factors and water stressed situation, sustainable production of rice in India with more rice eaters is a serious concern.

In short, implications of climate change and water scarcity in agricultural trade sector are multifaceted. The major objectives of this chapter are:

- To Quantify the impact of climate parameters on Water Availability,
- To explore the relation between climate change and water used for producing exportable rice, and
- To capture the indirect impact of climate change mediated by water availability on water usage for rice crops for export.

Data Sources

Secondary data is obtained from Government reports, websites, government statistics and international data sources. Compilation of time series data for a period of thirty-two years (1986-2018) was done on climate parameters namely temperature, rainfall, special events, economic variables, quantity of export in India, domestic production, yield, and irrigated area for rice. Data on export quantity was collected from The Agricultural Food Processed Products Export Development Authority (APEDA). Information on Domestic consumption of rice, population is obtained from Handbook of Statistics, Reserve Bank of India (RBI) and World Bank. Statistics on domestic water availability, water requirement and agricultural share have been collected from Central Water Commission (CWC) and *indiastat.com website.* Water availability is estimated and projected by using per capita water availability and population. Crop water requirement in India has been obtained from a report by Brahmanand (2016). Time series data on annual rainfall (rainfall) and mean temperature have been obtained from Indian Meteorological Department. Number of occurrences of extreme events (floods, droughts, heat waves, cold waves, wind blows etc.) were estimated from EM-DAT database and National Disaster Management Authority, India (NDMA) for India.

Methods

Data on various parameters selected for these studies are analyzed using different statistical methods like, trend analysis, Wilcoxon ranked test for comparing mean, Pearson's correlation and multiple regression with interaction terms. Bootstrap method has been used to capture Indirect effect or Mediation effect. Based on existing data interpolation and extrapolation have been done for getting missing years for some variables viz. consumption of rice, water availability, water demand for irrigation. Water usage (mm-ha/lit) for producing rice for exportable amount has been calculated using export of rice (tons), yield (kg/ha) and crop water requirements (mm/year). Unit conversions are done accordingly. All statistical analysis is performed using Excel and SPSS 14. PROCESS .4 in SPSS is also used to conduct BOOTSTRAP mediation effect analysis. Each of the methods used in the study is explained below.

Trend Analysis: Analyze the Past 30 years Trend

To capture the trend of climate parameters (Average temp, annual rainfall, no. of extreme events) over the chosen 30 years (1988-2018), linear time series analysis has been done taking time period as independent variable and rest as dependent variables.

Average Temperature (standardized) = $\beta_0 + \beta_1$ Time +Error...(1)
Annual Rainfall (standardized) = $\beta_0 + \beta_1$ Time +Error....... (2)
Mean no. of occurrence of extreme events = $\beta_0 + \beta_1$ Time +Error... (4)

Where β_i represents coefficient value for independent variable, time, for each of the model. This indicates, how average value of dependent variable will change as one more year would be added.

Wilcoxon Signed Rank Test (WST)

Wilcoxon Signed Rank Test is performed on water related variables such as, water availability, domestic water consumption for irrigation and water used for producing exportable rice. Before selecting this method, normality test (Shapiro-wilk) was done on study variables. Based on findings, WST, non-parametric statistical hypothesis test is chosen to be conducted to see the differential impact of time variable on all three water related variables. This is used to investigate change in water variables from *pre period* to *post period* where "year 2003" has been decided as the cut of year for deciding *pre* and *post* as this has been notified by IPCC and UNFCC as "climate base year". *Pre* is defined as (1986-03) and Post is (2003-2018). Descriptive statistics have been used to elabourate mean and standard deviations of the selected variables. The alternative hypotheses for Wilcoxon rank test are:

H1: there are no difference in *pre* and *post* period water availability

H2: there are no difference in *pre* and *post* period water usage for producing export able rice.

Correlations Matrix

Pearson correlation analysis is done among climate variables. The objective was to identify the association between mean temperature, annual rainfall, and extreme events. A correlation matrix is a useful tool to select necessary variables for choosing models for regression analysis.

Multiple Regression Analysis and Empirical Models

To identify and quantify the significant impact of climate change on water availability and water used for export quantity of rice in India, we have used two linear regression models. Multiple regression analysis is generalized form of simple regression analysis, where two or more variables are used to explain a dependent variable. Coefficients of "interaction terms" are important for all two models which capture the combined impacts of climate variables on dependent variable. Stepwise regression is used to get the significant and best fitted model.

Model 1: Mean Water availability = β_0+ β_1 rainfall + β_2 temp+ β_3 Extreme events + β_4 Temp*rainfall + β_5 temp*rainfall* extreme events+ β_6 extreme event*rainfall + β_7 extreme events*temp+ (error term)

Model 2: Mean Water usage for export (stand) = β_0+ β_1 rainfall+ β_2 temp + β_3 extreme events + β_4Temp*rainfall

+ β_5 temp*rainfall* extreme events + β_6 extreme event*rainfall+ β_7 extreme events*temp+ β_4 GDP+ $\in$
Where,

$\beta_{i=1\ to\ 3}$ implies one-unit increase in independent variable how impact on mean water availability when other variables are constant

$\beta_{i=4\ to\ 7}$ implies given one variable how change in another has impact on mean value if dependent variable.

Model with Mediator (Indirect Effect)

Mediational analysis tests a hypothetical (presumed) causal chain where one variable X affects a second variable M and, in turn, that variable affects a third variable Y (MacKinnon, 2012). In present context, Mediational Analysis is employed to have better understanding of the nature of relationship between the impact of climate variables on export is direct or indirect impact mediated through domestic production. Bootstrap method (Preacher and Hayes, 2004) has been used to capture the presumed mediation impact of domestic water availability on water usage for exportable rice controlling climate parameters. *PROCESS version 3 for SPSS was used (Hayes, A, 2013) to conduct Mediation analysis.*

Impact of Climate Variables (IV) on Quantity of Export of rice (DV) in India *mediated by production (MV)*

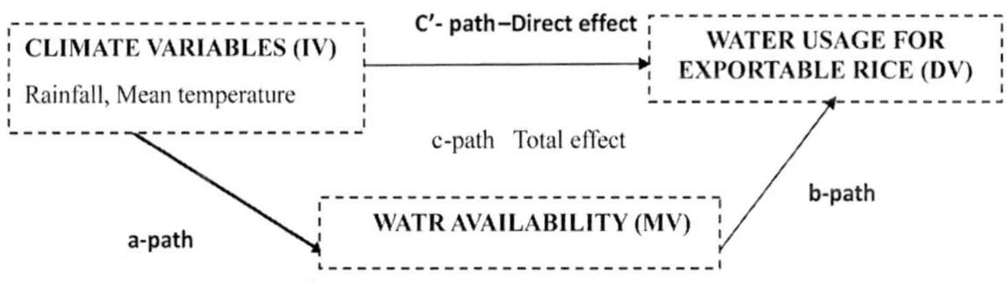

Path Analysis Diagram: Mediational Analysis.

Source: Aron, A., Coups, J.E., Aron, N.E. (2013). The General Linear Model and Making Sense of Advanced Statistical Procedures in Statistics for Psychology, chapter 15, 636, 6th Ed.

a-path: Mean Water availability = β_0+ β_1 rainfall+ v_2 temp+$\in$.

b-path: Mean of Water usage for Exportable rice = β_0+ β_1 water availability +$\in$

c-path: Mean of Water usage for Exportable rice = $\beta_0 + \beta_1$ rainfall+ β_2 temp + …. *Direct Effect*

Mediation Effect (b and c' path): Multiple regression predicting DV from MED & IV

Water usage of exportable rice= $\beta_0 + \beta_1$ rainfall+ β_2 temp+ β_3 production+ (error term)

Significance level of Indirect Effect will determine if country's water availability behaves as mediator in explaining climate impacts on Export of rice. Significance determines if "0" lies outside the range between lower bootstrap CI and upper bootstrap CI.

Results

Findings are presented in following five sections.

General trend of Climate Change: Trend Analysis

This is evident from (Table 7.1) average earth temperature is increasing over the years with more extreme events and uneven declining rainfall. Annual rainfall shows decreasing trend (0.56) in last thirty years. However, annual rainfall does not reflect the actual variation in precipitation as India is divided in different agro-climatic zone with and different weather pattern. Moreover, amount of rainfall varies across regions and within months. July to September is the time when heavy rainfall is experienced by most of the region. Therefore, instead of annual rainfall, monthly rainfall may give clearer picture about the pattern and amount of rainfall in India.

Table 7.1: Trend Analysis for Rainfall, Temperature, Extreme events

Variables		Adjusted R-square	Coefficients	T-value	Sig
Climate	Average Temperature	0.73	0.85	9.07	.000**
	Annual Rainfall	0.30	-0.56	-3.74	.001**
	Extreme Events	0.56	0.76	6.46	.000**

**P<01.

Table 7.2: Analysis on water availability with water usage for export of rice

Parameters	N	Mean	Std. Deviation	Minimum	Maximum	Percentiles		
Water Availability before	20	1878.3	19.65	1864.24	1933.15	1869.2	1869.43	1878.7
Water Availability after	12	1988.3	18.7	1946.22	1999.61	1975.9	1999.33	1999.5
Water usage export before	20	13.2	10.43	0	31.83	3.86	11.09	23.73
Water usage export after	12	36.02	16.84	11.16	56.05	16.77	39.17	49.23

**P<.01 1% error

Water Situation in India and water usage for production of export amount of rice: Wilcoxon Rank Test

Shapiro-Wilk test gives significant result for water availability (.762**) and water usage (.911*) which indicate data are not normally distributed. Therefore, non-parametric test is done and reported in Table 7.2 and Table 7.3. Table 7.2 shows about 6% growth rate of water availability in India after the year of 2003 whereas, water needed for exportable rice recorded above 170%, imply a tremendous pressure on water resources in India and indicate an uncertain export of rice in future years where latter would outweigh the former if adequate water related measures are not taken. However, standard deviation shows a more stability in water availability in post climate period compared to water usage for export. Results are statistically significant at 1% error (Table 7.3) which confirms that both the variables show significant differences between pre and post climate periods.

Table 7.3: Significance test

	Water Availability before Water availability after	**Water Usage before (ex) water usage after**
Z	-3.059^{b}	-3.059^{b}
Asymp. Sig. (2-tailed)	0.002	0.002
a. Wilcoxon Signed Ranks Test.		
b. Based on negative ranks.		

Dynamics Between Climate Parameters: Correlation Matrix

Correlation matrix (Table 7.3) shows higher association between average temperature and extreme events (.60) and annual rainfall and extreme events (-.45) which are statistically significant at 1% level. In addition to this temperature and number of extreme events shows a significant positive association whereas, later shows a negative association between them. Mean temperature and annual rainfall present negative significant association between them (-.38). Results do not reveal the exact direction of the association as relationships are complex and have differential impact on different parts in India.

Table 7.4: Correlation between Climate Parameters

Pearsons-Correlation	Rainfall	Temperature	Extreme Events
Rainfall	1	-.380*	-.455**
Temperature	-.380*	1	.602**
Extreme	-.455**	.602**	1
N	32	32	32

*P<.05 **P<01.

The contribution of Climatic Factors on Water Availability and Water usage for Exportable Rice: Multiple Regression analysis

Table 7.5 depicts the most important findings of the study, that frequency of extreme events and interaction term of temperature and rainfall have significant impact on water availability in India. One more occurrence of extreme event can cause increase in water availability by 0.9 million litre besides, given temperature, 1 mm rise in rainfall can cause increase in water availability by 0.36 million litre. However, the interpretation needs special care here as, extreme events might be flood, drought, more heat waves, or cold waves. This study chose to include the parameters "extreme event" as year-wise total number of 'natural calamities' rather type-wise number of events. The column containing 'standardized values' of each variable show a reduced level of collinearity. Larger Adjusted R square implies that 81% variation of water availability in India might be explained correctly by the chosen independent variables in this model.

Table 7.6 demonstrates impact of climate variables on usage of water for export of rice. Results revealed that, temperature (0.63), rainfall (0.33) both are separately having significant impact on usage of water for exportable rice. Interaction term (0.28) shows that, given rainfall temperature has significant negative impact on water usage. Direction of impacts of climate variables on water usage are ambiguous especially for rainfall. One of the reasons is, crop breeding to maturity period requires a range of temperature and precipitation amount. Discrete statistics on climate parameters may not rightly capture the impacts on dependent variables. Analysis under different

Table 7.5: Climate Variables on Water Availability

		Standardized Coefficients	t test	Sig.	Collinearity Statistics		Adjusted R square	F Value
		Beta			Tolerance	VIF		
Climate water Availability Model (Standardize)	(Constant)		262.01	.00			0.81	19.7**
	Rainfall	-.14	-1.06	.30	.34	2.93		
	Temperature	.33	1.89	.07	.21	4.83		
	Extreme Events	**.90**	**4.32**	**.00**	**.14**	**7.03**		
	Rainfall* Temperature	**.36**	**2.60**	**.02**	**.32**	**3.16**		
	Rainfall* extreme event	-.28	-1.57	.13	.20	5.03		
	Rainfall* Temperature* extreme event	.44	1.95	.06	.12	8.37		
	Temperature* extreme event	-.17	-0.63	.53	.09	11.29		
a. Dependent Variable: Water availability								

*P<.05 **P<01.

Table 7.6: Climate Variables on Water Usage for Export

		Standardized Coefficients	t test	Sig.	Collinearity Statistics		Adjusted R square	F Value
		Beta			Tolerance	VIF		
Climate Variables	(Constant)		10.07	.00			0.63	19.08**
	Rainfall	-.33	-2.61	**.01**	**.73**	1.37		
	Temperature	.63	5.42	**.000**	**.84**	1.18		
	Rainfall* Temperature	-.28	-2.39	**.02**	**.85**	1.18		
a. Dependent Variable: Export water								

*P<.05 **P<01.

climate models proposed by IPCC or UNFCC may be the next step of this study.

Therefore, present analysis only confirm that the causal relation exists between water availability and water consumed for exporting rice with climate factors such as annual rainfall, average temperature and total number of extreme events in India.

Indirect Impact Analysis of Climate Change: Model with Mediator

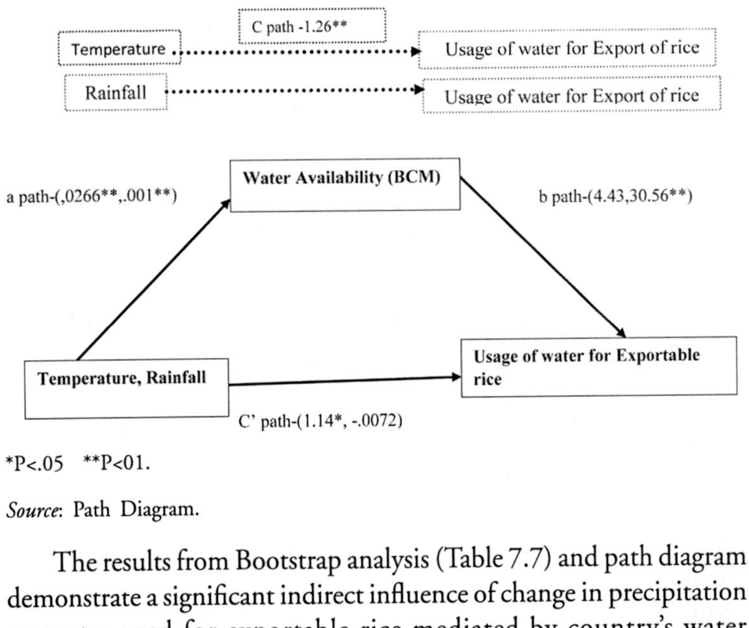

*P<.05 **P<01.

Source: Path Diagram.

The results from Bootstrap analysis (Table 7.7) and path diagram demonstrate a significant indirect influence of change in precipitation on water used for exportable rice mediated by country's water availability but temperature shows an insignificant indirect impact on usage. For rainfall "0" lies between the lower CI and upper CI. However, effect is small (-.0043) and direction is ambiguous. One of the reasons for this output is inadequate data on rainfall. As India is characterized with different agro-climatic zones with differential amount of precipitation in different seasons, annual average rainfall may not provide the correct and desirable estimations. State level analysis using monthly rainfall statistics would be further analysis to get in-depth understanding of impact of climate on water usage for export of rice mediated by water availability.

Table 7.7: Mediation Effect (Indirect effect)

	Indirect effect(s) of X on Y:			
	Effect	**Boot SE**	**Boot LLCI**	**Boot ULCI**
(a) Water Availability (Temperature)	.1180	.2737	-.5327	.5192
(b) Water Availability (Rainfall)	-.0043	.0026	-.0114	-.0031

Conclusion, Recommendation and Policy Implication

Sustainability of export of rice in India depends on its production and availability which in turn depends on India's climate type and water situation. Studies indicate a water stress situation is already experienced by various zones in India. Our analytical findings indicate that, **First,** average surface temperature is increasing over the years combined with declining trend of rainfall and more frequent natural calamities such as floods, droughts etc. **Second,** water availability rate is significantly low compared to water needed for agricultural irrigation and water usage for producing exportable rice where latter shows an extremely higher trajectory during last thirty years. The results stipulate that considerable amount of water usage is taking place in India to fulfil international rice demand without considering the present water situation in India and calculating future risk towards sustainability of rice production and food security. **Third,** substantial expansion of groundwater irrigation triggers a possibility of depletion of water tables which in turn causes huge financial burden on farmers in terms of irrigation cost. **Fourth,** the crucial findings of this study that significant causal relationship exists between water availability and water used for producing exportable amount with climate parameters. Moreover, temperature and rainfall have a combined impact on both the dependent variables which are highly statistically significant. However, direction of these relationship is ambiguous and need further study and detailed analysis.

Based on findings, this can be inferred that, agricultural trade, water and climate sectors are interdependent. A country's water situation and occurrence of climatic changes may have impact on the flow of export or import of water intensive crops. Sustainable production and export of water intensive rice and food security need adequate infrastructure, efficient water management, right cropping pattern, change in agricultural practices and suitable export import policies.

While an expected revenue loss may occur as a result of decision to reduce export of water intensive rice, an integrated climate-water-trade policy is the need of the hour. This will help secure sustainable production and export of rice without putting much pressure on water resources in India. On one hand, promoting stress Tolerant rice, climate smart seeds, introduce robust crop varieties which provide improved nutritional values, various agro-investment opportunities for farmers are required to be implemented to address climate adversities, on the other hand water management policies such as increasing water recharge, promote waste water management, practicing more micro or drip irrigation, reducing overexploitation of groundwater resources, improve infrastructure are need to be put in first priority during policy implementations. In this context, Government of India already announced a hike in minimum support prices (MSP) for all 14 "water efficient" and "highly nutrition" cereals such as Jowar, Bajra, Ragi, Edible oils, soybean to promote climate resilient and less water consuming crops to replace water guzzling crop rice.

Government may need to reconsider the long-term impact of a certain trade policy or international law on various sectors and evaluate benefit and cost not in monetary terms but on ecological conservation, securing biodiversity, and sustainability of resources like water and clean environment.

References

Alcamo, J., Florke, M., Marker, M. (2007). Future Long term changes in Global Water Resources Driven by Socio-Economic and Climatic Changes. *Hydrological Science Journal.* Vol. 52, No. 2, pp. 247-275.

Amarasinghe, Upali A. & Shah, Tushaar & Anand, B.K. (2008). "India's water supply and demand from 2025-2050: business-as-usual scenario and issues", IWMI Conference Proceedings 235165, International Water Management Institute. http://www.iwmi.cgiar.org/Publications/Other/PDF/NRLP%20 Proceeding-2%20Paper%202.pdf.

APEDA (2018). India Export Statistics (APEDA Products). Agricultural and Processed Food Products Export Development Authority (APEDA).

Aron, A., Coups, J.E., Aron, N.E. (2013). The General Linear Model and Making Sense of Advanced Statistical Procedures in *Statistics for Psychology*, chapter 15, 636.6th Ed.

Asariotis, R., Benamara, H., Naray, M.V. (2018). Port Industry Survey on Climate Change Impacts and Adaptation, UNCTAD Research paper no. 18. Division on Technology and Logistics, UNCTAD. United Nations.

Auffhammer, M., Ramanathan, V., Vincent, J.R. (2012). Climate change, the monsoon, and rice yield in India, *Climate Change*, Vol. 111, pp. 411-424. https://doi.org/10.1007/s10584-011-0208-4

Brahmanand, D.P.S. (2016). *Design Crop Water Requirement: Indian Scenario*, ICAR, Bhubaneswar, available at: https://aphrdi.ap.gov.in/documents/Trainings@APHRDI/AEEs/syllabus/Crop%20Water%20Requirement.pdf (accessed 18th July 2019).

Central Water Commission, CWC (2002). Projected Water demand (by different uses) in India. Water Related Statistics, Central Water Commission. Government of India. Retrieved on 12th Jan 2019 from https://www.indiastat.com/per-capita-availability-data/24/water supply/18198/stats.aspx

Central Water Commission, CWC (2018). Reassessment of water availability in basins using spatial inputs, basin planning and Management Organization, New Delhi, India.

Centre for Research on the Epidemiology of disaster, CREED. The International Disaster Database (EM-DAT.). Disaster of the week retrieved on 19th November, 2019 fromhttps://emdat.be/

Dellink (2017). "International trade consequences of climate change", *OECD Trade and Environment Working Papers*, 2017/01, OECD Publishing, Paris. http://dx.doi.org/10.1787/9f446180-en

Despande, T. (2017). State of Agriculture in India, Analytical Reports, PRS research.

FAO (2018). Rice Market Monitor. Food and Agriculture Organization of the United Nations, Vol. XXI, No.1. www.fao.org/economic/RMM. Rome.

FAO (2019): GIEWS Country Brief India.

Gandhi, J. (2017). Sharp spike in natural disasters impacting agriculture, data shows globally, disasters rose from 59 in the first decade of the last century to 4,479 in this century. *Hindustan Times*. Retrieved on July, 7, 2018 from https://www.hindustantimes.com/india-news/sharp-spike-in-natural-disasters-impacting-agriculture-data-shows/story-Wv5ywWXx6U1X4hwVjnVFZK.html

Goyol, S.S., Pathirage (2017). Climate change impacts on transport infrastructure in agrarian communities and policy implications for agricultural trade and food security in Nigeria. FAO. Corpus id: 171080565. Retrieved on 5th May, 2020 from www.fao.org/3/a-bu415e.pdf .

IMD (2018). All India monthly seasonal and annual rainfall. Indian Meteorological Department, Government of India.

Climate Change and Water (2018). Bates, B.C., Z.W. Kundzewicz, S. Wu and J.P. Palutikof, Eds. Technical Paper of the Intergovernmental Panel on Climate Change, IPCC Secretariat, Geneva, p. 210.

Hoekstra, A.Y. (2010). *The relation between international trade and freshwater scarcity, working paper ERSD-2010-05,* WTO working paper series; No. 5. Geneva, Switzerland: World Trade Organization.

IPCC (2018). Global Warming of 1.5°C, An IPCC Special Report on the impacts of global warming of 1.5°C above pre-industrial levels and related global greenhouse gas emission pathways, in the context of strengthening the global response to the threat of climate change, sustainable development, and efforts to eradicate poverty; Allen, M.R., O.P. Dube, W. Solecki, F. Aragón-Durand, W. Cramer, S. Humphreys, M. Kainuma, J. Kala, N. Mahowald, Y. Mulugetta, R. Perez, M. Wairiu, and K. Zickfeld. [Masson-Delmotte, V., P. Zhai, H.O. Pörtner, D. Roberts, J. Skea, P.R. Shukla, A. Pirani, W. Moufouma-Okia, C. Péan, R. Pidcock, S. Connors, J.B.R. Matthews, Y. Chen, X. Zhou, M.I. Gomis, E. Lonnoy, T. Maycock, M. Tignor, and T. Waterfield (eds.)]. In Press.

Kapil., S. (2019). Indian Rivers crossed highest flood level 25 times in August in 2019. This caused extreme floods in many states, according to Central Water Commission data. Down to Earth. Retrieved on 7th June, 2019 fromhttps://www.downtoearth.org.in/news/natural-disasters/indian-rivers-crossed-highest-flood-level-25-times-in-august-2019-66818

Mackinnon, P.D. (2011). Integrating Mediators and Moderators in research Design, *Res Soc Work Pract*, Vol. 21 (6), 675-681.

Maya, A.K., Sarker, R.A., Gow, J. (2019). Factors Influence Rice Farmers' Adaptation Strategies to Climate Change and Extreme Weather Events Impacts in Bangladesh, *Climate Change Economics*, Vol. 10, No. 03.

Mekonnen, M., Hoekstra, A.Y. (2010). The green, blue and grey water footprint of animals and animal products, Value of Water, Research Report Series No. 48, Twente Water Centre, University of Twente, Enschede, The Netherlands.

Ministry of Agriculture & Farmers Welfare, MoA (2019). Net Area Irrigated by Source in India, Government of India (on 1393) & Past Issues.

Mohan, V. (2017). Climate change costs India $10 billion every year: Government, *Economic Times*. Retrieved on 22 March, 2018. https://economictimes.indiatimes.com/news/economy/finance/climate-change-costs-india-10-billion-every-year government/articleshow/60113030.cms?utm_source=contentofinterest&utm_medium=text&utm_campaign=cppst

MOSPI (2007). Household Consumption of Various Goods and Services in India, 2004-05, NSS 61st Round (July 2004-June 2005), Vol. Major States and All-India, Report No. 509. Ministry of Statistics and Program Implementation, Government of India.

Mudur, S.G. (2012). India top virtual water exporter—Per capita domestic use half of us: study. *The Telegraph*. Retrieved on 7th August, 2018. Fromhttps://www.telegraphindia.com/india/india-top-virtual-water-exporter-per-capita-domestic-use-half-of-us-study/cid/450430

National Disaster Management Authority (NDMA). Some major Disasters in India, Disaster Data and Statistics. Government of India.

Nelson, G.C., Rosegrant, W.M., Koo, J., Robertson, R., Sulser, T., Zhu, T., Ringlker, C., Msangi, S., Palazzo, A., Magalhaes, M., Santos, V.R., Ewing, M., Lee, D. (2009): Climate Change: Impact on Agriculture and Costs of Adaptation, Food Policy Report. International Food Policy Research Institute, Washington, DC.

Nemry, F., Demirel, H. (2012). Impacts of climate change on Transport:A Focus on road and rail transport infrastructures, JRC Scientific and Policy Reports, Joint research Centre, Institute for Prospective Technologies Studies, European Commission. Spain.

Niti Ayog (2018): Composite Water Management Index: A tool for Water Management Niti Ayog, Government of India. < https://niti.gov.in/writereaddata/files/document_publication/2018-05-18-Water-Index-Report_vS8-compressed.pdf>

Oki, T., Kanae, S. (2006): Global Hydrological Cycles and World Water Resources: Freshwater Resources, Review Paper. *Science*, Vol. 313, pp. 1068-1072.

Pfister, S., Koehler, A., Hellweg, S. (2009): Assessing the Environmental Impacts of fresh Water Consumption in LCA, *Environmental Science and Technology*, Vol. 43, No. 11, pp. 4098-4104.

Postel, L.S., Daily, C.G., Ehrlich, R.P. (1996). Human Appropriation of Renewable Fresh Water. *Science*, New Series, Vol. 271, No. 5250, pp. 785-788.

Qazi, M. (2017): India's thirsty Crops are Draining the Country Dry: An Emphasis on Wtaer-Intensive Crops like Sugarcane and Rice is depleting India's Groundwater, *The Diplomat*, 06 April.

Roson, R., Sartori, M. (2010). Water Scarcity and Virtual Water Trade in the Mediterranean, Working Paper No. 38, The Centre for Research on Energy and Environmental Economics and Policy, Bocconi University, Milano.

Sharma, R.B., Gulati, A., Mohan, G., Manchanda, S., Ray, I., Amarsinghe, U. (2018): Water productivity Mapping of Major Indian Crops. Water Productivity, NABARD, ICRIER.

Singh, K. (2016). India's Water Crisis, *Bio Buzz*, Vol.1, 02.

Zhu, T., Xie, H., Wqas, A., Claudia, R., Muhammad, I., Goheer, M., Timorthy, S. (2014). Climate change and Extreme Events: Impacts of Pakistan's Agriculture. Report Number: IFPRI Policy Note 002, International Food Policy Research Institute.

8
Armed Conflicts, Military Pollution and its Environmental Hazards

An Overview

O. Nirmala

Introduction

The exploitation of natural resources is a serious concern for the security of nations. Exploitation is the selfish exploitation of a person or group in order to profit from them. Throughout history, it has been shown that the exploitation of natural resources and the environmental pressures associated with it can become a major factor in violence. In particular, when resources are scarce and competition for those resources increases, conflict-like situations are more likely to occur. The control and use of natural resources has always been a factor in armed conflict. The exploitation of valuable natural resources such as oil, gas, minerals, and timber is often cited as a key factor in starting, escalating, or sustaining wars around the world. Competition for increasingly scarce renewable resources such as land and water is increasing and being exacerbated by environmental degradation, population growth, and climate change. Researchers have recognized that members of armed forces and groups at the center of conflicts often rely on the exploitation of natural resources to fund their activities, including the payment of personnel and the purchase of weapons.

Environmental Degradation

One of the most critical issues for a nation's security in the 21st century is environmental degradation, particularly climate change and its impacts. Environmental degradation is a major factor in exacerbating and perpetuating poverty, especially among the rural poor, when it affects soil fertility, water quantity and quality, air quality, forests, wildlife, and fisheries. Global warming and climate change are hot topics in the news worldwide, and scientists are concerned about such climate variability in various places.

Environmental Security

Environmental security studies the vulnerability that environmental events and trends pose to specific people, groups, or entire regions. It may focus on how human conflict and international politics affect the environment or how environmental problems transcend national boundaries. Protecting the environment for its inherent moral value includes: preventing or restoring military damage to the environment; preventing or responding to conflicts caused by environmental factors. It takes into account how well people, communities, and countries can adapt to environmental hazards, change, conflict, and natural resource depletion. For example, the threat to environmental security posed by climate change could be analyzed. Agricultural production is changing as a result of regional and global climate and environmental changes caused by human activities that affect CO_2 emissions. Water scarcity and food shortages could result, which in turn could trigger political controversies, ethnic tensions, and social unrest. The ecosystem is significantly affected by military activities. War not only has a negative impact on the social environment, but also on the environment through the production of pollutants, greenhouse gasses, and depletion of resources.

Climate Change

Climate change has become critically important to global security in recent decades. Climate change-induced global warming is expected to have a cascading effect in which rising temperatures promote more frequent formation of hurricanes and storms in tropical regions and melting of the polar ice caps, which in turn will lead to rising sea levels and possible flooding of low-lying areas and island nations, threatening their existence. Rising temperatures may also favour the spread of communicable diseases such as malaria and cholera, as the number of airborne and waterborne vectors increases. Climate change is thus a serious cause for concern, as it is the source of several other natural and related phenomena that could threaten the existence of humanity in the coming decades. Climate change may also affect agricultural production as normal climates are disrupted by rising temperatures.

Food scarcity is an issue that has been called the most important problem that nations will face in the future if we do not take care of our environment. Food price inflation is already a reality, especially in developing countries that have high population densities. Although predictions of a food shortage have not yet materialized, it cannot be ruled out in the future, as a rapidly growing population will put additional strain on finite land resources and the overuse of fertilizers could lead to soil infertility due to a chemical imbalance. Environmental refugees could soon become a reality, as environmental degradation and food and water shortages could lead to mass population outflows from affected regions and contribute to instability in host countries. Protecting and nurturing the environment is an urgent need of the hour, as a destabilized environment can lead to a tipping point after which catastrophic and irreversible consequences, such as an increase in natural disasters, can threaten the survival of the state and its population.

Threat Multiplier

States already face myriad internal conflicts and social threats. Apart from this, climate change acts as a 'threat multiplier' that reinforces existing vulnerabilities in populations and existing threats to security, and may indirectly increase the risk of violent conflict. Environmental change, and climate change in particular, is most vulnerable in countries with weak or failed governments and/or existing conflicts. Climate change impacts are likely to disproportionately affect these more vulnerable societies.

Environmental security is the viability of the environment with three sub-issues: Preventing or remedying military damage to the environment, preventing or responding to environmentally induced conflict, and protecting the environment for its inherent moral value. The environment has no boundaries or it has no limits like a defined boundary for states. Humans cannot control nature. Any impact, no matter how small, on one part of the world will affect other parts. Degradation of the environment can lead to conflict and a reduction in security. Or conflict can destroy the resources and services provided by the environment, which also affects security. The environment has become hostage to wars or armed conflicts.

Table 8.1: Major Conflicts and Environmental Impact

S. No.	World Conflict	Year	Environmental Damage
1	World War-I	1914-1918	Reduction in flora and fauna, pollution, destruction of resources, Health related issues etc.
2	World War-II	1939-1945	Nuclear hazards, Reduction in flora and fauna, pollution, destruction of resources, Climate Change, Health issues etc.
3	Gulf War	1991	Oil Spill, coastline sediments, marine species and ecosystems, destruction of marine resources, Health issues etc.
4	Ukraine Russia conflict	Present	Reduction in flora and fauna, pollution, destruction of resources, Climate Change, Health issues etc.

The list of conflicts in world is more but to understand the criticality the few world conflicts were highlighted. Whether it is small or large scale conflict, the environment is the silent victim. To understand in much better way it is important to analyse how environment is degraded before, during and after conflicts.

Environmental degradation before wars or conflicts

Environmental problems at domestic military sites include noise pollution, explosives on the firing range, and contamination of drinking water when exercises take place in bodies of water. The environment near some military installations has been devastated by debris, industrial solvents, and fire fighting foams. Environmental consequences begin long before the actual conflict. Enormous amounts of resources are consumed to build and improve military forces. These include hydrocarbons, common metals, and rare earths for the manufacture of weapons and munitions. Training is essential in maintaining military readiness, but training consumes its resources. All forms of infrastructure, especially military vehicles, aircraft, ships, and buildings, require energy, and petroleum is usually the least efficient source of that energy. It is believed that the largest militaries emit more CO_2 than the majority of the world's nations combined. Like any other activity, the military requires large areas of land and sea, whether for testing, bases, or training. Military sites are thought to cover 1-6% of the global land surface. This is because they are used to preserve natural resources that are essential for the development of the state. In this case, many of these areas become ecologically important areas. Military training in these areas causes emissions, disturbance of landscapes and habitats on land and water, as well as chemical pollution and noise pollution from the use of weapons, aircraft and vehicles. Normally, environmental risks in these areas are analyzed after the conflict, but it is important to pay attention to our environment during the training period as well.

Military pollution is mainly due to the maintenance of existing military equipment. Disposing of obsolete equipment costs more and has a greater impact on the environment, especially when the equipment is filled with chemical, nuclear, and biological agents. This not only impacts the environment, but also the entire life cycle of the affected area. Sometimes excess munitions are also dumped in the ocean, weakening our environment and affecting public health, which in turn results in huge investments in environmental cleanup. These military spills will continue to increase in the international arena because state survival is critical. Sometimes, through treaties, states allow other states to build their military bases around their territory, which increases the risk, especially in terms of the environment. Military spending is important, but it indirectly diverts resources from solving environmental and other problems and affects the sustainable development of the state. Problems in international relations create severe tensions, leading to enormous military expenditures and neglecting climate issues. Access to and control over energy resources, especially coal, oil, natural gas, and nuclear substances, is changing the international situation. Therefore, it is important for nations to have high-level security policies and militarism should also be kept under control to protect the environment for future generations.

Environmental Degradation during Conflicts

Conflicts can have a variety of impacts on the environment. Even if they are short-lived, some international armed conflicts are very devastating. Some civil wars are fought at low intensity, while others can last for decades. Many modern confrontations are more ambiguous, lasting years but with regular intervals of intense fighting. The nature of the conflict—who is fighting, where, and how—has a significant impact on the environment. When there is war or unrest, environmental damage cannot be studied on a daily basis. However, it is reasonable to assume that the states involved in the conflict, whose scientific and technological development has already been assessed, can recognize environmental degradation during combat to some degree. Not only do they have an immediate impact on the environment, but they also have a long-term impact on the environment, especially when chemical, biological, and nuclear weapons are used. Nations affected by war or conflict will have their own time to recover from the economic and environmental turmoil. Humans are the game changers when it comes to climate change and effective use of natural resources. If nations cared about the environment and other important issues, they would not be at war. The long-term effects of conflict will teach people to care about the environment. The events before and during the battle can be decided, but the events after the war can only be analyzed.

Pollution, emissions, and the rapid depletion of natural resources are the immediate consequences of conflict. When the state's target is either a countervalue or a countervailing power, the environmental consequences are unpredictable. When states attack key infrastructure, especially military bases, the amount of carbon a bomb emits will damage the air and land. Surrounding biological organisms will be completely destroyed. If the priority of states is livelihood, especially water availability, the food security and health security of states is in question.

When fighting occurs in the oceans, the marine ecosystem is severely impacted by shipwrecks and attacks on offshore oil facilities. The displacement or migration of people during conflict has significant environmental impacts, primarily due to poor management and sanitation. During a crisis, it is difficult to introduce new projects. As a result, the ecology suffers greatly during a conflict.

Post-conflict Environmental Degradation

After conflict, states need time to recover before resuming activities. There is also a shift in the geographic pattern when neighboring states are enemies or at war. States may erect a wall or barbed wire to restrict the free movement of animals and people. Conflict or violence can isolate people from the resources they depend on, especially forests, minerals, and water. The new occupier may benefit from these resources, but the people who had access to them before the conflict are limited to the resources available. The new occupant can extract these resources more quickly, leading to natural resource depletion and environmental degradation. Post-conflict clearance of landmines and explosives is a major environmental problem. The costs that states must bear to clean up the environmental damage are enormous.

The Impact of War on the Environment

Constant strikes against refineries, chemical plants, energy facilities, industrial depots, or pipelines have caused toxic chemicals, fires, and building collapses to damage the nation's air, water, and soil, posing long-term health risks such as cancer and respiratory disease. Many of these problems are transboundary, so the consequences are felt not only in the state where the conflict is taking place, but pose a major health threat to the entire population. Military operations have also led to a significant increase in waste. This includes damaged or abandoned military vehicles and equipment, shell fragments, civilian vehicles, construction debris, and uncollected household or medical waste. Some of these materials are harmful, such as shell fragments, medical waste, or asbestos-containing construction debris, and require special handling, transportation, and disposal.

The use of firearms inevitably has serious negative consequences, including acute and long-term environmental and health effects. Exposure to hazardous compounds contained in ammunition residues that release toxic substances into the soil and alter the quality of surface and groundwater poses a direct threat to public health. Hazards include munitions-related heavy metals, energetic chemicals such as trinitrotoluene (TNT), hexogen (RDX), and rocket and missile propellants. The large number of abandoned or damaged military vehicles contain hazardous compounds that pose a danger to humans and the environment and require careful management for collection and disposal.

Environment Security

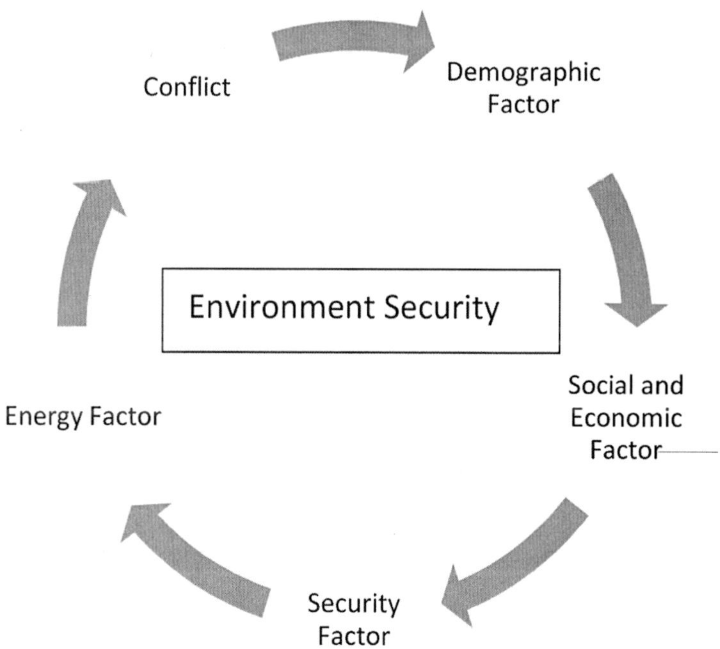

Fig. 8.1: Linkage between Conflict and Environment Security.

Conclusion

Post-war restoration will be a major task that will require extensive efforts. The environment can be restored if certain measures are taken, such as effective waste management in armed conflict areas, ensuring the sustainability of natural resources, and the restoration and development of conflict areas. International cooperation and coordination is needed for the restoration and development of conflict areas. Disposal, management, and recycling of the vast quantities of military and other wastes will help reduce acute health hazards. It goes without saying that it is better to maintain a peace-like situation through diplomacy than to wage war, especially when the environment is the victim.

References

https://ceobs.org/how-does-war-damage-the-environment/

https://na.unep.net/siouxfalls/publications/Conflicts.pdf

https://www.fawco.org/global-issues/environment/environment-articles/4767-impact-of-war-on-our-natural-environment

https://www.globalcitizen.org/en/content/how-war-impacts-the-environment-and-climate-change/

https://www.fcnl.org/updates/2020-11/environmental-cost-war-and-armed-conflict

https://nationalhumanitiescenter.org/education-material/the-environmental-impact-of-world-war-i/

https://www.economist.com/europe/2023/01/12/the-war-has-devastated-ukraines-environment-too?utm_medium=cpc.adword.pd&utm_source=google&ppccampaignID=18151738051&ppcadID=&utm_campaign=a.22brand_pmax&utm_content=conversion.direct-response.anonymous&gclid=Cj0KCQjwk7ugBhDIARIsAGuvgPZlgB0yMFoJuNSm7qz1gGArFfrFizY_7E4h2koM-ZhpjhCWZtKqy2waAvgDEALw_wcB&gclsrc=aw.ds

https://www.researchgate.net/publication/227574694_The_effect_of_warfare_on_the_environment

https://www.researchgate.net/publication/225379707_Prevention_of_War_and_Its_Environmental_Consequences

https://opendocs.ids.ac.uk/opendocs/bitstream/handle/ 20.500.12413/17466/1129_The_Environmental_Impacts_of_War_and_Conflict.pdf?sequence=1

https://research.library.fordham.edu/cgi/viewcontent.cgi?article=1070&context=environ_theses

https://www.unep.org/news-and-stories/story/rooting-environment-times-conflict-and-war

https://iopscience.iop.org/article/10.1088/1748-9326/7/1/015601

https://www.downtoearth.org.in/blog/climate-change/protecting-the-environment-in-times-of-war-66854

https://www.un.org/en/land-natural-resources-conflict/pdfs/GN_Renew.pdf

https://www.cmi.no/publications/file/1374-pressure-points-environmental-degradation.pdf

https://reliefweb.int/report/world/witnessing-environmental-impacts-war-environmental-case-studies-conflict-zones-around

https://warpp.info/en/m8/layers/environmental-safety/enviro-con#1/13/17

https://www.prio.org/publications/3686

https://pure.iiasa.ac.at/id/eprint/7427/

https://www.genevaenvironmentnetwork.org/resources/updates/protecting-the-environment-in-armed-conflict/

https://www.hrw.org/news/2022/11/04/curtailing-environmental-harms-armed-conflict

https://wedocs.unep.org/handle/20.500.11822/7813;jsessionid=372823C367B31843422A4375E98684BD

9

Energy Cooperation in Eastern South Asia to Strengthen Energy Security

Anita Elizabeth Mathew and *Santhosh Mathew*

Energy is one of the basic needs for development of any country. Being developing nations, Bhutan, Bangladesh, India and Nepal face a growing demand for energy. All the four countries are heavily dependent on energy. Energy holds a prominent position in their EXIM trade basket. Constant increase in imported energy sources such as coal, gas and oil have an adverse impact on the energy security of the sub-region. The energy demand in the region is expected to grow at an annual rate of 5%. (Rahman *et al.*, 2012) This sub-region is equipped in producing almost all kinds of energy (hydro, thermal, wind, solar). Some of these energy generation is affected seasonally. But the sub-region has the geographical advantage of being contiguous in nature. The willingness of subregional political regime is the most significant factor for enhancing sub-regional cooperation in supply of fossil fuel and energy trading.

A general analysis of the needs and potential of individual country would give a clear picture for assessing whether a cooperation as the sub-regional level is feasible and beneficial. The sub-region taken into consideration in this chapter includes India (especially eastern part of India), Bangladesh, Nepal and Bhutan. The study would delve into the potential that the Eastern South Asia hold for energy cooperation in order to strengthen energy security in the sub-region. The SAARC has come to a deadlock because of the Indo-Pak conflict. Strengthening ties among the countries of Eastern South Asia creates new hope in greater integration in the region.

Energy Overview of India

In April 2018, Indian government announced 100% electrification of its rural areas has been completed (The Wire, 2018). But electrification of all households is yet to be achieved. Moreover, electrification does not mean that there is 24-hours power supply in those areas. The duration of supply of electricity for domestic use in about 53% of the villages is less than 12 hours per day (Mishra, 2019). There has been an improvement in rural electrification, but the quality of energy supply is still very poor.

India is heavily dependent on coal for its energy needs. India has become a power surplus nation with no scarcity of coal or electricity, the power minister said in June 2017 (PIB, 2017). Thermal energy is a significant part of India's energy mix. But some of the thermal power plants are becoming NPA (non-performing assets) and one of the reasons is the shortage in the supply of coal (Mishra, 2019). In order to meet the growing demand, India imports coal.

India has a diversified energy mix to generate power. These include biomass, solar, wind, small hydro, hydro, natural gas, and nuclear power. As on February 2023, the generation capacity of India is 412 GW (CEA, 2023). India imports crude petroleum and refines it in the refinaries. The refineries have the capacity to process more than the demand in India. The surplus refined petroleum products is exported to Bhutan, Nepal, Bangladesh and other countries.

Energy Overview of Bangladesh

Natural gas and coal are the primary energy sources used to generate electricity in Bangladesh (Al-tabatabaie *et al.*, 2022). In Bangladesh, electricity is available for 85 per cent of the population (International Energy Agency, 2023). In Bangladesh, oil, gas and coal are the main fuels for electricity generation. Apart from that, natural gas is also used for fertiliser industry. Natural Gas has a majority share in the energy mix of Bangladesh. About 58% of the domestic power demand is met by natural gas (Bangladesh Power Development Board, 2019). The gas reserves in Bangladesh are depleting. In order to meet the growing demand, the country is importing gas from Qatar. At the same time, new renewable sources like solar, wind energy and hydro energy for electricity generation have been explored. Bangladesh imports coal from India.

The total electricity demand in 2021 was around 20 GW (Ministry of power energy and mineral resources). To meet the increasing demand and to address the depleting resources, Bangladesh has number of projects in its pipeline. In Bangladesh, renewable energy has advanced significantly in recent years. By 2030, the Bangladeshi government plans to produce more than 4100 MW of power from renewable sources (Al-tabatabaie *et al.*, 2022). With the commissioning of 360 MW Haripur and 450 MW Meghna Ghat and Power plants built by the private sector with foreign investment, Bangladesh achieved 100% electrification (*Dhaka Tribune*, 2022). It is constructing its first nuclear power facility in Rooppur with technical and financial support from Russia (Gyanwali *et al.*, 2021). It has an expected generation capacity of 2.4 GW by 2024. An LPG pipeline is being negotiated among India, Bangladesh and Myanmar (IBM). Hydro power in Bangladesh has very little scope because of its concern for land use and flooding. However, Bangladesh is planning to import hydro power from Nepal through India.

Energy Overview of Nepal

Being situated in the Himalayas, Nepal has abundant potential for hydropower. Hydropower is the main source of electricity in the country. About 94% of the population have access to electricity. Nepal has not yet fully harnessed its hydropower potential. It is capable of producing more energy than required within the country. Therefore, energy trading is a possibility for Nepal to earn forex by exporting energy to India and Bangladesh. Currently, Nepal is dependent on India for fossil fuels like petrol and diesel as it does not have fossil fuel reserves or production capacity.

Most of the hydropower plants in Nepal are run-of-river (ROR) projects. This makes Nepal vulnerable to irregular and erratic supply of electricity based on seasonal climatic changes. The electricity generation is less than 40% during winter. Nepal has four major rivers:

the Saptakoshi, Narayani, Karnali and Mahakali, and their tributaries originate either from the Himalayas or from the Tibetan Plateau (Jha, 2010). Nepal has a shortage of technical human resources and financial resources. Hence, it is unable to harness its hydro power generation capacity to its full potential.

Private sector enterprises and even foreign investments are being utilised for constructing hydro storage projects and power trade agreements are being established with neighbouring countries. For example, a trilateral cooperation mechanism consisting of Nepal, India and Bangladesh (NIB) has been agreed upon. The Upper Karnali hydropower project is a run-of-the-river hydropower project being developed on Karnali River in Nepal. The project will supply power to Nepal, India, and Bangladesh for a contracted period of 25 years. The Government of Nepal awarded the project to GMR Upper Karnali Hydro Power Limited (GUKHL), a subsidiary of GMR Group India in 2008. GMR is developing the project on a build-own-operate-transfer (BOOT) basis (*The Himalayan Times*, 2019). According to the agreement, Nepal will get 12% free power from the total power generated by the project, while Bangladesh will buy 56 per cent and India will buy the remaining 32%. This project is looked upon as a stepping stone towards enhancing cooperation in the energy sector which may have a dominos effect for similar collabouration in other sectors as well.

Energy Overview of Bhutan

The power system of Bhutan is dominated by indigenously produced hydropower with an installed capacity of 1.6 GW. The majority of potential sites are concentrated in the Wangchhu, Punatsangchhu, Mangdechhu and Drangmechhu river basins (Gyanwali *et al.*, 2021). All these rivers are perennial in nature. Its flow is determined by melting of snow from the high Himalayan ranges. Therefore, they have the potential for developing hydro-power projects. Bhutan is self-sufficient in meeting its electricity needs. It has achieved 100 per cent electrification of its households. It has utilised only 2 per cent of its hydropower capacity. It imports refined petroleum products, gas and coal from India. The Bhutanese people depend on firewood for primary energy and it contributes to 90% of energy consumption.

The Bhutanese government has adopted clean energy policy to develop its carbon-neutral hydropower in order to meet its domestic demand and to export the surplus power to neighbouring countries. Bhutan exports hydropower energy to the Indian state, West Bengal. In collabouration with India, Bhutan is developing numerous hydropower projects. One such project is run-of-the-river 1,020 MW Punatsangchhu-II Hydroelectric Project (PHEP-II). The project is expected to become operational by October 2024. It will generate 4357 million units of electricity annually increasing Bhutan's power generation capacity by 43 per cent (Kuensel, 2022).

Prospects for Sub-Regional Energy Cooperation

Mutual co-existence and intra-regional energy trading is the key to ensuring energy security in the sub-region. Access to steady supply of electricity is the fundamental aspect of energy security.

The average per capita energy use of BBIN is about 0.6 tonnes of oil equivalent (TOE) which is far below the global average (Gyanwali *et al.*, 2021). Petroleum products and gas in this sub-region is very limited. This compels the sub-regional countries to rely heavily on imported fossil fuels.

Nepal and Bhutan have abundant potential to meet their energy needs as well as engage in energy trading through hydropower projects. But Nepal has been able to accomplish only 89 per cent of electrification (World Bank, 2023). Bhutan has become fully capable of meeting its energy demands since 2016. India and Bangladesh are heavily dependent on coal based and other non-renewable energy resources. Among renewable sources, solar energy generation too has great potential in all these four countries especially Bhutan and Nepal. Lack of financial, technical and infrastructural facilities are the basic reasons for underutilisation of resources. These hurdles can be overcome by cooperation among the four countries in the sub-region.

Bhutan has used only 2% of its hydropower generating capacity. It has met all the energy needs of its population. Whereas Bangladesh which is downstream has energy shortage. Only 70% of its energy needs have been met. Thus, the potential to supply for the shortfall of energy exists within the sub-region. India is energy deficit during peak season and is mainly dependent on thermal energy which is not environment friendly. This deficit can be met by the excess supply of clean hydro energy from Bhutan and Nepal. Bhutan and Nepal are 100% dependent on India for coal, oil and gas.

The water and energy cooperation among the BBIN countries has two basic features: Firstly, Cooperation is based on bilateralism, with each of the countries entering into separate energy development and trade agreement with India. Recently, electrical grid interconnections and hydro-energy cooperation has emerged with governments increasingly shifting from bilateral to multilateral energy-sharing agreements. Bangladesh is willing to connect its power grid with Nepal and Bhutan and expand the existing transmission capacity in both the eastern and north-eastern parts of India. Secondly, the countries of the sub-region follow a solid approach in bilateral agreements, whereas water management and energy sharing are interlinked sectors. (Saklania, *et al.*, 2020). In water management and in energy trading agreements, the upper riparian state is in a dominant role. To ensure a win win situation, multilateral agreement is appropriate to give bargaining position to the smaller states than in bilateral agreements with India. India, on the other hand, can assure the smaller states who are suspicious of India's hegemonic tendencies.

Cooperation in the energy sector has two aspects—Water management and Hydro Energy trading. The two aspects are complimentary in nature. The BBIN countries are prone to flood and drought. There is a chronic shortfall of energy in Bangladesh, while Bhutan and Nepal are yet to use their energy potential. The BBIN countries share several transboundary rivers that are part of the Ganga-Brahmaputra-Meghna (GBM) basin. The GBM basin is home to around ten per cent of the world's population. Most of the people in the region are dependent on agriculture and other small-scale industries. However, water availability in this region is erratic and non-dependable. The quality of groundwater available is also low. Climate change is another challenge faced by the people in this region. Therefore, there is a dire need for better water management.

Conclusion

The current policy of bilateralism works good for India but is looked upon with suspicion by the smaller riparian states. This is the reason for fallout of some of the initiatives for cooperation. The four countries can manage the challenges faced in the energy and water management by cooperating with each other. This will help them to reduce the cost of electricity, deal with scarcity in peak season, diversify their energy basket and also shift to cleaner energy sources. However, tapping all of the hydro power potential of the Himalayan region may lead to environmental hazards as the region is prone to earthquakes and landslides. An environment impact assessment should be made before starting any such projects.

References

Al-tabatabaie, K.F., Hossain, M.B., Islam, M.K., Awual, M.R., Towfiqul Islam, A.R.M., Hossain, M.A., Esraz-Ul-Zannat, M., & Islam, A. (2022). Taking strides towards decarbonization: The viewpoint of Bangladesh. *Energy Strategy Reviews, 44*. https://doi.org/10.1016/J.ESR.2022.100948

CEA (n.d.). *Executive Summary on Power Sector*. https://cea.nic.in/wp-content/uploads/executive/2023/03/Executive_Summary_Feb_2023.pdf

Dhaka Tribune (2022). *PM Hasina: 100% electricity coverage a landmark success*. https://www.dhakatribune.com/bangladesh/2022/03/22/pm-hasina-illuminating-every-house-is-a-great-achievement

Gyanwali, K., Komiyama, R., Fujii, Y., & Bajracharya, T.R. (2021). A review of energy sector in the BBIN sub-region. *International Journal of Sustainable Energy, 40*(6), 530-556. https://doi.org/10.1080/14786451.2020.1825436

International Energy Agency. (2022). *WORLD ENERGY BALANCES 2022 EDITION—Database Documentation*. https://www.iea.org/subscribe-to-data-services/world-energy-balances-and-statistics

Jha, R. (2010). Total Run-of-River type Hydropower Potential of Nepal. *Hydro Nepal: Journal of Water, Energy and Environment, 7*(7), 8-13. https://doi.org/10.3126/HN.V7I0.4226

Kuensel (2022, December 22). *PHPA-II Dam is ready*. 2. http://phpa2.gov.bt/kuensel-paper-on-dam/

Mishra, P. (2019). *Overview of the Power Sector*.

PIB. (2017). *Three Years' Achievements & Initiatives of the Ministries of Power, Coal, New & Renewable Energy and Mines*. https://archive.pib.gov.in/archive2/erelease.aspx

Rahman, S.H., Wijayatunga, P.D.C., Gunatilake, H., & Fernando, P.N. (2012). *Energy Trade in South Asia*.

Saklania, Udisha, Shresthab, Padmendra P. Mukherjic, Aditi. Scott, C.A. (2020). Hydro-energy cooperation in South Asia: Prospects for transboundary energy and water security. *Environmental Science and Policy*, 22-34.

The Wire (2018). *Modi Announces 100% Electrification—But That Doesn't Mean Everyone Has Power.* https://thewire.in/government/narendra-modi-government-rural-electrification-power

10

Does Awareness on Climate Resilience Promote Peace Building Practices in Adolescents?

Tara S. Nair and *Anjali G.*

Introduction

Schools in several countries have started educating students on climate change as a vanguard that threatens human existence. Often integrated in the Earth Science curriculum it enables students to combat climate change in their efforts to find solutions. Building resilience among students and youth is one of the key measures that can be implemented by education sector to prevent the spread of violent extremism (UNESCO, 2017). Thinking of resilience as a capacity built through different practices gives individuals, communities and governments flexibility in deciding which measures make the most sense for building their resilience to the specific impacts of climate change they face. Climate resilience refers to the ability to anticipate, prepare for and respond to hazardous events or disturbances related to climate. Improving climate resilience involves assessing how climate change will create new or alters current climate related risks and taking steps to better cope with these risks (Climate resilience portal, 2018). The key focus of climate resilience is to encompass economic, social, political and technological strategies that are implemented at all levels of society in order to address vulnerabilities that communities, states and countries currently have. Heavily debated in both conceptual and practical terms, its key issues include how resilience relates to climate change adaptation, the extent to which it encompasses actor based versus system based approaches for improving stability and its relationship with the balance of homeostatic equilibrium or nature theory view of ecological systems.

Peace Education for Peace Building

Peace building, an essential component of the discipline Political Science, has become a guiding principle of international intervention since its inclusion in the UN Agenda for Peace in 1992 directed towards the eradication of root causes of violence with the objective of creating conditions of self-sustaining peace. The UNICEF Programme Report, 2016 views Peace Building as a multidimensional range of measures to reduce the risk of lapse or relapse into conflict by addressing both the causes and consequences of conflict and by strengthening national capabilities at all levels for conflict management in order to lay foundations for sustainable peace and development. Peace building involves political, legal, cultural, social and economic institutions and security practices which are seen as complementary and mutually reinforcing in a multifaceted manner. It facilitates the establishment of durable peace and prevents recurrence of violence by addressing root causes and effects of conflicts through reconciliation, institution building and transformation. This should be taught to prepare students for the future so as to develop peaceful climate change solutions even though STEM skills are on the rise. Many attempts to educate people about peace education integrate peace and resilience building approach for the Prevention of Violent Extremism (PVE). Yet there is a little understanding of how this can be utilized and embraced to enhance competencies of learners to ensure participatory learning experiences for resilience and peace building. Successful peace building activities create an environment supportive of self-sustaining, durable peace; reconcile opponents; prevent conflict from restarting; integrate civil society; create rule of law mechanisms; and address underlying structural and societal issues. To accomplish these goals, peace building must address functional structures, emotional conditions and social psychology, social stability, rule of law and ethics, and cultural sensitivities. Mohanty (2008) says peace education as an attempt to respond to problems of conflict and violence on scales ranging from the global and national to the local and personal. It is about exploring ways of creating more just and sustainable futures.

Environmental Peace building is an emerging field in both academic and practitioner communities that views environmental conflicts as an opportunity to build peace. It has gained popularity among many international organizations, NGOs and scholars creating new research and funding opportunities. Critical assessment of existing scholarship shows in peace and conflict studies, hydro politics, political ecology, and institutional-economical economics. As Peace building is an activity that aims to resolve injustice in non-violent ways and to transform, the methods included in peace building vary depending on the situation and the agent of peace building. Such efforts aim to change beliefs, attitudes and behaviours to transform the short and long-term dynamics between individuals and groups towards a more stable, peaceful coexistence. It involves a range of measures targeted to reduce the risk of lapsing or relapsing into conflict by strengthening national capacities at all levels for conflict management, and to lay the foundations for sustainable peace and sustainable development. Peace building strategies must be coherent and tailored to specific needs of the country concerned, based on national ownership, and should comprise a carefully prioritized, sequenced and therefore relatively narrow set of activities aimed at achieving the above objectives. This is a long-term process that should be essentially developed in our students to initiate appropriate attitudes, behaviour and norms to appreciate the factors that contribute to peace, the absence of which can potentially lead to conflict. Peace component should be included in the process of education as it is only antidote to the forces of war, terrorism, violence and aggression (NCERT, 2006).

Rationale

Higher secondary school students should have a basic awareness about climate and climatic changes. Awareness help the students to understand and address the impact of climatic changes, increase climatic literacy, encourage changes in their attitudes and behaviour and helps them adapt to climate change related trends. Awareness on climate resilience is essential to enable students to live according to the future perspective of Nature. As education is an essential element of the global response to climate change, it helps people understand and address the impact of global warming, increases climate literacy among young people, encourages changes in their attitudes and behaviour and helps them adapt to climate change related trends. Moreover, education and raising awareness enable informed decision-making which play an essential role in increasing adaptation and mitigation capacities of communities empowering people to adopt sustainable lifestyles. Climate change education is part of UNESCO's Education for Sustainable Development (ESD) programme. The scope is just too large to grasp and many of the most noticeable impacts are still too far removed from our daily lives. Encouraging climate change awareness in our students by focusing on local or regional impacts is unavoidable in order to be alert for climate change impacts in our specific region, to think about how they might affect our community and then, tying it all to climate change.

Objectives of the Study

1. To find out whether there is any significant relationship between Awareness of Climate Resilience and Attitude towards Peace Building Practices of Higher Secondary School Students in the whole sample and relevant subsamples based on gender, locale and type of management.
2. To find out whether there is any significant difference in the relationship between Awareness of Climate Resilience and Attitude towards Peace Building Practices of Higher Secondary School Students' comparable pairs of subsamples based on gender, locale and type of management.
3. To find out whether there is any significant difference in the mean scores of Attitude towards Peace Building Practices among Higher Secondary School Students based on gender, locale and type of management.
4. To find out whether there is any significant difference in the mean scores of Awareness of Climate Resilience among Higher

Secondary School Students based on gender, locale and type of management.

Hypotheses of the study

1. There exist significant relationship between Awareness of Climate Resilience and Attitude towards Peace Building Practices among Higher Secondary School Students in the whole sample and the relevant subsamples based on gender, locale and type of management.
2. There exist significant difference in the relationship between Awareness of Climate Resilience and Attitude towards Peace Building Practices among Higher Secondary School Students between the comparable pairs of subsamples based on gender, locale and type of management.
3. There exist significant difference in the mean scores of Attitude towards Peace Building Practices among Higher Secondary School Students based on gender, locale and type of management.
4. There exist significant difference in the mean scores of Awareness of Climate Resilience among Higher Secondary School Students based on gender, locale and type of management.

Methodology

The present study aims to find out the Awareness of Climate Resilience of Higher Secondary School Students in relation to their Attitude towards Peace Building Practices. Survey method was adopted on a sample of 400 Higher Secondary School Students studying Humanities. Test of Awareness on Climate Resilience and Scale of Attitude towards Peace Building Practices were developed to collect data. The data was analyzed and interpreted on the basis of descriptive and inferential statistics using arithmetic mean, standard deviation, Karl Pearson's Product Moment Co-efficient of Correlation, Fischer's t-test and Test of significance of difference between means.

Major findings

- There is significant relationship between Awareness of Climate Resilience and Attitude towards Peace Building Practices of Higher Secondary School Students in the whole sample (r=0.491).

- There is no significant difference in relationship between Awareness of Climate Resilience and Attitude towards Peace Building Practices in the sub samples based on gender, locale and type of management.
- There exists a significant difference between mean scores on awareness of Climate Resilience based on type of management of school (t=4.02). Aided school students are found to have high awareness of Climate Resilience than Government School students.
- There exists a significant difference between mean scores on attitude towards Peace Building Practices based on gender (t=2.36). Girls showed high attitude towards Peace Building Practices when compared to Boy Students.

Conclusion

The findings of the study reveals that awareness on climate resilience help adolescents to understand and address the impact of climatic issues to enable informed decision-making related to hazards, vulnerability and exposure. Thinking of resilience as a capacity built through different practices can give individuals, communities and governments flexibility in deciding which measures make the most sense for building their resilience to the specific impacts of climate change they face. Successful peace building activities create an environment supportive of self-sustaining durable peace; reconcile opponents; prevent conflict from restarting; integrate civil society; create rule of law mechanisms and address underlying structural and societal issues. Peace building must address functional structures, emotional conditions and social psychology, social stability, rule of law and ethics, and cultural sensitivities to accomplish its goals.

Educational Implications of the Study

Teachers have a key role to play in enhancing the Attitude towards Peace Building Practices in the classroom. This study helps the teachers to utilize their creativity in the classroom to practice peace building among students. This study helps teachers as well as the parents to understand the student's level of awareness on aspects related with Climate Resilience and take necessary steps to improve it. This study would also help practitioners of the education system to develop positive attitude towards peace building among school students by inculcating Peace Building Practices in the curriculum.

References

Climate Resilience Portal (2018). https://www.c2es.org/content/climate-resilience-overview/

Mohanty, A. (2008). Conflict Resolution through Peace Education, *University News,* 46(9).

NCERT (2006). Education for Peace, Position Paper of National Focus Group, NCERT: New Delhi.

UNESCO (2017). Building resilience through the development of Intercultural Competencies, https://en.unesco.org/themes/intercultural-dialogue/competencies

UNICEF Programme Report (2016). Peace building, Education and Advocacy in Conflict affected contexts programme, https://www.unicef.org/media/96556/file/UNICEF-PBEA-Final-Report.pdf

11

Zero Waste Management

A Key to Sustainable Development

Midatala Rani and *Natasha Raikar*

Introduction

"A clean India would be the best tribute India could pay to Mahatma Gandhi on his 150 birth annivarsary in 2019" said Shri Narendra Modi as he launched the Swachh Bharat Mission at Rajpath in New Delhi on 2nd October, 2014. The Swachh Bharat Abhiyan is the most significant cleanliness campaign undertaken by the Government of India till date. With citizens now becoming active participants in cleanliness activities across the nations, the dream of a 'Clean India' has begun to get a shape. People from different sections of the society have come forward and joined this mass movement of cleanliness. Right from Government officials to *jawans*, bollywood actors to sports persons, industrialists to spiritual leaders have all joined for the noble work. Swachh Bharat Abhiyan has become a 'Jan Andolan' receiving tremendous support from the people. In this context, the management of waste has assumed increasing attention by urban local bodies.

Civilization began and developed around river banks. People lived in harmony with nature and things were manageable. By the end of 19th century industrial revolution brought in number of changes with increase in population. In this process urbanisation posed many challenges. One such challenge before local administration is the issue of waste management (WM) at global, regional and local levels. Collection of waste, requirement of land, energy, human resources, NIMBY (not in my backyard) syndrome, its effect on environment are some of the major issues haunting the economies of the world. Increasing consumption, consumerism, population, urbanisation, changing lifestyle and depleting natural resources base indicate clearly that waste management has become a challenging task for a clean India.

Solid Waste (SW)

SW are those organic and inorganic waste materials produced by various activities of the society which have lost their value to the first user. It encompasses all kinds of waste such as Municipal Solid Waste (MSW), Industrial Waste (IW), Hazardous Waste (HW), Bio-Medical Waste (BMW) and Electronic Waste (E-Waste) depending on their source and composition. Due to rapid increase in urban population as well as constraint in resources, SWM poses a complex problem for any society and improper management of the same affects the public health and degrades environment.

Municipal Solid Waste (MSW)

MSW is an ever growing problem in India. Urban population generates tons and tons of waste every day. With the expansion of cities, the problem will only worsen. In many upcoming cities there is no proper waste management system. MSW can be categorised into five categories:

- Biodegradable waste: food and kitchen waste, green waste (vegetables, fruits, flowers, leaves).
- Recyclable material: paper, glass, bottles, cans, metals, plastics.
- Inert waste: construction and demolition waste, dirt, debris.
- Composite wastes: Waste clothing, tetra packs, waste plastics such as toys.
- Domestic hazardous waste and toxic waste: medication, e-waste, paints, chemicals, bulbs, fertilizer, etc.

The civil authorities with their age old techniques and practices proved to be a failure in managing these wastes. The result is overflowing *dhalaos* and clogged drainages in the cities. Incineration and landfills are no more a solution in expanding cities. The former is not environmentally friendly nor is it cost-effective. The latter is difficult in a city as it needs wide uninhabited area and contaminates groundwater and soil. The scenario is grim in most cities.

In this context, Decentralized Waste Management (DWM) becomes important. The 1999 Burman Committee appointed by the Supreme Court to assess the issue of Municipal Waste also recommended composting mandatory in every municipality. Current politics of WM have not solved the problem. New strategies and alternatives which go beyond the conventional approaches have to be explored. Zero Waste (ZW) is one of the options which aims at elimination rather than managing of waste.

Zero Waste Management (ZWM): Need of the 21st Century

ZWM system is a philosophy and design principle that goes beyond recycling by taking a whole system approach to the flow of resources and discarded materials. In nature everything is a resource or home for something else. ZW does two fundamental things. It redesigns our systems and resource use from product design to disposal, to prevent wasteful and polluting practices. It then captures, discards and uses them, instead of natural resources to make new products creating less pollution and feeding the local economy. A working group of the ZW International Alliance in 2004 defined ZW as, "a goal that is ethical, economical, efficient and visionary to guide people in changing their lifestyles and practices to emulate sustainable natural cycles where all discarded materials are designed to become resources for others to use. ZW means designing and managing products and processes to systematically avoid and eliminate the volume and toxicity of waste and materials, conserve and recover all resources and not burn or bury them. Implementing ZW will eliminate all discharges to land, water or air that are a threat to planetary, human, animal or plant health".

ZW can represent an economical alternative to waste systems where new resources are continually required to replenish wasted raw materials. It can also represent an environmental alternative to waste since waste represents a significant amount of pollution in the world. The term ZW was first used publicly in the name of a company ZW Systems Inc which was founded by Paul Palmer in mid-1970s in

Oakland, California. The mission of ZW was to find new homes for most of the chemicals being excessed by nascent electronics industry. They soon expanded their services in many other directions. The movement gained publicity and reached a peak in 1998-2002 and since then has been moving from "theory into action" by focusing on how a "zero waste community" is structured and behaves.

There are many cities in India which have adopted the ZW concept into their Urban Local Bodies (ULBs) policies. They include Kovalam Project in Kerala, Miranda House in Delhi, Indian Tobacco Company in Bhadrachalam, Andhra Pradesh, Sarita Vihar in South Delhi, Vellore in Tamil Nadu, Pune in Maharashtra and Mysore in Karnataka. The ZWM is a brain child of EXNORA GREEN CROSS—VELLORE, a non-governmental organisation that is being successfully implemented in Vellore and Hyderabad.

Zero Waste Management in Mysore City

Mysore City is one of the historical tourist places in India, well-known all over the world for its rich heritage, culture and tradition. The city was the capital of "Wodeyar" dynasty and is also known as the city of palaces and gardens. It is known as environmentally sustainable city and second clean city in the country and first best clean city in Karnataka State. The city is spread over an area of 128.75 sq kms (Municipal limit) with a population of 9.38 lakhs (2011 Census). The city has a literacy rate of 84.5% (2011 Census). The State Government has prepared several plans to develop Mysore as the second IT city of the State, next to Bangalore. Mysore is the only city in Karnataka where ZWM is being implemented successfully. The administrative area of Mysore City Corporation (MCC) is 128.6 sq kms. The city has been divided into 65 Municipal Wards, and has 61 notified slums. The solid waste generation and collection is 402 tons per day. ZWM is an initiative in Mysore City as a pilot plant project. This is a decentralised waste management where the citizens, Self Help Group (SHG) members, Federation of Ward Parliament and MCC together are handling the waste.

Table 11.1: Quantity of Waste Generation

Sl. No.	Generator	Number	Unit Generation per day	Estimated Quantity (MT)
1	Population	9,38,386	360 gram/ capita/day	338
2	Commercial Establishments	20,000	1 kg per unit per day	20
3	Hostels and Restaurants	410	50 kg/unit	21
4	Marriage and Function Halls	124	50 kg/unit	6
		Total MT		385
		Street sweeping		17
		Total MSW generated per day is		402

Source: MCC, 2012.

Municipal Solid Waste Management (MSWM) is an obligatory function of the Urban Local Bodies (ULBs) under the Karnataka Municipalities Act, 1964. MSWM was carried out by many ULBs when the Supreme Court passed an order in the Almitra Patel Case in the year 2000. In the same year, the Court ordered the implementation of the SW (management and handling) Rules, 2000. The Rules were the guidelines that were provided to the ULBs. In pursuance of MSW Rules, 2000, a compost facility of 200 TPD capacity was setup for treatment of MSW in the year 2001 in Mysore.

The Jawaharlal Nehru Urban Renewal Mission (Jn NURM) scheme which encompassed Bangalore and Mysore in Karnataka funded the extensive process of Zero Waste Management (ZWM) in Mysore in 2010. The proper stabilised system of decentralised SLRM has been functioning since 2011. Earlier there was only one centralised unit which has now been increased to nine decentralised ZWM units and one centralised dry waste unit.

Methodology

The process begins with waste collection in two different bins (red and green) provided by MCC by SHGs in push carts and auto tippers by door to door collection.

The collected waste undergoes further secondary and tertiary segregation. The secondary segregation is divided into four basic categories:

- Wet waste segregation,
- Dry waste segregation,
- Food waste segregation, and
- Segregating highly degraded materials.

The tertiary segregation includes:

- Processing and storage unit (organic items),
- Reusable items processing and storage unit (egg shells and citric fruits powder, etc.),
- Storage (non-recyclables, organic manure, vermi cast/vermi wash),
- Cattle related products processing and storage (*panchgavyam, amritpani*, etc.), and
- Responsible for sale of all end products.

The segregated waste is sent to the

- Cattle shed,
- Tertiary segregation and processing and storage unit, and
- Drying unit.

The organic waste which is transferred to the cattle waste is treated in two stages, namely,

- Cattle dung microbial decomposing, and
- Vermi composting to produce rich organic manure.

The organic waste is laid on a composting tank in different layers. This process takes 45-60 days to complete. At the end of the process the whole manure are sieved and can be used. Cattle eatable items can be fed to cattle and through this process waste will be converted into dung in less than 24 hours time and the same dung can be fed to Bio-gas plant to trap Methane gas (Bio-gas plant) for generating electricity and the slurry can be used for vermi composting to get best organic manure. The residue is later sent to composting, vermi composting, drying unit, liquid waste management and further tertiary segregation.

walls. The four pits are to be used one by one in a cyclic manner. Each pit has a capacity to accommodate garbage for 15 days. Thus, the total duration of one cycle is nearly 60 days. When the fourth pit is full, the vermi compost in the first one is ready for harvesting

Arrangement is made by providing a small pipe connection with a tap at the bottom of the vermi tank for collection of thick brown liquid known as vermi wash in a small pit adjacent to the vermi tank. Vermi wash contains a variety of plant growth promoting enzymes. It is an important by-product of vermi composting process which are being carried out in hale Kesare, Mysore University campus and other units of Mysore.

Waste to Energy

When biodegradable organic solid waste is subjected to anaerobic decomposition, a gaseous mixture of Methane (CH_4) and Carbon dioxide (CO_2) known as Biogas could be produced under favourable conditions. The decomposition of the waste materials is mainly done by the fermentation process which is carried out by different group of micro organisms like bacteria, fungus, actinomycetes, etc. The process involves a series of reactions by several kinds of anaerobic bacteria feeding on the raw organic matter. In anaerobic conditions, anaerobic bacteria disintegrate the biodegradable solids by a biochemical process shown below.

Programme of waste-to-energy

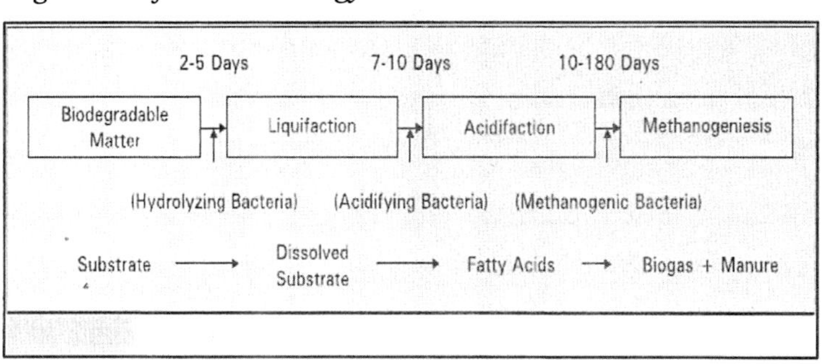

This programme of waste to energy is done at Pinjarapole Society in Mysore.

Liquid Resource Management

Disposal of waste water is a major public health problem in rural areas. Stagnant waste water acts as breeding place for mosquitoes, resulting in spread of various diseases. Proper disposal and reuse of waste water will help in combating diseases. In Mysore this has been introduced in Kesare STP (Sewage Treatment Plant) Project. Two methods are put into effect:

- Aerators (30 hp motor), and
- Natural Aerators (Ducks).

Aeration is the process of bringing water and air into close contact by exposing drops or thin sheets of water to the air or by introducing small bubbles of air and letting them rise through the water. For both procedures the processes by which the aeration accomplishes the desired results are by sweeping or scrubbing action caused by the turbulence of water and air mixing together, oxidizing certain metals and gases. The scrubbing process caused by the turbulence of aeration physically removes undesirable gases from solution and allows them to escape into the surrounding air. Aeration can help remove certain dissolved gases and minerals through oxidation. Once oxidized these chemicals fall out of solution and become suspended material in the water. The suspended material can then be removed by filtration.

Natural aerators are the Ducks which are the most efficient and naturally effective mechanism that helps in purifying grey water. Their unique padding pattern and action helps in pulling down the unwanted filth and dirt to the bottom of the water and this helps in forming the suspended silt, thereby helping to bring about fresh and reusable water on the surface. Grey water stabilised and cleaned can be used for irrigation for agricultural use, irrigation for horticulture and fish farming.

Dry Leaves Compost Beds

Dry leaves beds are sprayed with cow dung slurry and continuous moisture maintained by covering the beds with gunny bags. Each bed of size 10 feet by 5 feet consists of 600-750 kgs of dry leaves. Moisture maintaining is done for 60 days. After 60 days, the dry leaves compost bed is harvested. Each bed yields about 1.2 to 1.4 tons of compost. The cost of dry leaf compost is Rs. 6000 per ton. There is lot of demand for this compost sold under the brand name 'Mysore Gold'.

Table 11.2: Dry Leaf Waste Management

No. of beds	Total expected compost (1.2 tons/bed)	Total expected income (cost = Rs. 6000/bed)	Expenditure incurred
278	334	20.00 lakhs	5.10 lakhs

Source: MCC, 2012.

The leaf compost is also beneficial for planting of kitchen garden.

Special Project of Wet Waste Management at Pinjrapole

The stray, injured, hungry, destitute, weak and abandoned animals in Mysore city get shelter at 'The Society For The Promotion Of Kindness To Animals' called 'Mysore Pinjrapole Society'. It was established in 1938 by Maharaja Jayachamaraja Wodeyar. Pinjrapole is situated in 62 acre land in Mysore-Ooty road at the foot of Chamundi Hill, has a serene atmosphere in the midst of nature.

The MCC has taken up the issue of disposing wet waste by providing the waste from Devaraja market to Pinjrapole Society. Every day there are five trips that carry wet waste (fresh greens, vegetables and fruits) to Pinjrapole. With the help of SHG employees the wet waste is categorised, cleansed and given to cattle as food. The cattle feed is converted into cow dung within 12 hours. The dung is used for bio gas plant for bio gas generation. The by-product, the cow dung ash is further used for vessel washing powder. It is also used for vermi-wash and for dry leaves compost beds. The urine of the cattle is used for medicinal purposes and also for creation of products like *panchagavyam*, *amritpani*, etc. The peels of citrus fruits are used to prepare cleaning powder. *Amritapani* and *panchagavyam* are used as pesticide and enzyme for plant growth.

Table 11.3: Products from Cow Dung and Citrus Fruits in Pinjrapole

Sl. No.	Product	Ingredients	Rate/ kg or Rate/ltr	Remarks
1	Eco-friendly vessel washing powder	Citrus fruits peels, cow dung ash, soap nut, shikakaih	40	For 10 kgs expenditure is Rs. 70 and the selling price is Rs. 40/kg (Income = 10 × 40 = 400) (Profit = 400 – 70=330)
2	Panchagavyam (for effective plant growth)	Cow dung, cow urine, ghee, milk, curd, sugarcane juice, ripe banana, jaggery, tender coconut	20	For 10 ltrs expenditure is Rs. 10 and the selling price is Rs. 20/liter (Income = 10 × 20 = 200) (Profit = 200-10=190)
3	Amruthapani (enzyme for roots of the plants)	Cow dung, cow urine, jaggery, sugarcane and juice water	10	For 10 ltrs expenditure is Rs. 20 and the selling price is Rs. 10/liter (Income = 10 x 10 = 100) (Profit = 100 – 20=80)

Source: MCC, 2012.

The SHG members have been provided with self-employment. There are 3600 cattle in Pinjrapole for which Rs. 59,700/day was spent for cattle feed. By transporting wet market waste to Pinjrapole, the expenditure has reduced by Rs. 15,000/day.

Occupational Safety

Procurement of Personal Protection Equipments for workers like mask, helmet, gloves, rain coat, gum boot, etc. The workers are also provided with tools and equipments to avoid direct contact with the waste and medical check-up once in 3 months.

SHGs/Community Participation

Each SHG leader is entrusted to guard 300 houses and each SHG member guards 5 houses. The SHG member ensures that waste is segregated into wet and dry waste and is put into the push carts/auto tippers. The SHG member also ensures that waste is disposed off daily from the households, that there is no open defecation and there is no burning of wastes. Capacity building training programme is given to all the SHG members, leaders and workers.

Cost Benefit of ZWM

Envisaged revenue from ZWM unit of 3 MTPD plant with 70% collection efficiency is:

Total O&M charges incurred per month which is inclusive of 30 workers + 2 supervisors + fuel cost is Rs. 1,99,000. The savings is Rs. 2,93,430.00–1,99,000 = Rs. 94,430 per month.

Problems Involved

There are various problems in implementing the ZWM process. They include the following:

- Excessive generation of waste.
- Lack of proper infrastructure for waste management.
- Lack of long-term investment planning.
- Lack of clean institutional mechanism for implementation of projects.
- Problem of co-financing of the project.
- Lack of proper collection and systematic segregation of waste at source.
- Weak public involvement.
- Complexity of the implementing process.

MCC's New Initiatives

MCC has come up with innovative measures to address the problems related to ZWM. They include the following:

- Launching of Information Communication and Education (IEC) activities to sensitise the citizens in Mysore about segregation of waste at the grassroots level. The officials and representatives from MCC visit various localities and explain the need to take up segregation activities at individual home. Public announcement and street plays by artists on ZWM are adding to the awareness programme.

- Use of new technology to address problems related to ZWM.
- Setting up of bio-gas plants in various localities.
- Set up projects to produce electricity using waste collected from the city.
- Plan to produce crude oil using plastic waste.
- Setting up of ZWM units at various zones.
- Developing networking process with Agriculture, Horticulture Departments and Raitha Samparka Kendras located in villages surrounding Mysore to sell the compost.

End Note

To make recycling economy of the 21 century a reality, behaviour change and educational programmes to raise awareness are needed. Compromising present lifestyles and limiting economic growth might be the most critical challenges for all cities all over the globe. It needs to be realised that we are living on a planet with finite resources. Therefore, efficient use of resources and recovery of resources from waste are vital for global sustainability. Zero waste management initiates a healthy, hygienic and cost-effective method to manage the waste. It ensures community participation, revenue generation, hygiene, low expenditure and safeguards the environment with minimal use of resources for a better sustainable management and development. A city that can grow its own food, use water from its own areas, produce energy from its own system, create jobs and economic activities, regulate the whole system efficiently and recover all resources from waste can be a true sustainable "Zero Waste City". Zero Waste Management is not only a key to sustainable development but an essential requirement for Swachh Bharat Mission.

References

C. Srinivasan, Exnora Green Cross, 2000 www.homeexnora.org/green_exnora.html (http://www.exnoragreencross-vellore.org/zero.html)

City Development Plan for Mysore City, Mysore City Corporation, 2012.

"City's Garbage Woes—Zero Waste Management", *Star of Mysore*, 8th December 2012.

Detailed Project Report—Zero Waste Management, Mysore, Mysore City Corporation, 2012.

Dry leaves compost beds, Mysore City Corporation, 2012.

http://en.wikipedia.org/wiki/zerowaste

M. Ravindra, K. Dhir (2003). *Sustainable Waste Management*, London, Thomastelford Publishing.

Manual on Municipal Solid Waste Management, Central Public Health and Environmental Engineering Organisation, Government of India, 2000.

"Months Long Campaign on Waste Segregation Begins", *Star of Mysore*, 5th December, 2012.

"Mysore City Corporation First Step for a Cleaner City", *The Hindu*, 19th November, 2012.

"Mysore City Corporation Zero Waste Management Scheme Takes Off", *Star of Mysore*, 18th November, 2012.

"Mysore Launches Door to Door Campaign on Zero Waste Management", *Star of Mysore*, 18th February, 2012.

Products from cow dung and citrus fruits in Pinjrapole, Mysore City Corporation, 2012.

Project Report on Integrated Solid Waste Management for Mysore City, Mysore, Karnataka, 2010.

R.K. Somashekar (2008). *Environmental Science and Technology in India*, New Delhi, Daya Publishing House.

"The Transformation from Waste to Power", *The Hindu*, 29th September, 2012.

V. Rajashekar (2008). *A Perspective of Zero Waste in Urban India*, New Delhi, Daya Publishing House.

"Waste should be considered as a resource", http://www.cleanindiajournal.com

12
Power and Soft Power
Theoretical Developments

S. Loganathan

Power and its characteristics

Wind blows in many directions, from east to west, from north to south, dust laden or dustless, fierce gales or gentle breezes, and hot or cold. In the same way, power flows in all direction. It touches all and never discriminates anyone on the basis of sex, sect, creed, colour, region, religion and so on. Sometimes, it is laden with useful or useless things and brings pleasant or unpleasant results. Power is notorious for its extreme form whether it is good or bad, that is, gentle and fierce. As different forms of winds produce different phenomena, one can understand power and its different behaviour. Power is not static and its behaviour is highly dynamic and changing and flows continuously with different form and with different structure, like a wind. Most of the time we are not aware of wind, similarly, power is always not observed and sensed—objectively. Power and its different behaviour is tangible or intangible, visible or invisible, measurable or immeasurable, observable or non-observable, fungible or non-fungible; it never lost its importance in the realm of human existence. Power matters the most. Scholars like Michel Foucault and Steven Lukes succinctly argued that power is most effective when it is least observable. They tried to unfold the least observable character of power and even attempted to locate or unlock the elusiveness of intangible, invisible, unmeasurable and non-fungible character of power. Their effort was worthwhile. Even though, Lukes admitted to his critiques: "every way of seeing power is also a way of not seeing the power."[1]

Human being without power and power without humanity is unthinkable and unimaginable; human being and power are similar to the two wings of the bird, it is the source for the flow of life or human existence. Since power is a driving force for human relationships, it plays the central and important role in analysing human behaviour. Human behaviour and motivation is too complicated to predict the outcomes. Why is human behaviour and motivation too complicated? Because human relationship is conducted in endless ways in different settings, sequences, arrangements, contexts, environments, timelines, knowledge and information and so on. Every moment (relationship) is unique and one cannot easily identify and compare. The outcome of the uniqueness of every single moment is absolutely unique. This is the reason why many thinkers fail to understand the uniqueness of every moment of human relationships.

Power does not have any defined structure on its own. It is structureless. Power works always in structureless settings, sequences, arrangements, contexts, and environments. Though the power is structureless, many people argued that power is vague and meaningless concept because of its structurelessness but its effect and affect is very real and meaningful in a structureless setup. Power relationship is a continuous process and each and every stage of process takes different shapes, structure, character and behaviour. Power is endless. Power is always a means to an end but it is not end in itself. Thus, power is so polymorphous and amorphous in its character and structure.

Power in a relationship is always based on the value, what is the meaning of value in a power relationship? It is all about weightage in a relationship which means outcome of the event. The outcome may be apparent or non-apparent, visible or invisible, tangible or intangible, and fungible or non-fungible, stronger or feeble in character. But the outcome of the power relationship is always value dependent, that is, the outcome is positive or negative, pleasant or unpleasant, good or bad, useful or useless, meaningful or meaningless but always laden with value but very rarely is the outcome neutral. Every relationship is made up of power with ineradicably value dependent. Power and value assumptions are intricately tied in a power relationship.

Hitherto, there is no acceptable agreement about the concept of power in a totality. Scholars from different walks of life, never agreed or coexist, never calm and composed together when it comes to power and its different forms, especially on definition, conception and measurement of power and its cognates. Lukes correctly pointed out that "there is complete disagreement about how to define it, how to conceive it, how to measure it."[2] Power is ubiquitous in nature. It cannot be conceptualised or captured in all its form in a human relationship. Human relationship is itself endless. Every moment in a power relationship is very much unique and cannot be observed thoroughly. The search for single conceptualisation of power will become completely illusory and parochial. Power has more than one meaning and it is highly polysemy in character.

According to Robert Gilpin, power is essentially troublesome in the field of international relations. Why is power more troublesome? Lukes clearly pointed out three reasons for power, and it is more troublesome, and a matter of much controversy. Firstly, he argued that, power is one of the most primitive and volatile concepts in the specific sense, which means that power with reference to any other notions is always controversial. For example, interest and freedom are always aligned with power. In this case, how interest and freedom are understood properly is not less controversial than the power itself. Secondly, power is essentially a contested notion. The traditional algorithm of power is always contested because it involves endless disputes about their proper uses on the part of their users. Thirdly, contestedness—not agreeable agreement on what counts as power and what weighs as being a more powerful is not a less contested phenomenon.[3] Power always depends upon individual intuition, cognition, perception and conceptualisation. Individuals always differ from one another. It leads to perpetual contestedness on the part of power. Moreover, different ways of conceiving power are natural to different perspectives and purposes.

Power relationship is endless. It affects each other in myriad ways all the time. Power becomes meaningful whenever the relationship is taking place. From birth to death, human existence is driven by endless power relationships. Every human encounter is made up of power. Identifying and observing, evaluating and estimating, comparing and controlling and contemplating the power and its different nuances is really enigmatic. It cannot be complete in itself and it is a continuous process. According to Lukes, "in daily life and scholarly works, people discuss its location and its extent, who has more and who has less, how to gain, resist, seize, harness, secure, tame, share, spread, distribute, equalise or maximise it, how to render it more effective and how to limit or avoid its effects."[4]

Skeptics rejected the notion of power as an elastic and empty term. They strongly argued that, power is not at all useful for any practical purpose and the idea of power should be abandoned. Is power really empty and malleable? Power is real, actual, absolute and practical in our day to day life, in all aspects of human endeavour, but for human inability to identify, locate, define, measure, and conceptualise it precisely. Robert Dahl strongly stated that "no temerity to say the study of power is a bottomless swamp."[5] Michel Foucault always emphasised that the subtlest aspect of power should be observed objectively and asserted that subtlest form of power is more powerful and more effective. In the same line, Lukes argued that, "power is real and effective in a remarkable variety of ways, some of them indirect and some hidden, and that, indeed, it is at its most effective when least accessible to observation, to actors and observers alike, thereby presenting empirically minded social scientist with a neat paradox."[6] Power is a pure science of relation between people those who are involved in it but it is always elusive than observed objectively.

However, Foucault and Lukes strongly rejected the skeptics' notion of power that power is an empty and folk term and not useful for analysis. At the same time, Lukes politely admitted that, "thinking clearly about power is not easy and it gets more difficult, offering more opportunity for confusion, when we try to think about power in social life, not least because we all talk and write about it all the time and in confusingly different ways."[7] It is very clear from the above statement that power and its many faces cannot be captured, characterised and categorised thoroughly because it is believed that power is beyond the human absorption and imagination (but power is true). Power is meta-physical concept. That is why scholars from across the world are always confused about the existence of power and its real effect. This accumulated confusion has formed a big heap in the minds of scholars and act like a barrier not permeating the finest aspects of power. This barrier leads to different ways of confusion about power and its cognates. Unifying power theory is very difficult because formation of an opinion on incomplete information is a difficult task.

Power cannot be compared or equated with any concept or material (animate or inanimate resources) because power is beyond the material wealth, that is, power is a capacity of actors involved in the process. Most of the time, it cannot be observed by human mind. Power in a situation cannot be the same in another situation even in the same relationship. Power is constantly changing its position or state. It is more ephemeral that it changes shape under different circumstances.

Any attempt to develop a single index of power is doomed to fail because power depends upon human relationships that vary in different contexts. Like many basic ideas, power is a contested concept. No one definition is accepted by all who use the word, and people's choice of definition reflects their interests and values. Power is the capacity to do things and in social situations affect others to get the outcomes one wants.

Scholars believed that power also can be derived from the complex interdependent forces, that is, social forces or structural forces, in which social powers can be obtained and visible or direct forces—active power can be derived. How can social powers be derived? Our society is driven by a web of inherited forces. Social power is closely associated with behavioural aspect of the society. It is shaping the society by underlying social structures, knowledge system, belief and value system and general environment surrounding the society. For instance, temple, church, mosque and other places of worship act as preconditioned beliefs and value systems. These are the main shaping forces and operate beneath the behavioural level or subconscious level of the society—one of the main causes of social power. These social forces are very important to understand the society in totality. It is also useful for policy analysis. For instance, British Empire survived in India and elsewhere because they understood the pulse of social forces inherited in the society which helped them to establish their empire for many centuries.

Power is very old and widespread concept. There are many definitions revolving around the concept of power. Power is defined as a will, ability, intentionality, potentiality, capacity and actuality. Robert Dahl's definition of power is widely acknowledged by many. He defined power in his earlier article, 'the concept of power', "A has power over B to the extent that he can get B to do something that B would not otherwise do." In the same article he also clarified his definition further that, "power involves a successful attempt by A to get 'a' to do something he would not otherwise do."[8] He defined power in terms of a relation between people. He believed that power is all about relations among the people. If you look very closely at Dahl's two kinds of definition, a clear cut deviation can be identified, that is, from the A's capacity to A's actual power.

Max Weber observed power as the realisation of the will of the powerful despite resistance. Weber understood that power of the powerful person always draws resistance naturally, when he uses power at his will. In the similar tone C. Wright Mills talks about power and its realisation only through the will of the powerful. Mary Parker Follett defined "power as the ability to make things happen, to be causal agent, to initiate change."[9] Her definition of power is one way and general but it is wider than earlier. John Locke's definition, "having power as able to make, or able to receive, any change". His definition, a more generic one, but two way, that is, agent able to make change in others, at the same agent able to receive response or any change from others. According to Lukes, Locke's definition lacks power to resist change. Lukes extended Locke's definition of power, that "having power is being able to make or to receive any change, or to resist it. It implies that power is a dispositional concept. It identifies capacity: power is a potentiality not an actuality—indeed a potentiality that may never be actualised."[10]

Different Faces of Power

Over the millennia, power and its synonyms widely and commonly used and embedded in all civilised society in the world. An array of scholars, starting from Plato and Aristotle, Hobbes and Spinoza to Pareto and Weber, to name a few, intensively and extensively discussed, debated and disputed about the concept of power. They identified, conceptualised, illuminated and diversified the concept of power and its cognates. Generally they were sporadic in their approach but lack any systematic and coherent approach when it comes to theoretical formulation or theory building. Their approach to power is more generic in sense than the specific and systematic one. The beginning of Robert Dahl and his community study has opened up a systematic and methodological study about power. Later, his approach is dubbed as the first dimension of power. His approach is very famous because he made an unusual attempt to see power as concrete, practical and measurable and mainly in contrast to the then prevailing notion of power, that is, elitist approach to power, in which power is more generic in sense.

The first face of power is built on the assumption that A participates in decision and thus adversely affects B. Here, conflict is very clear and observable, suppression of the conflict is the source of power and it is very specific and direct.[11] This face identifies clear, visible and direct use of power when there is an observable conflict which is detrimental to B's set of preferences. This face identifies the clear idea of binary relationships between actors and observes behaviour very carefully. The second face of power is constructed and developed by the important missing element of power, which is not captured in the first face of power, that is, mobilisation of bias in favour of the power wielder or non-decision making power of the actor. The main contribution of the second face of power is identifying the existing indirect power-relationship, which is an indirect communication between power wielder and receiver. The second face very clearly identifies that, power to decide what is decided; that is, A participates and works to sustain the value system embedded in the institutional setup, it acts as a shield against potential threats to the authority of power. Indeed, this entire process, neither involves nor identifies with any decisions arrived at on specific issues. This face identifies overt and covert control of power or agenda setting power. It is less visible than the first face of power identified by the pluralist. This face believed that power is always identified when there is overt and covert conflict of interest, it is as same as the assumption from the first face of power that involves only overt act of power. In other words, this face has wider interest than the pluralist. At the same time, the second face involves subjective interest rather than solely concentrating on objective interest by the pluralist.[12]

Lukes, in his analysis of power, identified the least observable character of power which is missed entirely by earlier analysis (I and II dimension) of power. The subtle aspect of power is most effective than the most visible aspect of power. He argued that power is not only exercised if there is a conflict of interest overtly and covertly, power is also exercised by shaping the very preferences of the people and thwarts the arising of the conflict in the first place. This is the most important dimension of power, that is, the third dimension of power. He says that "power is supreme, when most insidious exercise of power to prevent people, to whatever degree, from having grievances to, by shaping their perceptions, cognitions, and preferences in accordance with existing order of things or accept their role in the existing order."[13] Here, complete recognition and resignation of the people to the exercise of power may reflect no more alternatives and no more grievances. It is the genuineness of power to shape the very preferences of the people without having a trace of conflict of interest and attempt to prevent the conflict arsing in the first place. The requisite and needs of the people is genuinely represented and understood by the authority of the power. Third face of power is entirely subject oriented than the earlier first and second dimension of power.

Third dimension of power is thorough going critique of earlier two faces of power. The first and second dimension of power believed that conflict of interest is source of power. The power to suppress the conflict may be overt or covert control. The overt and covert control can be taken by the actor with different forms of power, ranging from coercion to co-optation. Even the overt and covert action by the actors is readily observable in nature in the first two faces of power, they both committed with behavioural aspect in their theory. The behaviour of the binary relationship is very important in their analysis. In binary relationship, the spirit of the powerful always prevails and both faces of power entirely reflect the Weberian concept of power. According to Lukes, power is not confined to binary relationship between actors and binary relationship is always assumed to satisfy actors' unitary interest. This fails to consider that interests are comprehensive and conflicting and multiple and of different kinds. Lukes observes that "the pluralist considers interests as the policy preferences exhibited by the behaviour of all citizens who are assumed to be within the political system, in little difference over first face, Bachrach and Baratz also consider the preferences exhibited by the behaviour of those who are partly or wholly excluded from the political system, in the form of overt or covert grievances."[14] Lukes observes that, two dimensional view of power is inadequate to identify the subtle aspect of power. The main theme of their study is non-decision making power, they argue that non-decision making power exists only where there are grievances which are denied entry into political process in the form of issues. If the observer is unable to uncover any grievances, then the second face of power categorically assumes that there is genuine consensus on the prevailing allocation of values, put it in different sense, if people do not have any grievances, then their interest is not harmed by the use of power.[15] According to Lukes, this view of second dimension is highly unsatisfactory because it does not consider the genuine consensus that can be achieved by insidious effort of the power wielder.

Power is the essential source of controlling and suppressing others' immediate interest is only one aspect of power. Actors can be more powerful by shaping, satisfying and advancing others' interests. In the best sense, securing consent is the critical source of power by averting both conflict and grievances arising in the first place; it is an important dimension of power. Airing of policy conflicts in the public domain can be prevented by different power determinants such as social forces and institutional procedures or through individual decisions. In the same way, Lukes argued that consensus can be achieved without any overt and covert conflict interest by through social forces and institutional value system or through individual choice of decisions.[16] Dahl, in his later writings, readily agreed that leaders not only respond to the preferences of constituents; they also involve and shape their immediate preferences. For a long time, many scholars mistakenly believed that power is always essential to settle the actual and observable conflicts in favour of the power wielder. This was missing face of power identified by Lukes and he shows the very subtle and effective face of power.

When Lukes identified the third dimension of power, in his book, *Power: A Radical View* (2005), he tried to bring the very subtle aspect of power into practical reality, actuality, specificity, observability and usability. He argues that, third dimension of power is researchable and seeing power in all-embracing direction than for not doing so.

Third dimensional view of power concerns that specificity of power as domination within the wider conceptual field of power in general. Here, he observes the real and specific use of power to achieve domination in wider aspect of power. At the same time, the focus is on how to get domination by the willing subjects by the complete resignation towards the authority of power by their own freedom, autonomy and real choices without any latent conflict of interest—for example, when submission and intellectual subordination are absent or diminished, when the apparatus of power is no more. One of the best examples of intellectual subordination or voluntary subordination in the society is related to religious faith. Unquestionable faith leads to persistently insubordination to the apparatus of the religious authority (Temple, Mosque, Church and other religious institutions). In this situation power always prevails; here, domination is the continuous phenomenon. In this case domination is achieved through the false consciousness and thus apparatus of power is indirectly driven and gets domination in favour of the religious authority.

Power in International Relations

Power is the most important concept in the field of International Relations (IR). There are many theories that relate the conduct of international relations. There are two broad important groups to study IR theory. One group of theorists is called as Realist and other side of spectrum is known as Idealist, Liberalist, and Constructivist and so on. They are diametrically opposite in their analysis especially when it comes to power and its cognates. The study on power is only a sole province of realist tradition in the analysis of international relations but not monopolise the study completely.[17] Many theorists who mainly dedicated to study about international relations without touching the salience of power in their concept, they want to show their theoretical features and advancement in IR theory without understanding the properties of power in their analysis. They never understand the original characteristics of power, every relationship and its causal effects made up, ineradicably value laden that is the source of power. Protracted tradition of scholars (realist) strongly endorsed the concept of power in the field of international relations. They understand that every political action deeply fabricated by power relationship or power variables. In realist tradition, to study about power in international relations are differ from one another by different formulation in their analysis but they are all united at a single point, that is focus on power politics or states' competitive struggle for power. They are known as classical realist, neorealist, offensive realist, neoclassical realist, modified realist and so on.

Some of these realist traditions of power formulations in IR theory need to be looked at. First, classical realist, begins with, Thucydides, his famous dictum is that let the strong prevail in the society, and the weak endure the consequences. In the simple sense, the powerful can do whatever they want and others in the society accept the determination of the power holders. Their methodology of power analysis stems from the law of human behaviour or human nature, and assumes that human motivation is to accumulate power and desire to dominate others. For Thucydides and Hans J. Morgenthau, their analysis of power is very similar to the behaviour of state continuously driven by power seeking, which is clearly rooted in the biological drives of human beings. Morgenthau argued that men always have an insatiable lust for power and man is *animus dominandi,* which means that human being is a political animal by nature, they try to seek more power or desire to maximise power. He viewed that the state always involves an unending struggle for power, and states' utmost priority lies heavily on power maximisation. Kautilya's *Arthashastra* and Machiavelli's *Prince*, strongly advised their king that survival of the state is only achieved through by maximisation of power variables (capacity). They encouraged their respective kings to go for pre-emptive war and support expansionist policy to ensure survival to become most powerful in the comity of nations. Classical realist always emphasised that international relations is all about to continuous efforts to maintain the inequality of the allocation of shares, that is to increase one's own wealth and try to reduce or check other nation's wealth. They also believed that power is the immediate aim and viewed power as the end in itself.

They defined power on the basis of resources. They equated power with the possession of both material and ideational (non-material) resources. Morgenthau identified material resources into two broader categories; one is more stable quantitative resources and the other is subject to constant change or qualitative resources. The quantitative resources, largely stable over time, which is country's geography, natural wealth, population, industrial and technological advancement, and military shining strength. Other ideational resources or qualitative resources are very unstable or inconsistent in their nature, which are national character, quality of national government, national morale and quality foreign policy or nation's diplomacy. They argued that among the material and non-material resources, military strength is *primus inter pares* or *ultima ratio* of the state power. Military power is the mostly recognised as the political strength. According to classical realist, the power of the powerful states can be adjudged the shining capability of the military power. Military strength is the main apparatus of the state power.

E.H. Carr, slightly in advance over other classical realist, he argued that power is invisible, yet for the purpose of analysis, he defined a country's power on the basis of military power, economic power and power over opinion.[18] His distinction of country's power is very clear and specific than any other classical realist. According to Carr, opinion making is the important source of power. He explains how Hitler used his ability to shape the opinion of the mass to become very popular in a very short time. Power over opinion is all about propaganda, it is mainly aimed at mass appeal. He further claims that "The art of persuasion has always been a necessary part of the equipment of a political leader, rhetoric has a long and honoured record in the annals of statesmanship."[19] He clearly argues that organised use of power over opinion as a regular instrument of power in the quality nation's diplomacy. For example, Communist International, the first and foremost organisation of the kind, was established in Soviet Russia. Further, he adds that international relations no longer deal with purely material factor alone but also deal with ideas and ideology and thoughts and feelings of the human beings. Carr rejects the notion of power over opinion cannot be disassociated from military and economic strength. It should not be a separate entity of power, it should be complimentary to each other. Though he much highlighted the importance of power over opinion, but he avowed military is the supreme importance in his analysis of state power structure. The important source of power always lies in the relative military strength of the countries. Also, he believes that force and popularity are the two pillars of the state.

Kenneth Waltz is a major proponent of neorealism or structural realism or defensive realism. The idea of classical realist, which is insatiable lust for power, is the human law of nature. It slowly and steadily faded away. This period was marked by rise of many organisations such as international, regional etc. Therefore, the locus of power, clearly shifts from human behaviour to structural aspect of the institution. Waltz argues that power seeking behaviour of states lies in the anarchical international institutional setup and further added that source of power derives from the anarchical structural system and it is the structure of the systems' environment that inhibits states to seek power. Waltz argues that power as a resource which is highly fungible and endorsed the elements of the national power approach. The vehicle of state of power is all about the total aggregates of national material resources. The core idea of structural realism is not power maximiser rather than security maximiser. Why is it called defensive realism? The survival of the state lies in the aspect of security and not power mongering. It simply keeps with state's ability to protect from others' aggressive policy. Thus, according to defensive realism, state's prime interest is security maximisation to defend their state from the aggressor. According to neorealism, force or military power serves not only ultima ratio and in fact the first and foremost one. State power is measured on the basis of military capabilities and roughly equivalent to military power. Waltz entirely differs from Morgenthau's aspect of power, for him, power is a means not an end but it is contrary to Morgenthau, who viewed power as an end in itself.

Offensive realism articulates that the structure of international institution (mainly anarchical system) urges the states to maximise their relative power position in the international arena. It is contrary to the defensive realism, which argued for security maximisation. According to Mearsheimer, the study on state's power mainly lies in the calculations about how to maximise more power and its cognates the world around them. States appraise others relative power positions (resources) at the regular basis, because it always continues to be more powerful at the costs of other states.[20] The bedrock assumption of the offensive realism is nothing but power maximisation. Based on this assumption, the survival of the state heavily depends upon the accumulation of more power variables than anyone else and supports expansionist policy to amaze more power and wealth. Like Waltz, Mearsheimer, in his analysis of power, endorses elements of national power approach or resource based approach. He defines power as all about the specific material assets in the state or material resources which are available to the state. He was first in the realist tradition, made a clear cut attempt about how to measure the state's power in a reliable way. He concurs the view of other realist tradition, that is, power is largely in terms of military strength and further ahead with other realist, he supports aggressive or expansionist policy to become more powerful in conducting international relations.[21]

Neoclassical realist is different from other realist tradition. First, they agree with classical realist that power can be derived from the both material and ideational resources. Further, they extended their analysis of power into foreign policy behaviour and decision on specific issues. They argue that it must be observed objectively and elements of national power are not sole province of power and the perception of the decision maker and his behaviour matter the most. The main difference between classical realist and neoclassical realist is that, locus on power, former believed that power seeking effort of the state draws conclusion from the human law of nature and later, arrived at the anarchical structure of the system, that compels states to seek power. Second, they concur the view of defensive and offensive realism, locus of power, state power seeking is mainly caused by structural setup in the international relations. Both the defensive and offensive realism, they critically differ from the focus of power, that is, former believed that power seeking effort of the state is mainly from the security perspective or security maximisation and latter, concluded that power maximisation is the ultimate effort of the state to become more powerful among the nations.

But neoclassical realist strongly believed that state's continuous struggle for domination from others mainly draws from the both security maximisation and power maximisation, which is 'influence maximisation'. Both offensive and defensive realist, have only seen one aspect of the state power seeking capacity, none of them are seen both as part and parcel of state building with strong intention of dominating other states. They are in favour of amalgamation of locus of power in pursuit of both individual and structural level. They endorsed the lump concept or elements of national power approach, but they argued that relative power position alone cannot explain the foreign policy behaviour of the states. According to neoclassical realist, "one of important obstacles to providing a reliable way to measure power originates from the fact that it is not national power per se that is crucial importance but the perception of the decision maker. It is highly intangible in nature, therefore, any analysis of state power in realist tradition fails to capture the intangible aspect of power."[22]

Neorealism argued that, the relative distribution of power in the international system has an objective existence that directly influences the behaviour of states. This argument was strongly rejected by the neoclassical realists that they much emphasised on the role of political leaders and their perception is central to power. But they agree with neorealist that is pursuit of power is not the end per se rather it is one of crucial means in which state has control and shape the environment in favour of their own needs and wants. The quest for power is subject to cost-benefit analysis, they reject other realist view that, "there is no direct transmission line linking material capabilities to foreign policy behaviour and must be incorporated domestic variables and decision makers perception in their calculation of state power."[23]

However, Brian C. Schmidt argues there is a degree of consensus on how they define power. Classical realists, Morgenthau in particular, defined power both in terms of relational and elements of national power approach, the overwhelming majority of realists in all three categories endorse the latter view. In general, he criticised realist theory that in totality lacks to identify a variety of problems and inconsistencies (in many of its central tenets) especially define, measure and utilise the concept of power and also ambiguity of the conceptualisation of power.[24] In the same line, Michael Barnett and Raymond Duvall argued that there is a general lack of consensus on the most appropriate manner to conceptualise and measure power.[25] Nye criticised that realist theory does not consider changing nature of power and inadequate understanding of power.[26] Baldwin observed that realists always equate power with resources, and by insisting that power is fungible across diverse issue areas, realists continue to be vulnerable to a wide range of criticisms.[27] In addition to defining power in terms of possession of material resources, there is a general tendency among realists to associate power with military might, realist fully obsessed with war fighting ability to be essence of state power.

Realists studied and gave importance to the concept of power in international relations. They believed that the power is *numero uno* in international relations, and it is the sine qua non of international politics. They strongly believed that conflict and competition are the two pillars of the state's implicit practice of international politics. Except realist, there is no alternative approach to power in world politics. Other theorists in international relations have failed to show the essence power variables in their analysis. They always carefully explained their theory to avoid the critical importance of power and not try to expose power variables which are inherent in nature.

This paved the way for the discipline of international relations to treat power as the exclusive province of realism. Those opposing realism, always distance themselves from power considerations. Barnett and Duvall, in their analysis about power in international politics, clearly argued that "neoliberal-institutionalist, liberals and constructivist have attempted to demonstrate their theoretical salience by demonstrating how power variables are not causally consequential in their explanations of empirical outcomes."[28] Scholars from different schools of thought in IR, never understand different face and its behaviour of power, every theory in IR has its own power behaviour but it is not analysed in terms of different characteristics of power and even they solely obsessed and equated with power for realism.

Evolution of Soft Power Theory

The properties (attraction) of soft power is nothing new in the world. It is age-old phenomenon and immortal concept. Soft power is a form of power, like any other power, it can be used for both good and bad intentions. It can be identified in the form of material and non-material resources but the characteristics of soft power remains intangible, invisible, immeasurable, and non-fungible in nature. It can be used to shape the behaviours of others in the form of attractive measures. These characteristics are not less strong than the any other form of power. It is least observable for analysis but it is most effective. It has direct and indirect effects, intentional and unintentional effort, shorter and longer sustenance, less and more powerful tool, immediate and gradual aim, nearest to deepest engagement and static and dynamic behaviour and etc. But it is all about individual perception, intuition, and cognition and heavily relies on subjective interest. Before Nye, "thinkers no less significant than Foucault, Bourdieu, Gramsci, Lukes and others articulated the version of soft power and recognise that power can be expressed without making threats, or promising payments, or inducements."[29]

However, for Nye, soft power theory has been built on the realist tradition. Especially scholars like Carr, Morgenthau and neoclassical realist, their works shed some lights on intangible aspect of power, such as power of ideational resources or non-material resources, power over opinion (mass popularity), leader's perception and foreign policy behaviour but they never conceptualised the entire realm of intangible aspect of power behaviour. The roots of the soft power stem from the realist tradition, when Nye coined the term soft power in 1990. He draws his soft power from Carr's idea of power over opinion, which was a strong base for Nye's notion of soft power theory. He opines that "there is no contradiction between realism and soft power. Soft power is not a form of idealism or liberalism. It is simply a form of power, one way of getting desired outcomes."[30] Nye's theory can be combination of liberalism and realism, he himself floated the idea of his theory (soft power) can be genuinely called as neoliberal-realism. He intended that soft power is real and it can be nourished by the combined features of liberal and realism thought.

The newness of Nye's theory lies in the aspect of identification of the changing nature of power resources in international relations and also clearly come out with the spectrum of power behaviour ranging from hard power to soft power. Realist tradition really missed what Nye identified in his analysis of power. Almost all realist traditions, much emphasis was given to military strength as main source of state power but they never saw the *ultima ratio* of military power declining and losing its relevance and position in international relations to get the desirable outcome. Nye's soft power is really a continuity of realist tradition. He thoroughly captured the missing link from the realist view of power. He also followed the realist tradition of national elements of approach in his power analysis which depicts power as a material and non-material resource and calculates a country's relative power position among the nations. Nye's candidates are mainly non-material resources or soft resources, that is, countries' culture, values, ideals, foreign policy and so on because he wants to explore the intangible aspect of power stems from the cultural aspect of resources.

Nye differentiates power behaviour into two broader categories namely hard power and soft power based on resources. According to Nye, hard power mainly derives from military and economic strength and soft power obtains mostly from the country's culture, values, ideals, institution and foreign policy effort. This difference clearly indicates the existence of spectrum of power behaviour. It is very clear denomination identified by Nye, earlier, realist had viewed only one side of the spectrum of behaviour—that is hard power, and completely ignored the other end of spectrum, that is soft power or soft use of power in international relations. Initially he projected that soft power is benign power than the other power but in the later works he accepts that soft power is a form of power like any other power. It (attraction) can be used both to deceive and for the good of others.

Nye is the sole proprietor of soft power theory. During 1990s, he coined the term, conceptualised, wrote numerous articles and many books, to support and to build his theory. Since then, slowly and steadily, the evolution of soft power theory is taking place very deeply and getting more and more strength. At every stage, he clarified and rectified many aspects involved in the theory. Over the period, the scope and domain of soft power has spread its wings beyond imagination and it touches all the aspects of resources and events. Soft power moves beyond from specific soft power resource to all kinds of resources (including military and economic) available in the circumstances for effective use of soft power. Analysis of soft power can be incorporated in all the events of international politics, ranging from small to complex issues. Issues may be related to both non-military and non-economic and also military and economic domain. In all the events, how the elements of attraction can be explored to shape the positive opinion and subside the negative opinion. Nowadays, soft power is the main source of power to project a country's image and also important tool of diplomacy to reduce the negative image. It is not necessarily seen as zero-sum game and negative-sum game but generally seen as a positive-sum game and win-win situation because interplay of soft use of power. Here there is no space for coercive power. However, in some situations, it encourages zero-sum game and the resultant favours some and disfavours others.

How and why soft power become more prominent in international relations?

This is the age of information, this era marked the beginning of global information revolution, Nye aptly called this period belongs to third industrial revolution. The locus of power is on information, it is less coercive and less tangible in nature. In this circumstance, use of military is not an easy task to get desirable outcome, it requires an elabourate moral justification and getting popular support become a difficult task. The major technological breakthrough in the computing and communication has changed the nature the sovereignty of the government, creating more space for non-state actors, and enabling environment to have cheaper and deeper communication. It enhances the role of soft power in foreign policy making (it involves deeper digital diplomacy and more communicative public diplomacy) and cyber domain always gives equal opportunity for all, full freedom with anonymity.

Information Communication Technology (ICT), plays an important role in reducing military power into ceremonial power. No country is willing to use military power to get outcome one wants, because its impacts are very high in political, economic and social life, for both who use the force and who receive the force. The space for communication is wider, longer and deeper, it enables greater knowledge about what is going around the world, it gives more power to the common people to say about policy making of their own country and also affects others. The socially awakened population cannot be controlled easily and in this situation, use of military is irrelevant and more difficult. Soft power is more useful when information is more diffused and horizontal in nature (flow of information).[31] These technological advancements give boost for socially awakening population and reduce the warlike situation in modern democracies. According to Nye, "power today is a less tangible and less coercive among the advanced democracies than it was in the past."[32]

However, military strength remains a critical tool in international arena, but today it reduces to less vital because other powers and different players are getting their own share to shape the international politics, it is no more the sole dictator of world politics. There are different factors, such as the more economic interdependence, cheaper and deeper communication, growing regional and international institutions, powerful transnational actors and wealthy and charismatic individuals, are collectively influencing the behaviour of the state. They sometimes play a larger role than money and force.

In modern days, warfare becomes increasingly about intelligence system, communications and electronic warfare. The age of conventional war fading away, now, more emphasis on cyber warfare, economic and propaganda tools, to reduce other states' strength to gain relative power. Many developed, developing, and even under-developed countries are engaging and increasing their relative power position in cyber domain. For example, the '*love bug virus*', developed and circulated in internet by a man from Philippines, a piece of coding costs billions of dollars all around the world. Now, these kinds of activities keep occurring on a daily basis. Today, electronic espionage is most important to curtail others' national interest, in the form of stealing other countries' valuable and official information, information relating economic, military, and strategic assets. Both individuals and states also have the capacity to carry out offensive cyber-attacks in other countries. For example, America's tenth fleet and twenty fourth air force have no ships or planes, their battlefield is cyberspace.

Soft Power has both Material and Non-material Resources

Power is conceived as one's ability to obtain what one wants, to channelize one's ability often linked with the possession of certain tangible and intangible resources. Realist tradition mainly believed that the wielder of the power mainly represents the possession of the large amount of material resources such as natural resources, population, territory, economic and military capability and political stability. But, Nye's soft power potentials initially lies in the intangible aspect of resources such as a country's dynamic culture, ideals, values, institutions and foreign policy. These resources are highly non-fungible and immeasurable in character. Later Nye writings, in further, he forced to delve the attractive elements in all material resources especially resources like military and economic in which he argued that these resources can be attractive when the softness of these resources explored. Even these material resources have the elements of attractive qualities if used for the good of others.

How did he shift his focus from ideational to material resources in his soft power analysis? Before looking into the above question, how he formulates his idea of power in the initial period? At the early stage of his analysis, his soft power candidates are dynamic culture, admiring values and ideals, skilful diplomacy and so on. Culture of a country is one of the potential sources of power because many aspects of culture has an influential and attractive qualities. It also transmits knowledge and value system. Culture can be seen as important intangible resources. It is divided into two broader area of resources namely high culture and popular culture. High culture includes a country's powerful literature, art and quality education and so on. The country's high culture is always a tool for diplomacy in the form of cultural programmes, such as various forms of dance and music concert perform in other countries, and art and literary festival and book and educational exhibition conducted to expose a country's superior art and literary heritage in other nation, and also academic and scientific scholarship programmes, to exchange ideas and knowledge and share a country's values and ideals to other country. It produces and enhances country's soft power and also a critical source of attraction of the host countries. Popular culture is widespread than the high culture (art, literature etc.). It includes country's cinema, television programmes and mass entertainment. This popular culture always carries the message of individual freedom, freedom of choice and other values and ideals which create a positive image in the minds of the viewer.[33] It affects the attitude in the subliminal level which generates favourable opinion. Nye sets the condition for popular, that is, "it should be exiting, exotic, rich, powerful, trendsetting—the cutting the edge of modernity and innovation, then only it can able to attract others."[34]

Values and ideals are important resources of soft power. Nye argued that values like promoting human rights, individual freedom, tolerance, opportunity, open markets, liberty, openness, upward mobility, feminism, promoting peace and so on and ideals such as democracy, federalism, secularism, liberalism etc., both contribute broader and deeper intangible national interest and to shape one's identity towards others. These attractive qualities are a major advertising point in view of others. A country's policies at home and abroad are one of the critical sources of soft power. For example, India's caste based discrimination in the society undercuts India's soft power and also is a major threat for India's soft power projection abroad. In his article, Nye accepted economic power straddle between hard and soft power. While sanction and restriction of trade comes under hard power strategy and the positivity of economic resources comes under soft power realm such as grants, developmental aid, low interest credit facility, and promoting trade and investment. He argues that "economic prowess contributes not only to wealth but also reputation and self-confidence and thus contributes attractiveness."[35]

In latest writings, Nye delves deeply the attractive elements in the military resources. He examines the various activities of military resources such as emergency assistance during national calamity like Tsunami, safety and security reassurance, peace keeping, reconstruction, assistance programme in peace time, joint exchanges, joint training, joint exercises, educational training programmes, military to military contacts, preventive defence, countering terrorism, sharing intelligence, coordinating police across the borders and so on. These events and activities of military power reveal the humane, cooperative and common good of others in military resources which contains the strong elements of soft power. Finally, about soft power resources, he concludes that "a country's concerns for soft power, it has to explore better ways and prudent use of all resources."[36] He has developed a spectrum of behaviour for both economic and military resources but fails to develop a spectrum of attractive behaviour ranging from less attraction to stronger attraction from all kinds of resources.

In addition, he argues that power resources, whether hard or soft, have their own spectrum of behaviour ranging from coercion to attraction. How resources (hard or soft) generate soft or hard power, he arrived with conclusion that depends upon the context but he failed to view that, softness or hardness of power primarily flows from the perception of the individual capacity and knowledge system which plays an important role to decide whether the particular resources can be viewed as softness or hardness, not the context alone. When he replied to his critiques about his resource based approach, he argued that people tend to confuse with resources with the behaviour of attraction.[37] But he never viewed power as a subjective matter, he only gave much emphasis on resources and forgot the fact that resources never generate attraction; attraction only flows from the mind of the perceiver. How it is good or bad for him/her, this evaluation decides fact that whether the use of power resources become hard or soft.

The Effect of Soft Power (Direct and Indirect)

In general, the effect of power may be direct or indirect form. In direct form, power and its effect is specific, clear, visible, calculable, fungible, tangible and also measurable. While in indirect form, power is not aimed at immediate effect, it is more diffusive in nature and works on a longer period. It cannot be measured very specifically and it lacks clarity about specific outcomes. However, the indirect effect of power is more powerful than direct effect. Nye's soft power analysis has taken the intangible aspect of resources to observe the more subtle effect of power behaviour. He argued that more subtle aspect of power is more powerful, it affects the sub-conscious mind and this will be a useful tool to shape and mould the opinion of others. Like any other form of power, soft power has both direct and indirect effects to influence the behaviours of others. Though soft power resources are highly intangible in nature, but it has tangible, immediate, fungible and measurable effect in which soft power can be clearly observed objectively. Efforts to affect the civilians of other countries have long roots both direct and indirectly. For example, Emperor Ashoka had sent ambassadors to other countries carrying the message of *Dhamma*.[38] These messages were direct and specific effect on the people's opinion in neighbouring states and generated goodwill, tranquillity, attraction, amity, co-optation, emulation. Simultaneously, his messages spread across his own kingdom and neighbouring states in the form rock and iron pillar edicts. These edicts were the source of indirect effects in the mind of others.

Criticism on Soft Power

The bedrock assumption of soft power theory lies in resources especially intangible aspect of cultural resources. This resource based approach creates a lot of confusion, misunderstanding and theoretical fuzziness. Nye's soft power theory invites criticism from many quarters. Criticism can be clubbed into two categories. Initially, criticism on surface of the concept or lack of proper understanding of the concept and latter criticisms mainly on the depth of the concept or validation of the Nye's theory building on the basis of material and non-material resources. In the initial period, the word soft power stretched and twisted in all directions because lack of proper understanding. Historian Niall Ferguson has described that "soft power is a non-traditional forces such as culture and commercial goods."[39] Josef Joffe, in his article, *Perils of Soft Power*, has argued that cultural resources are not much influential factors in world politics.[40] In the same line, realist tradition, objected the notion of soft power in the realm of international politics because their conception of power is narrow in terms of force and money power. They never acknowledged that the power of attraction emanates from the non-fungible resources like one's culture, values and ideals and so on and argued that these resources are not useful for any policy outcomes.

Somehow, they all misunderstood the concept in two different ways. First, they never thought that soft power is a form of power like any other powers, one way of getting desired outcomes through attraction by intangible resources. Second, soft power is misunderstood in a way many believe that it is an alternative to hard power and holds an ethically superior position than hard power. Even this misunderstanding floated different schools of thought on soft power such as cultural school and political school or narrower and broader views. Cultural school equated with softness of power only to be derived form of cultural resources, they rejected military and economic resources, while political school included economic and cultural aspect of resources is an important source for attraction and neglected command and control power which emanates from the military prowess.

Before Nye, Walter Russell Mead argued that elements of attraction is deep-rooted in the economic resources. In 2005, Nye also accepted the economic resources straddle between hard and soft power. A little later, many articles and books were floated by many scholars, focussing especially on country's economic resources and how these economic resources generate attraction in other countries. Joshua Kurlantzick argued that "soft power means anything outside of the military and security realm, including not only popular culture and public diplomacy but also more coercive economic and diplomatic tools like aid and investment and participation in multilateral organizations."[41] His analysis helped China and India to project their strong economic growth and millennia old cultural civilization as source for attraction or as tool for diplomacy to advertise their positive image in international politics. Many like-minded scholars come out with numerous analyses on soft power on economic diplomacy. This extended scope of soft power resources leads to greater confusion and misunderstanding because according to Mingjiang Li, "much of the confusion and misunderstanding of the concept of the soft power is due to, it being undertheorized, lack of academic refinement and analytical fuzziness."[42] In the same tone, Brantley Womack, argued that Nye's event or issue driven approach (including economic and military sphere) to soft power theory is an important cause for greater misunderstanding and further added that he explains his theory based on some international events with identified by some material and non-material resources which is cause for attraction or detraction, that is soft or hard power.[43]

Later criticism on soft power theory building or validation of soft power theory, mainly on three grounds namely resource or vehicle fallacy, the absence of conceptual clarity on attraction, persuasion and lacks in subjective interest. Nye's analysis on soft power has faith in resources. First, Lukes rejects the resource based approach on power. Lukes argued that Nye equated power with power resources, that is, whatever goes into effect or affect the process when power is activated. He further added that power is a capacity and not the vehicle of the capacity. Merely possessing or controlling the means of power is not the same as being powerful. In addition, he argued that "power need not be blunt or behavioural; it can operate socially in ways that subconsciously affect the formation of preferences."[44] In the same way, Janice Bially Mattern criticised Nye's view of power, saying, "power is a relationship rather than a 'hard thing'; a process rather than a hard condition; and an idea or belief rather than a hard fact of truth."[45]

Second, lies in the conceptual aspect of soft power, that is, attraction and persuasion are two wings of the Nye soft power theory but it lacks conceptual clarity. According to Lukes, "Nye makes no distinction between different ways in which soft power can co-opt, attract and entice those subject to it, and between different ways in which it can induce their acquiescence". In addition, he argued that hearts and minds of the subject are never won by pure persuasion alone but at the same the masked or deceived face of black art of rhetoric.[46] In short, concealing of information and trimming of information invariably go together with seduction. Bially Mattern has identified two ontological discrepancies attached with Nye soft power theory (attraction)—"one as an essential condition and the other one as a result of social interaction or persuasion." If attraction were natural, one would not need to cultivate soft power in the first place. She further argued that persuasion as a normal practise in international relations through representational force leads to be socio-linguistically constructed reality or verbal fighting, it is not evidenced or fact based reality, fact can be concealed and trimmed by the representational force.[47] This lead her to conclude that soft power is not so soft.

Third criticism mounted on Nye's agent centred approach, his theory completely discarded subjective interest of the subject. Lukes criticised that Nye's soft power theory, has taken the subjective interest as a given. He further argued that "the ability to shape the preferences of others is a troublingly obscure phrase which fails to discriminate between those causal processes which limit and sometimes undermine individual capacities."[48] On the other hand, Bially Mattern argued that "attraction is a rather subjective experience, which raises the question of what makes something or someone alluring to some and not to others."[49]

A Power Currency Approach to Soft Power

Alexander Vuving argued that Nye fails to identify the subtle aspect of power process in a relationship. Power does not flow from the resources rather it flows from the power currencies. Power and its softness are not derived from the resources; they are mainly derived from power currencies. Nye has given a clear distinction of power behaviour. For hard power he unknowingly used hard power currencies like threat, coercion, payment, inducement and sanction in which hardness is derived from the resources like military, economic, technological strength. For the soft power, he relied heavily on resources like culture, political values, foreign policy and institution but Nye also mentions attraction; it is a form of power currency and it has wider meaning and not a very specific in nature. This created confusion and misunderstanding of the concept. To overcome Nye's resource based approach on soft power, since soft power is the power to attract, there are two questions which are raised: what constitutes soft power? And what generates attraction?

To solve this problem Alexander Vuving has introduced the concept called soft power currencies, which causes attraction. For soft power he proposes three sets of power currencies namely benignity, brilliance and beauty in which both power and its softness derived. Before going into analysis of soft power currencies, one should have an understanding about power resource and power currencies, both are sources of power, the difference between power resource and power currency, according to Vuving, is a subtle distinction only comparable to the one between a structure and its architecture. He further adds that "a power currency is a property that causes power. Power currencies are usually properties of resources or activities."[50]

Vuving has explained in detail the basic soft power currencies. Firstly, benignity is an aspect or attribute of agent's relations with others, especially targeting the client of soft power. It refers to positive attitude of the agent to express and treat the client in the form of kind, gentle, benevolence, compassion, goodwill, generosity, magnanimity, and so on. Benignity as a soft power currency works closely on the inclination of reciprocal altruism; one can witness this in the day to day life of human being. It generates soft power through the "production of gratitude and sympathy". Secondly, brilliance is an aspect or attribute of agent's relations with its work, it refers to the property, strength, and high performance of agent that is the capability and ability to succeed of the agent. Brilliance as a power currency attracts client in the form of learning from the success of the agent. Human beings are always attracted towards the success story of the others. It generates soft power through the "production of admiration." Thirdly, beauty is an aspect or attribute of agent relations with ideals, values, causes or visions. It refers to the agent's tendency or strong desire to represent or promote the ideals, values, causes or visions. In this power currency, client gets attracted towards the agent, because of the selfless motive of the agent and his ability to represent the ideals, values, causes or visions for common good and development of the society. Beauty generates soft power through "the production of inspiration."[51]

Concluding Remarks

Power currency approach for soft power analysis has given a clear cut picture of the way in which soft power and its softness can be nurtured through prudent use all the resources like military, economic, culture and so on. This concept makes very clear that softness of the power can be generated from all kinds of resource available in the circumstances. Beauty, benignity and brilliance power currencies not only cause softness from resources like culture, values, policies and institution but also softness can be driven by diligent use of military and economic strength. This approach gives more importance to the individual perception and perception leads to behaviour. So it ends confusion over resources with its behaviour.

Notes

1. Steven Lukes (2007). "Power and the Battle for Hearts and Minds: On the Bluntness of Soft Power", in Felix Berenskoetter and Michael J. Williams, *Power in World Politics*, p. 90.
2. Steven Lukes, *Power: A Radical View*, New York, Palgrave Macmillan, 2005, p. 61.
3. Lukes, n.1, p. 83.
4. Lukes, n.2, p. 61.
5. Robert Dahl, "The Concept of Power", New Haven: Yale University, 1962, p. 201.
6. Lukes, n.2, p. 64.
7. *Ibid.*, pp. 70-71.
8. Robert, n.5, p. 204.

9. Peter Bachrach and Mortan Baratz, "Power and its Two Faces Revisited: A Reply to Geoffrey Debnam", *The American Political Science Review*, September 1975.
10. Lukes, n. 2, p. 68.
11. Dahl, n. 5, p. 204.
12. Prasad and Prasad (2007). *Administrative Thinkers*, New Delhi, p. 74.
13. Lukes, n. 2, p. 28.
14. Peter and Mortan, n. 9, pp. 900-905
15. Lukes, n. 2, p. 28.
16. *Ibid.*, p. 35.
17. *Ibid.*, p. 45.
18. Barnett and Duvall, in their article, Power in International Relations, argued that power is not monopolised by realist tradition because Nye analysis of soft power, has taken away power analysis from the realist. *Source*: International Organization, Vol. 59, No. 1 (Winter, 2005), pp. 39-75.
19. E.H. Carr (1981). *The Twenty Years' Crisis (1919-1939): An Introduction to the Study of International Relations,* Macmillan Press Limited, p. 135.
20. *Ibid.*, p. 145.
21. Schmidt C. Brian, "Realism and Facets of Power in International Relations", in Felix Berenskoetter and Michael J. Williams, n. 1, p. 56.
22. *Ibid.*, p. 57.
23. *Ibid.*, p. 58.
24. *Ibid.*
25. *Ibid.*, p. 62.
26. Michael and Raymond (2005). "Power in International Relations", *International Organisation*, Winter, p. 40.
27. Joseph S. Nye (1990). "Soft Power", *Foreign Policy,* Autumn, p. 154.
28. Schmidt C. Brian, "Realism and Facets of Power in International Relations", in Felix Berenskoetter and Michael J. Williams, n.1, p. 61.
29. Barnett and Duvall, n. 26, p. 40.
30. Janice Bially Mattern, "Why Soft Power isn't So Soft: Representational Force and Attraction in World Politics", in Berenkoetter and Williams, n.1, p. 101.
31. Joseph S. Nye (2011). *The Future of Power,* New York: Public Affairs, p. 82.
32. Joseph S. Nye (2002). *The Paradox of American Power: Why the World' only Superpower Can't Go it Alone*, New York: Oxford University Press, p. 47.
33. Joseph S. Joseph (2004). *Soft Power: The Means to Success in World Politics*, United States: Public Affairs, p. 30.
34. *Ibid.*, p. 35.
35. *Ibid.*, p. 12.

36. *Ibid.*, p. 33.
37. Joseph S. Nye, n. 31, p. 82.
38. Joseph S. Nye (2008). *The Powers to Lead*, New York: Oxford University Press, p. 28.
39. *Dhamma* (includes four noble truth and eightfold path to come out suffering), which covers entire moral teachings of Buddha.
40. Niall Ferguson, "Think Again: Power", *Foreign Policy*, February 2003.
41. Josef Joffe, "The Perils of Soft Power", *New York Times Magazine*, May 14, 2006.
42. Joshua Kurlanzick (2007). *Charm Offensive: How China's Soft Power Transforming the World*, London: Yale University Press, p. 6.
43. Li Mingjiang (2010). *Soft Power: China's Emerging Strategy in International Politics*, Pentagon Press, Lexington Books, Maryland, p. 4.
44. Brantly Womack (2010). "Dissecting Soft Power: Attention, Attraction, Persuasion," Chapter-III in the *China among Unequals: Asymmetric Foreign Relationship in Asia*.
45. Lukes, n. 1, p. 95.
46. Janice, n. 30, p. 100.
47. Lukes, n. 1, p. 94.
48. Janice, n. 30, p. 100.
49. Lukes, n. 1, p. 95.
50. Janice, n. 30, p. 102.
51. Alexander L. Vuving (2009). "How Soft Power Works", paper presented at the panel "Soft Power and Smart Power", *American Political Science Association annual meeting*, Toronto, p. 5.

13

Digital India Initiatives in Transforming Governance to Achieve Sustainable Development Goals

Sanjeev Kumar Mahajan and *Anupama Puri Mahajan*

"Humanity has the ability to make development sustainable to ensure that it meets the needs of the present without compromising the ability of future generations to meet their own needs" (WCED). Hence, the motto of Sustainable Development Goals (SDGs) is to finish the job that was expected to achieve the target of 'leave no one behind' by Millennium Development Goals. It apparently failed to achieve the targets and therefore the focus shifted to SDGs with the aim that the task may be fulfilled by 2030. The broad objective is to resolve to free the humanity from poverty, secure a healthy planet for future generations, build peaceful and inclusive societies as a foundation for ensuring lives of dignity for all. Therefore, the aim of SDGs is to ensure mental and physical health for people and the planet. The thrust of SDGs is to address the social, economic and environmental dimensions of sustainable development. The success of SDGs largely depends upon the effective implementation and monitoring process adopted by the nation.

Objective of this Article

The focus of this chapter is to study how the capacity-building of a government can be enhanced to adopt and transform the governance to reduce vulnerability and build resilience to achieve the targets laid by SDGs by 2030. This is only possible when the institutional arrangements of any country can handle the new challenges on time with the technological advancement around the world coupled with enabled fast access to citizens through information and communications technologies (ICTs). ICT is a tool to monitor the performance of the policies in real time. Digitization, as a phenomenon, has made its presence integral to the advancement of a society. Initially, digital initiatives were carried out for the processing and preservation of the official data to help the policy makers to identify the trends and pattern in policy-formulation. Digital revolution has opened a whole new set of opportunities to the nations in reshaping the scope of development. ICTs have given an opportunity to the average person and the governments to boost economy at the individual and at the national levels.

Digital initiatives at different levels, has helped India in transforming governance, especially, in achieving SDGs. The SDGs are integrated and balance the three dimensions of sustainable development viz. economic, social and environmental. The interesting fact about SDGs is that these are not legally binding on any nation since the member nations of the UN have pledged to achieve the targets. The 17 SDGs have been designed to encompass all areas of development that the governments have to work on. It has systematized and widened the scope of the government budgets. In this chapter, an attempt will be made to study how the digital initiatives at the policy level have been implemented by India to help in transforming the government and governance to improve delivery of public services and goods for the benefit of the people.

India is poised at the brink of becoming one of the world's largest and fastest growing economies. The second decade of the twenty-first century has witnessed a major shift in administration. India has a history of moving from the colonial period to the post-colonial era which was beset with Socialist ideals and then glided into a post-socialist correction albeit with many economic and structural reforms. The nation state is the only organization that can initiate and execute a change in the society politically, socially and economically.

A State, in today's world is the only enabler to bring about sustainable development, strengthen the democratic structures, adopt a sensitively comprehensive approach to security—internal and external—and synthesized forms to civil and responsive governance.

The New Economic Policy, 1991 and subsequent economic policies in India laid stress on the reduction in the interference of the Government in unwarranted sectors, as was the new approach in the world of withdrawal of Government from the market economies. This has resulting an ever-growing state of privatization, liberalization and globalization in India.

The Sustainable Development Goals (SDGs) have given a new turn to governance in India. Since the SDGs cover almost every objective which a Government intends to achieve through its budgetary appropriations, India has linked the two quite successfully. India's premier policy and planning agency, NITI Aayog, has prepared its Action Plan and Strategy for New India accordingly. The documents are not just a formal exercise but also a tool to transform governance. The Union Budget since 2017 has incorporated the SDGs as recommended by the NITI Aayog while it has directed all State Governments to follow suit by including the SDGs into their State Budgets.

The world is transforming through the Industrial Revolution 4.0 to 5.0, which India has to adopt all latest technological advancements to be a major player in the global competition and subsequently increasing its socio-economic growth. Digital India is the only methodology to transform the Governance in India to achieve the SDGs. It ensures transparency, accountability and accessibility which all lead to client-satisfaction, in this case, the citizens of India.

It is apparent that a Government has a vital role to play in manifarious aspects of the lives of its citizens. It involves policy-making and efficient resource-utilization and management. It employs all instruments through which policy stakeholders exercise legal rights with an aim to achieve political, economic, social and cultural objectives (Anil Kumar Dhiman, 2017). Citizens are considered the cornerstone of every Government in the modern period around whom all the Governmental activities revolve for their better standards of lives. Every policy formulated by the Government is aimed at improving the living conditions of its citizens directly or indirectly (Sweta Mishra, 2012).

Good Governance is an indispensable instrument for facilitating faster development in developing countries reeling under poverty and inequality largely because of the bad governance (B.K. Pattanaik, 2017).

Journey from Millennium Development Goals (MDGs) to Sustainable Development Goals (SDGs)

The term, 'governance' is used in different contexts. At geo-political levels, for instance, it is used to characterize global governance, national governance, local governance and so on (WPSR, 2015). The State is a key factor in providing responsive and accountable public governance to look after its citizens. The international development agenda has been actively led by the United Nations and its technical agencies ever since its inception after the Second World War. Till the 1990s, the approach was fragmented and disjointed, either initiated by the specialized agencies or funds at various World Summits or Conferences to address three dimensions of development—economic, social and environmental. The Millennium Development Goals (MDGs) saw the convergence of development agenda of the United Development Programme and other development (Sanjiv Kumar, 2013).

In September 2001, based upon the Millennium Declaration, the United Nations presented the MDGs as a list of common goals for the world community to achieve by 2015 (Maya Fehling, *et al.*, 2013). India, as a part of the world movement, has vigorously strived to achieve the different MDGs since the adoption of the Millennium Declaration. Figure 13.1 explains that the MDGs consist of eight broad goals dealing with multiple development issues.

It is clear from Figure 13.1 that India has made a considerable progress in meeting the targets laid down by the MDGs. Nearly, half of the indicators have achieved the targets and the rest are making satisfactory progress. However, the targets have been unevenly achieved across the rest of the countries and a need was felt to restart the discussions about the usefulness of the MDGs and to explore an improved mechanism to guide cooperation for sustainable development beyond 2015 (Government of India, 2017).

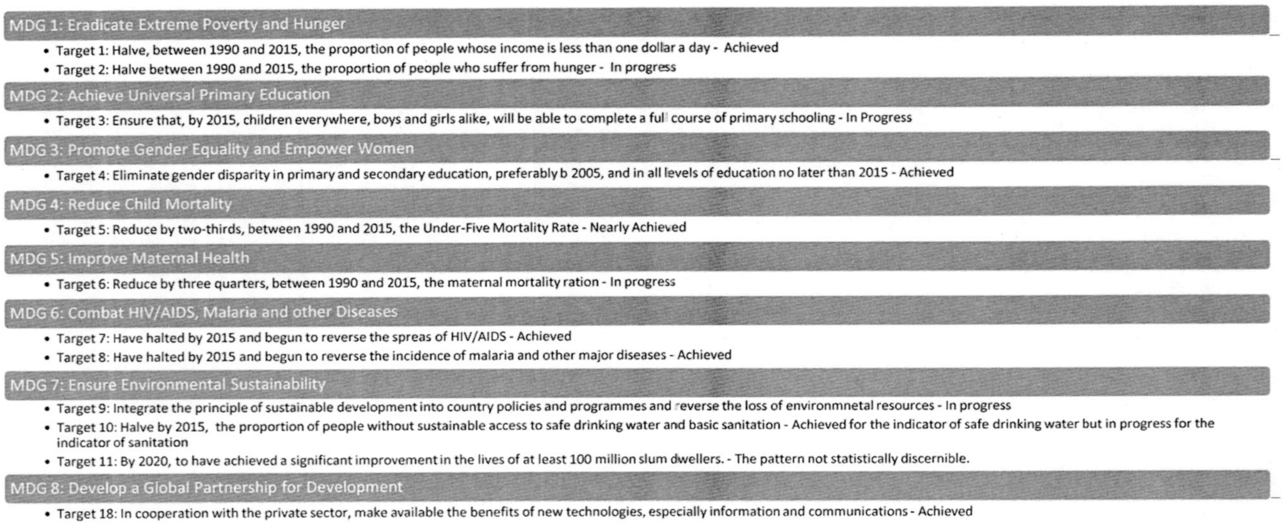

Fig. 13.1: MDGs and Targets—Summary of Progress Achieved by India.

Source: http://www.mospi.gov.in/sites/default/files/publication_reports/MDG_Final_Country_report_of_India_27nov17.pdf as retrieved on 29-04-2019

On the commemoration of the twentieth anniversary of the 'Rio Earth Summit, 1992'; 'The United Nations Conference on Sustainable Development' in 2012 initiated the debate and discussions towards post-2015 development agenda targets. Finally, the 17 Sustainable Development Goals (SDGs) came into force with effect from January 1, 2016. This is an enhanced and comprehensive approach to achieve peaceful societies. All member nations are expected to lay down the framework, grossly depending upon its own sustainable development policies, plans and programmes. Further, it is the responsibility of the individual country to monitor the progress of SDGs from time to time.

In India, there is already some convergence between SDGs and developmental goals in the country as the Government of India has been pursuing the path of '*Sabka Sath, Sabka Vikas*' (Together with all, development for all). Accordingly, the National Institute for Transforming India (NITI Aayog) has been assigned the task of identification of national targets assigning them to the concerned Ministries for their implementation. Overall, the Ministry of Statistics and Programme Implementation has been given the task of developing the National Indicator Framework (NIF) for measuring the advancement of the SDGs and associated desired plans. Hence, the 2030 Agenda for Sustainable Development places emphasis on the role of the Government and its responsibility for the follow up and review. In this context, digital revolution can empower the nation for inclusive growth and to ensure regular evaluation and monitoring of progress.

Digital revolution has helped in revolutionizing the pace of progress opening countless avenues to transform the society, culture and lifestyle. India, the fastest growing economy in the world, has undergone complete transformation with the rapid uptake of digital technologies. The journey to digitalization has been one of inclusive growth, transforming India into a global economy (Deepika Kaushal, 2018). The entire gamut of Digital Transformation is to provide innovative products and services to improve productivity and efficiency (R.S. Sharma, 2010).

Digital India Initiatives

India is the sixth largest economy in the world, poised to become a $5 trillion economy by 2022 and aspiring to be a $10 trillion economy by 2030. Integration of digital technologies and innovation is bringing about disruptive transformation in the country making a land of immense opportunities (NITI Aayog, 2019). India has been known as a powerhouse of software around the globe but has always had a deficit in its availability and applicability in the delivery of government services to its citizens. The digital revolution began in India as a well-planned strategy with demonetisation in November, 2016. The shortfall of currency notes in the economy forced people to rely on digital methods to make transactions which led to a wider base of financial inclusion. People who had never used a debit or a credit card and did not even have a bank account rushed to the banks to avail of these facilities. Moreover, the Government of India's adoption of Direct Benefit System, based on UIDAI (Unique Identification Authority of India) pushed the digitalization even further in the realm of common people. Given below are the digital initiatives in India which are instrumental in transforming governance to achieve the SDGs.

Digital India

The Digital India Programme was introduced in India as the Government's flagship programmes. Its main objective is to transform the entire ecosystem of public services through the use of information technology. The services are provided to the people with the help of mobile phones, personal computers, laptops, tablets, television, radio and internet. The vision is to transform India into a digitally empowered society and knowledge economy electronically (McKinsey Gold Institute, 2017). Post-demonetisation and February, 2017, there were 3,264 million digital transactions and it is expected that by 2020, the percentage will go up by 45% of retail transactions with a digital payment ecosystem has been estimated at Rs. 3.3 trillion with the help of business organizations like Federation of Indian Chambers of Commerce and Industry (FICCI) and the International Chamber of Commerce (Ratnadeep Banerjee, 2017). The various programmes and initiatives that have been taken and planned regarding digitalization of Government services for better delivery, in India, shall be studied here.

***Inde EA Project*:** The IndeEA (India Enterprise Architecture Framework) project, under 'The Open Group Architecture

Framework' (TOGAF), has been praised by the United Nations as a work of reference for other global governments looking to invest in digital technologies to achieve the SDGs. TOGAF is an enterprise architecture methodology for business that defines the business goals and their alignment with architecture objectives around enterprise software development. The Open Group, the vendor and technology consortium, announced that it had been working with the Indian Government and in November, 2018, IndeEA was formally notified as an Indian national standard. It has the best-in-class architectural governance, processes and practices using ICT, infrastructure and applications. It is instrumental in giving a singular experience in availing Government services which is cashless, paperless and faceless and is enabled by 'Boundaryless Information Flow' (The Open Group, 2019).

The Nine Pillars of 'Digital India' Programme

The Digital India is an umbrella programme that covers multiple Government Ministries and Departments to weave together the ideas and thoughts into a single, comprehensive vision so that they can be integrated into a larger goal. The Digital India Programme is based on the following nine pillars:

1. Broadband Highways: The Broadband Highways covers three sub-components—rural, urban and the National Information Infrastructure (NII). The Plan has begun its work to connect all rural area Panchayats under the National Optical Fibre Network (NOFN) with the Department of Telecommunications as its nodal Department. The new urban areas and developments are being covered as a mandatory requirement by virtual network operators for service delivery and communication infrastructure. The NII has the responsibility to integrate the network and cloud infrastructure in the country for high speed connectivity and cloud platform originating from the government departments and going down till the Panchayats.

2. Universal Access to Mobile Connectivity: There are still more than 43 thousand villages in India (*Economic Times,* Aug .1, 2018) which do not have mobile coverage in India. This project will be completed in a phased manner.

3. Public Internet Access Programme: Under this programme, there are two sub-components which are—

i. Common Services Centres (CSCs), and
ii. Post Offices as multi-service centres.

The target is to make available one CSC for each Gram Panchayat with multiple end-points for the delivery of Government and business services. The Post Offices have been proposed to be converted into multi-service centres.

4. E-Governance: Government processes re-engineering needs to be reformed through the use of technology in all its Departments and agencies. Under the Digital India Programme, some guidelines have been prepared for E-Governance, which are:

- Form simplification and field reduction,
- Online applications and tracking,
- Online repositories for certificates, educational degrees, etc.,
- Integration of services and platforms, for example, Aadhar, payment gateway, mobile data sharing, etc., and
- Improvement of all databases by making them online so that the workflows within the Government Departments.

5. E-Kranti: Computerization in India began in the 1980s with some State specific initiatives, the National E-Governance in 2006 and finally, E-Kranti Programme was initiated in 2014. Its motto is 'Transforming E-Governance for Transforming Governance' with the following guidelines:

- Transformation and not translation of services through E-Kranti to improve the quality, quantity, manner of delivery of services and significant enhancement of productivity and competitiveness.
- Integrated services and not individual services with a common middleware and integration of the back-end process and processing of systems to facilitate integrated service delivery to citizens.
- Government Process Reengineering must be mandatory in every Mission Mode Project.

- ICT infrastructure on demand must be provided to all Government Departments, such as, connectivity, cloud and mobile platform.
- Cloud by default must be leveraged while designing and hosting applications in all Government Departments and private cloud must be permitted to them only after its security is assessed.
- All applications must be designed for mobile phones so that services can be delivered through them.
- Fast tracking approvals must be put in place.
- Standards and protocols must be mandated with the use of E-Governance in all of their projects.
- Language localization must be facilitated.
- National GIS (Geo-Spatial Information System) must be leveraged as a platform and as a service,
- Security and Electronic data presentation must be ensured by following the National Cyber Security Policy, 2013.

There are 44 on-going Mission Mode Projects under the E-Kranti programme which are grouped into Central, State and Integrated projects (Ministry of Electronics and Information and Technology, 2019).

6. Information for All: An Open Data Platform facilitates release of datasets in an open format by the ministries/departments for use, reuse and redistribution. The Government is pro-actively engaging through social media and web-based programmes to interact with the citizens. The Government of India initiated a platform, https://www.mygov.in/, especially, for citizen engagement in governance. It is a two-way communication between the Government and the citizens and there have been frequent instances where the Government response to the citizens has literally surprised them. This transform reflects 'maximum governance' through digital initiatives.

7. **Electronics Manufacturing:** The seventh pillar 'Electronics Manufacturing' has a target of NET ZERO Imports by 2020 as a striking demonstration of intent. Its focus areas have been 'Big-ticket items' like FABS, Fab-less design, set top boxes, etc. India has inadequate resources at the moment to bring in this manufacturing revolution but the Government is working towards it. If India can

manage to get one manufacturing unit of a FAB for chips in the semiconductor industry, it will revolutionize the electronics industry. The demand for electronic goods is growing with a Compound Annual Growth Rate (CAGR) of 22% and is expected to touch 400 billion USD by 2020 (Ministry of Electronics and Information and Technology, 2019).

8. IT for Jobs: The eighth pillar emphasizes on providing training to youth in the skills that are needed to take advantage of job opportunities in the IT/IES sector. The Ministry of Electronics and Information and Technology has outlined eight sub-components that need focus under this pillar, which are:

i. IT training to people in smaller towns and villages;
ii. The target fixed in this regard is to train one crore students over five years in smaller towns and villages;
iii. IT/IES in the North-eastern States;
iv. Setting up of BPOs in every North-eastern State to promote ICT enabled growth;
v. Training Service Delivery Agents;
vi. Training three lakh service delivery agents as part of skill development to work for enterprises that are providing IT services;
vii. Training rural workforce on telecom and its related services; and
viii. Training five lakh rural workforce to develop the telecom sector.

9. Early Harvest Programmes: IT comprises of a cluster of projects with a short timeline, which are:

i. *IT Platform:*The portal has been active since 2014 which disseminates information to all elected representatives and all Government employees.
ii. *Government Greetings:* All greetings to be sent on important days like Independence Day, Teacher's Day, etc. are sent as e-greetings through crowd sourcing. Templates have been made available for easy access and the portal is live since 2014.
iii. *Biometric Attendance:* Over 40,000 Government employees from 150 organizations have already been registered on the common biometric attendance portal.

iv. *Wi-Fi in Universities:* The Ministry of Human Resource Department is ensuring that all universities have wi-fi installed.

v. *Secure E-mail:* The Government IT infrastructure has been upgraded for a secure e-mail system as a primary mode for communication for 60 lakh employees and efforts are on to cover all employees.

Other programmes to make processes easier in the Government through digitization are standardization of e-mail design, installation of public wi-fi spots, conversion of school books to e-books, SMS based weather information and disaster alerts through Mobile Seva Platform and a National Portal for lost and found children in real time.

The above given nine pillars of Digital India form the basic infrastructure and initiatives that have kickstarted the revolution encompassing the entire ecosystem in India.

Tools leading to a transformed Governance in achieving SDGs

India is transforming governance through very robust tools which are termed as digital initiatives serve as the infrastructure on one side to deliver services and empower the citizens of India on the other. They are many but some of the major ones are given here:

AADHAR: Aadhar is a unique identity platform through which each and every Indian resident of the country gets a unique identity number which is called, 'Aadhar'. It has been acknowledged as the largest biometrics-based identification system in the world. Its real benefit is the disbursement of Government benefits directly to the bank accounts of the persons of vulnerable sections. It also acts as a strategy policy tool for social and financial inclusion, public sector delivery reforms, managing fiscal budgets to achieve a people-centric governance and transformed Good Governance. It has the ability to weed out fake identities and illegal migrants while serving as an authentication mode for banking for customers to access their Aadhar linked bank accounts online.

Agrimarket App: It is a mobile app that informs the farmers about the current crop prices to avoid any distress-sales by them. The information is limited within a scope of 50 kilometres around the farmer's location which is determined by the app through GPS.

Beti Bachao, Beti Padhao (Save the Girl Child, Educate the Girl Child): India has a distressing social evil of aborting the girl-child as the male child is given more importance. The online campaign and app have been very useful in making interventions to save, nurture and educate the girl-child.

BHIM (Bharat Interface for Money): BHIM is an app that has made financial transactions simpler, easier and quicker using Unified Payments Interface (UPI). Its advantage is that direct bank to bank payments and collections are made instantly using a mobile number or a payment address.

Centre for Excellence for Internet of Things (COE-IT): The COE-IT has been the pillar of strength for digitization in India as it is entrusted with the duty of giving a jump-start to the IOT (Internet of Things) ecosystem by creating innovative applications and domain capability. It is actively involved in building industry-capable talent, start-up community and an entrepreneurial ecosystem for IOT.

Crop Insurance Mobile App: It can be used to calculate the Insurance Premium for notified crops based on area, coverage amount and loan amount in case of loaned farmer. It provides information regarding normal sum insured, extended sum insured, premium details and subsidy information of any notified crop in any notified area. This is helping the farmers to a great deal.

Digilocker: It is also another flagship programme of the Government of India to transform India into a digitally empowered society and knowledge economy. The citizens get a shareable private space on a public cloud and make all certificates available on the cloud. This will end to a paperless economy abolishing the need for paper certificates and documents. The documents are verified digitally through this platform and the people can access them when needed from anywhere.

E-Panchayat: The Government of India is making forceful strides in making the grassroot democratic institutions, Gram Panchayats (Village Councils), connected with the electronic system strengthening local governance. It provides a comprehensive software solution which enables the Panchayat functionaries to connect with the rest of the world to improve their social, economic and cultural lives.

There are various other digital initiatives like e-Basta (accessible school e-books); e-Granthalaya (an integrated library to help online members); etc.

PRAGATI: One cannot end the enumeration of digital initiatives being taken in India for its transform India without mentioning the project PRAGATI. The Prime Minister of India launched a multi-purpose and multi-modal platform PRAGATI (Pro-Active Governance and Timely Implementation). It is a unique integrating and interactive platform to address common man's grievances and simultaneously monitoring and reviewing important programmes and projects of the Government of India as well as projects flagged by State Governments. The PRAGATI is a step towards making India's governance more efficient and responsive.

All Government programmes and initiatives can be tracked and monitored through this project by putting the Chief Ministers, Ministers or bureaucrats concerned on video conference call and real time video of the projects under inspection. It is a credible mechanism to deliver timely implementation to achieve the desired outcomes. It combines Data Management and Analysis, Geo-spatial applications and video-conferencing. The system has been designed by the in-house PMO team with the help of National Informatics Centre (NIC) bringing e-transparency and e-accountability with real-time presence and exchange among the key stakeholders.

Series of Indices: The Government of India has formulated a series of indices through the NITI Aayog to rank all states in India across social sectors like the School Education Quality Index, Digital Transformation Index, SDG India Index and other sectors like health, water, etc. The NITI Aayog has identified 115 Aspirational Districts which have shown relatively slower progress in key social areas and are pockets of underdevelopment. They shall be developed on the basis of 49 Key Performance Indicators (Economic Times, 2018).

From the above given account of major digital initiatives, it can be safely observed that India is transforming governance into achieving SDGs. However, there are some challenges that India is facing to do so.

Impact of Digital Initiatives in India

The Digital Revolution is called the Fourth Revolution which is moving towards the Fifth Revolution called 5.0. Industry 5.0 is already on the horizon which rings back the human element to the manufacturing sector. The impact of Digital Revolution has affected the socio-economic and technological growth of humanity in the entire world. The story of India's Digital journey has been one of transformation and inclusion. Technology has been intrinsic in this transformative evolution by enhancing transparency, inclusion, productivity and efficiency (Simmi Chaudhary, 2018). This has helped to transform good governance outlook from government-centric to citizen-centric. India, being the largest democracy in the world, needs to create an environment of empowering citizens through their involvement in the decision making and policy initiatives.

India is one of the largest and fastest growing market for the digital consumers, with over 560 million internet subscribers in 2020, second only to China. As per the analysis of 17 mature and emerging economies finds India is digitizing faster than any other country in the world (Digital India: Technology to transform a connected nation, March 2019). Digital initiatives have a potential of being an enabler of socio-economic and political activity in designing the value creation for the individuals and institutions.

It is evident that there is 95% decline in data cost since 2013. Almost 94% of small business enterprises accept credit/debit cards or pay apps on the mobile phones like Paytm, amazon pay, etc.. The digitalization has empowered the Indian economy by moving from cash-based economy to cashless economy. This has resulted in saving of Rs. 90,000 crores by the Central Government (*Times of India*, June 20, 2018). Further, the total transaction value in the Digital payment segments amounts to US$81,197m in 2020 and expected to show an annual growth rate of 23% by 2023 (Statisca.com).

Challenges being faced by India in implementing SDGs

India, along with other developing nations, faces a similar set of challenges in the transformation of governance to achieve SDGs. The SDGs cover such a wide variety of goals and targets that if the governments strive to achieve them, they can move towards development. The following issues need immediate attention if the countries across the world are serious to meet the deadline of achieving SDGs by 2030:

1. Digitalization and Development and Internet of Things: There are over 400 million cellular IoT subscribers all over the world. Improving data collection and analysis through digital technology is crucial for achieving SDGs and so is measuring their progress in implementation (www.eu 2016.sk). Telecommunications and digital technologies can act as a facilitator to achieve different dimensions of development, for example, environmental sustainability, improving access to basic services, etc., resulting in the promotion of good governance, transparency and accountability. Hence, ICT can act as a catalyst to achieve sustainable growth, however, the only issue involved is investment. Investing in digital solutions via Public Private Partnership can help the nation to achieve SDGs targets on time (Mahajan, 2019).

2. Job Creation in the Fourth/Fifth Industrial Revolution: Digital revolution carries a real risk when it comes to jobs. Automation and artificial intelligence threaten to replace workers in routine-based occupations. Many service jobs like driving a taxi or working in a fast food restaurant could simply disappear. About two-thirds of jobs in developing countries, according to UNDP, could be at risk (UNDP, 2019). To counter this problem in the Age of the Fourth and now Fifth Industrial Revolution, the UNDP is working with the youth to develop the skills they need to navigate the information economy to create their own opportunities and design their own solutions.

3. Gender-Digital Divide: Less than one-third of internet users in India are women and additionally, there is an urban-rural divide with only 2 per cent of rural Indian women estimated to use the internet. There is almost a 50 per cent gender gap in mobile phone ownership (www.cgdev.org, 2019). The reasons for this gender-digital divide is lack of access, lack of awareness and lack of agency, cultural and social norms. There can be involvement of local agencies and civil society organizations to provide solutions to bridge this gap.

4. Lack of Data: Implementation of schemes to achieve the SDGs is hindered by lack of data because it hinders the course of mid-term correction. The goals need to be tracked at disaggregated levels by the identification of systematic constraints that hamper evidence-based decision-making. India needs to find solutions by employing data-driven analytics and monitoring solutions to strategize course correction (www.orfline.org, 2018).

5. Problem of Financing: The implementation of the SDGs in India and other developing countries is based on the available Government funds. India consistently requires huge amounts of funds for fifteen years to achieve this mammoth task.

6. Technology and Capacity-Building: Science, technology, innovation and knowledge sharing are the main drivers of economic growth and prosperity. India will have to strive to pursue with the developed countries for taking benefits of the innovative and affordable technologies regarding the attainment of SDG 17, which is, easy access to innovative and affordable technologies.

From the above issues and challenges, it cannot be deduced that it is a picture of misery in India. There are rigorous measures being taken to alleviate these issues.

Solutions to meet these Challenges

The Parliament of India, *Lok Sabha,* is uniquely positioned to influence the shape and content of national development agendas and ensure the implementation of the SDGs through the following:

Law-making: Each country has pledged to achieve the SDGs and are not binding in any legal sense. Hence, it is up to each country how it plans its roadmap by adopting the main principles in national Legislatures. The Parliament can make legislations by creating ownership and taking the responsibility of formulating credible laws and institutional framework keeping in mind the national and local realities (Lok Sabha Secretariat, 2017).

Parliamentary Oversight: The Parliament has the power to exercise oversight through its agencies over the SDG implementation at all levels. It can closely monitor through programmes like PRAGATI which can be initiated at local levels also for the local governments for the successful execution of the programmes.

Committees, Debates and Discussions: Parliamentary debates and discussions in the question hour or the zero hour can be used to highlight the SDG programmes and their implementation. On the other hand, the opposition Members of the Parliament can ask questions regarding any lapses that have been made to keep the Government in check. The Parliamentary Committees of Public Accounts, Estimates and Public Undertakings can further focus on specific sectors and SDG related schemes.

Collabourative Work: The SDGs are not only for the ruling Government in power. All parties have to collabourate and make shared efforts as a cross-party platform to achieve the SDGs. An Empowered Group of Ministers can be formed to come together to work out better solutions for transforming Governance.

Budgetary Allocations: The Indian Parliament is aligning its budgetary allocations with the SDG schemes and programmes. It can oversee which goals are lagging behind and in which States so that more funds can be allocated for them.

Cooperation with the Executive: The State agencies have to execute the Government's plans and policies. Their cooperation is very vital to do that so that the Parliamentarians include such programmes in their member of Parliament Local Area Development Schemes.

The Parliamentarians and senior bureaucrats attend International Conferences and Seminars and they must exploit this information to promote the SDGs when they come back. The UN E-Government Survey 2018 has ranked India at 96 position for its performance in development and execution of information technologies, up from 107 in 2016 and 118 in 2014—a massive leap over the years. The survey measures e-governance index (EGDI) on three dimensions, namely, online service index (OSI), Telecommunication Infrastructure Index (TII) and human capital index (HCI) and ranks 193 member nations every two years (United Nations, 2018). Despite of all the challenges that a vast nation like India is facing there is ample evidence to believe that it is well onto the path of transformation of governance through digital initiatives.

Conclusion

This study of digitalization initiative being taken in India by the Government has elicited tremendous cooperation from its citizens in India. People are happy because human interface has considerably reduced which has resulted in a hassle-free and corruption-free dealings on a day-to-day basis. Services like online banking and licensing have facilitated ease-of-doing business and India has jumped ranks on the ease-of-doing index. It has increasingly allowed foreign financial institutions and investors to come to India to make its economy robust. However, the recent coronavirus pandemic spread has changed things and when the world will emerge on the other side, there will be numerous changes that may have to take place. To sum up, India has been doing a good job in implementing digital initiatives and these practices may be followed in other struggling developing nations.

References

Amitabh Kant (2019). *Challenging Conventions to build a New India,* http://niti.gov.in/content/challenging-conventions-build-new-india as retrieved on 05-04-2020.

Anil Kumar Dhiman (2017). *E-Governance Good Governance Using ICTs*, New Delhi, S.K. Book Agencies, p. 2.

B.K. Patnaik (2017). *Issues and Challenges of Development: An Introduction*, New Delhi, Sage Publications India Pvt. Ltd. p. 416.

Deepika Kachhal (December, 2018). "Reshaping Development", *Yojana*, p. 5, www.yojana.gov.in as retrieved on 26-04-2019

Department of Economic and Social Affairs (2015). "Responsive and Accountable Public Grievances (2015 World Sector Report)", New York, United Nations, p. 387.

Government of India (2017). *Millennium Development Goals—Final Country Report of India,* Ministry of Statistics and Programme Implementation, New Delhi, pp. 172-173.

https://digitalindia.gov.in/content/ekranti as retrieved on 26-04-2019.

https://digitalindia.gov.in/content/electronics-manufacturing as retrieved on 26-04-2019.

https://economictimes.indiatimes.com/industry/telecom/telecom-news/over-43000-villages-in-india-without-mobile-services-telecom-minister/articleshow/65230856.cms?from=mdr as retrieved on 11-04-2020.

https://economictimes.indiatimes.com/news/economy/policy/niti-to-rank-states-on-school-education-quality-digital-transformation/articleshow/67075773.cms?from=mdr as retrieved on 29-04-2019.

https://feature.undp.org/global-goals-technology/as retrieved on 29-03-2020.

http://sri.nic.in/sites/default/files/SDGs-challenges%20of%20Implementation%20and%20Role%20of%20Parliament.pdf as retrieved on 29-04-2019.

https://timesofindia.indiatimes.com/business/india-business/centre-saved-rs-90000-crore-through-digital-transfer-niti-aayog-ceo/articleshow/64660208.cms as retrieved on 09-04-2020.

https://www.cgdev.org/blog/women-social-entrepreneurs-and-tech-can-accelerate-sdg-5-india-worlds-largest-democracy as retrieved on 29-04-2019.

https://www.orfonline.org/research/accelerating-growth-and-development-in-the-sdg-era/as retrieved on 29-04-2019.

https://www.statista.com/outlook/296/119/digital-payments/india as retrieved on 09-04-2020.

IndeEA Project based on TOGAF, a Standard of The Open Group, recommended by UN to Governments looking to achieve SDGs, https://www.opengroup.org/indea-project-based-togaf-standard-open-group-recommended-un-governments-looking-achieve-sdgs as retrieved on 26-04-2019.

Maya Fehling, *et al.* (2013). *Limitations of Millennium Development Goals: A Literature Review*, Global Public Health. www.ncbi.nlm.gov/pmc/articles/PMC 3877943/#s3title as retrieved on 21-04-2019.

McKinsey Global Institute (March, 2019). *Digital India: Technology to transform a connected nation*, U.S., p. 8.

Mckinsey.com, 2017. *India's economy: Why the time for growth is now available at* https://www.mckinsey.com/featuredinsights/india/indias-economy-why-the-time-for-growth-is-now/as accessed on 26-04-2019.

R.S. Sharma (December, 2018), "Regulating the Regional Revolution", *Yojana*, p. 18, *ibid.*

Ratnadeep Banerjee (2017). *Digital India for Inclusive Growth and Sustainable Development,* http://pib.nic.in/newsite/printrelease.aspx?relid=161724 as retrieved on 26-03-2020.

Sanjeev Kumar (2013). "Health in International Development Agenda: Present, Past and Future", in *Indian Journal of Community Medicines*, Vol. 38, Mumbai, Medknow Publications and Media Pvt. Ltd. p. 129.

Sanjeev Kumar Mahajan and Anupama Mahajan (2019), "Attainment of Sustainable Development Goals with Information and Communications Technology" in *South Asian Journal of Socio-Political Studies*, Kerala, India.

Simmi Chaudhary (December 2018). "Transformative Impact of Digital India" in *Yojana*, Ministry of Information and Broadcasting, New Delhi, p. 28.

Sweta Mishra (2012). *Citizen-Centric Public Systems,* Delhi, Pearson, p.1.

World Commission on Environment Development (WCED) (1987). *One Common Future*, New York, Oxford University Press, p. 8.

14

Upsurge of Indian E-Commerce Industry in the Era of Post-Demonetisation

M. Sarngadharan

Introduction

Technically speaking, E-Commerce is not a new industry, but it is creating a new economic model in the present context in India. There is a consensus view that e-commerce would positively impact the economic sector in the forthcoming years. E-commerce industry is capable enough of bringing out numerous social benefits. For instance, the cost of running an e-commerce business is lesser in comparison with the running of a physical store. The business processes are simple and only minimum manual hours are required to run a typical business smoothly. In areas, such as law, education, and culture, e-commerce industry would accelerate affirmative aftereffect. It can genuinely shape an information society with a modern outlook.

Demonetisation is the procedure in an economy, in which the currency unit is stripped of its status as legal tender. 'Demonetisation' has been the most popular phrase extensively used in India since the Union Government pulled the 500 and 1,000 Rupee currency notes out of circulation in November 2016. It was stated by the Government at the time of demonetisation that this move was initiated to: discourage tax evasion on undeclared income; check terror financing; promote a cashless economy; reduce inflation; eliminate the circulation of fake currency from the nation; facilitate trade; and eradicate the propensity for money laundering. These specifications made it obvious that the rationale behind demonetisation was to ensure a stabilized impact on social, political, legal and economic activities in the economy. However, it is conspicuous that the aftermaths of demonetisation are positive as well as negative in the Indian economy, when viewed from social, economic, political and legal dimensions. In this regard, economic impact on e-commerce industry is considered momentous, on account of the boost foreseen in digital deals and online payments.

It is in this backdrop that the current paper attempts to examine the enrichment of e-commerce industry in India, consequent on the decision for demonetisation. It needs emphasis, in this regard that the current study explores only the outcome of demonetisation in the Indian e-commerce industry, that too, relying mostly on secondary data. The required data, congregated from the research reports and articles published in research journals were bestowed for drawing conclusions of the study. In addition to this, the data gathered from business houses and consumers involved in online trading, through discussions were also made use of for the study.

At a glance, it is sensed that demonetisation has supported the e-commerce industry in India screamingly to flourish by buoying up the people to practice more cashless transactions in day-to-day life and enabling them to carry only a nominal quantum of money in currency even for normal shopping. This has contributed positively to the banking sector to expand the business to rural areas quickly and do more business to reach the general public for multiplying their regular activities. Lesser level of inflation, affordable rates of interest for loans and advances and declining budget deficits are likely to be the long-term positive macroeconomic effects that are expected to stimulate economic growth in general and expansion of regional business deals in specific. This move will definitely bring about drastic changes in e-commerce transactions carried out in India.

Periodical reviews carried out by the Reserve Bank of India have made indicated that demonetisation has led to several changes in the financial sector, such as shift in currency demand; significant growth in bank deposits; greater financial inclusion; detection of suspicious transactions; improved monetary transmission; increase in mutual fund investments by households; higher collections under life insurance schemes; accelerated digitisation of retail payments; and higher rate of detection of fake Indian currency notes. Based on these findings arrived at by the supreme body in the Financial Sector of India, it is evident that there has been a favourable effect of demonetisation decision on e-commerce industry, which is chiefly dependent on online business transactions and online payments. Despite bringing chaos in its initial days, demonetisation in the long run is considered beneficial to the growth of e-commerce in India. One of the long-term benefits for the e-commerce industry is sharp decline in payments via cash on delivery (CoD).

In order to ascertain the validity of the statement that demonetisation has favourably contributed to the proliferation of e-commerce industry in India, it is felt appropriate to examine the issue in question from four different dimensions: Online Retailing; Online Payments; Logistics; and Hyper-local E-Commerce.

Online Retailing

The Indian e-commerce industry has been on an upward growth orbit and it is expected to outperform the US to become the second largest e-commerce market in the world by 2034. It is poised to be worth $36.7 billion by 2020, from $3 billion in 2014. It is expected to reach Rs. 13,97,800 crore (US$ 200 billion) by 2027 from Rs. 2,69,076.5 crore (US$ 38.5 billion) in 2017. India's e-commerce market has the possibility to flourish more than four folds to Rs. 10,48,350 crore (US$ 150 billion) by 2022 supported by rising incomes and surge in internet users. Online shoppers in India are expected to reach from 120 million in 2018 and to 220 million by 2025.

The online retail sector in India has attained laudable progress since demonetiastion and has been building up strength and value. The Indian market is driven by factors such as increased penetration of internet and smart-phones, advertising, ease of shopping for customers, innovative payment options, imperative commercials and discounts combined with the comfort; hike in the number of urban households; avenue and array that online shopping offers, and the rapidly changing lifestyle needs. Large players are diversified across categories and are building their capabilities to service several of these categories. In the upcoming years, the e-commerce retailing industry is expected to witness the consolidation and emergence of a few big players. Further, changes in the FDI Regulations could also boost the penetration of major players and help them gain higher market share rapidly.

Internet penetration has been expeditiously growing in India year by year. Market research agency Kantar IMRB has reported that India's internet users registered double digit growth to reach 627 million in 2019, driven by fast internet growth in rural areas. Internet usage in the country eclipsed half a billion people, for the first time clinching 566 million in 2018, driven by rural internet growth and use. The top four metro cities have a 23 per cent penetration, while the other four metros have gained 11 per cent internet penetration over the years. There has been a steady increase in internet and mobile penetration, producing gorgeous space for e-commerce retailers. Further, modifications in the FDI Regulations could also boost the penetration of major players and help them in securing higher market share in the forthcoming years.

It remained a fact that electronics endured the largest segment in e-commerce retail industry in the economy with a CAGR of approximately 43 per cent till recently. However, the share of electronics in online retail was bypassed with higher growth by apparels with CAGR of about 50 per cent for the past four to five years. Yet another emerging competition is forecast for home furnishings, holding a CAGR of about 68 per cent. The e-commerce retailing industry has been witnessing approximately 1 to 1.2 million transactions per day, led by three categories including apparels, electronics, and furnishings.

Online Payments

The digital wallet and payment segment has turned up luminous champion of post demonetisation era in India. Payment gateways have already seen 80 per cent growth annually since 2017, marking significant growth in low-value transactions too. Strictly speaking, this sort of a change was witnessed in the economy in consequence of the cash catastrophe confronted by the society inclusive of low-income group in the initial months of demonetisation. A large section of them had money in their banks and the cash crunch prompted them to opt for payments relying on online options such as pay tm, credit/debit card, online banking, NEFT and RTGS, UPI and others.

The official statistics as revealed by the RBI confirms that the transactions through cards got flourished by more than 300 per cent in terms of number and more than 500 per cent in terms of value of transactions immediately after the decision for demonetisation was executed. Of this, the growth of transactions through mobile wallets was more than 200 per cent in terms of number and value of transactions. In fact demonetisation produced colossal impact on small tier 2 and 3 cities/towns in regard to online payment habit. The online transactions in Tier 2 cities escalated by 150 per cent and in tier 3 cities by 157 per cent. It is stated in a report published by the Internet and Mobile Association of India (IAMAI) that at end of 2019, India stands only to China in terms of the number of internet users. The report demonstrates that of the monthly active users numbering 451 million, a cardinal fraction has been executing online payments through mobile phones.

There are various options for devising payments through electronic modes in India, such as Banking Cards; Unstructured Supplementary Service Data (USSD); Aadhaar Enabled Payment System (AEPS); Unified Payments Interface (UPI); Mobile Wallets; Bank Pre-paid Cards; Point of Sale (PoS); Internet Banking; Real Time Gross Settlement System (RTGS) and National Electronic Funds Transfer (NEFT) System, Mobile Banking; and Bharat Interface for Money (BHIM) app. Digital payments present faster, easier, convenient; economical and less transaction fee. Besides, there are many rewards and discounts offered to the customers using digital payment apps and mobile wallets. Government of India promote for online payments by offering up to 10 per cent off on insurance policies, highway usage and concessions on train travel, besides waiving service tax on online transactions below Rupees 2,000. This leads to the outcome that one of the preeminent intentions of demonetisation to build digital payment habit among the consumers of all sections in the society irrespective of their economic status has been positively accomplished. It is also settled that the digital surge in consequence of demonetisation generates bright future for Indian e-commerce industry in the forthcoming years.

Logistics

The amplification of digital technologies has been benevolence to the human society as it has oscillated the earth into a consolidated marketplace. A study carried out by the KPMG India (Klynveld Peat Marwick Goerdeler) about online shopping behaviour, depicts that the basic reason to shop online was the readiness of round the clock shopping beyond bickering. About 58 per cent of the respondents interviewed for the study indicated it as their prime attraction for shopping online. It was also mentioned that online shopping facilitated them easy comparison of prices, fluctuations in ongoing and upcoming sales, and crack the best deal available.

In this backdrop, the exponential growth that the e-commerce industry, especially online retail industry, has been experiencing in India cannot be treated a miracle. The ongoing development has been providing favourable climate to the economy to come up as a dynamic market. The digital framework makes it accessible to anticipate individual processes, and the snags thereon, that would adversely cause customer satisfaction. This would help the trader to take corrective measures well in advance. For instance, if a delivery is not carried out on time, it is going to put the customers annoyed. It is in this context that logistics assumes greater significance for the growth of e-commerce industry in India.

Logistics is a decisive facilitator of the prosperity of e-commerce retail industry and has been progressively looming as a differentiator in terms of customer service and satisfaction. The logistics sector-specific to the e-commerce retailing in India was figured at $0.2 billion in 2014 and it has come out to witness a CAGR of 48 per cent in the subsequent years to reach about $2.2 billion in 2020, to be more specific, rampant expansion during post-demonetisation years. The logistics system provides support through warehousing, inventory, delivery, invoicing, handling sale proceeds and product-returns. It enables the e-commerce industry to scale down the risk that arises from the virtual relations and operates as an intermediary between the seller and the buyer by arranging the delivery of right product, to the right customer, at the right place and at the right time.

Since demonetisation, a large number of e-commerce retailers have collabourated with logistic service providers and this has tempted logistics service providers to invest more in edifying in-house logistics facilities. About half of the e-commerce logistics market is managed by the in-house logistics players, whereas the other 50 per cent is controlled by the third-party logistics service providers including traditional logistics service providers, e-commerce focused logistics providers and the India Post. It is expected that the rising demand from tier 3 cities and towns and remote locations would be instrumental in the growth of the volume of business by about 45 per cent of the total volume by the end of 2020, in comparison with the figures in the inception of demonetisation.

The focus is also shifted from standard to specialised deliveries and this demands huge investments in building new capabilities and infrastructure. The industry experts have put forward a claim that tier 2 and 3 cities are expected to contribute more than USD 10 billion to e-tailing shipments by the terminal of 2020. In order to take advantage of this demand, it is essential to develop a network of branches and delivery points that would enable servicing of these high-growth geographies. The introduction of goods and services tax (GST) has been providing a big push for the sector with a single nationwide rate for commercial tax and thereby enabling the supply chain to become far more cost-effective.

E-commerce retail companies have been labouring to offer new business models and technology-driven approaches. Handy payment options, customer-friendly policies, expeditious deliveries and easy returns drive customers to online channels. Besides, concepts such as, 'online and application (app) only' sales; 'by invite only'; discounts; special discount coupons; cash-back policies; and special online festivals, continue to drive customers to shop online.

The encouraging growth potential in India's e-commerce logistics industry has paved the passage to several new generation logistics start-ups, the setting up of new verticals by older logistics companies, as well as investments into a separate logistics arm by e-tailers. The sector has also recently seen a wave of interest by investors. It is a universally accepted fact that more than 80 per cent of the customers look for delivery of the desired goods on the same-day of shopping. A large number of them are willing to pay extra for the faster delivery of the items ordered. Delays in delivery, that is supply chain movement, are normally induced by factors like muddiness of cargos, plunging back in freight transfer, slow-down processe of a courier operator, and so on. Such challenges frequently cropped up earlier on account of inadequate transparency within the logistics procedures. The fast-moving digitization has been concurrently facilitating preeminent visibility and control over the logistics processes. Further, it has phased out a number of dilemmas arising from supply chain operations and smoothened the marketing processes.

Hyper-local E-Commerce

Hyper-local covers community, organisation, and service and so on, compassed to a specific geographical area. Although this concept originated years back, the 'Hyper-local e-commerce' has become one of the prominent marketing options in all the parts of the country since 2015. The decision for demonetisation coupled with the huge surge of internet users, expansion of payment options, commendable improvement in geo-location aware devices and heightened demand for quick delivery, opened the right passage and smooth track for hyper-local e-commerce in India. The consumers are extremely happy that they get deliveries of desired products such as, cooked food items, fish, vegetables, groceries and household items, medicines, laundry, and similar facets at their doorsteps as quickly as possible.

This sector in the e-commerce industry has witnessed colossal growth since demonetisation. The number of new customers that this segment receives has been expanding constantly and with the adoration of online payment modes there has been commendable rise in the pre-paid orders. Stirring up the curiosity and interest of a huge chunk of entrepreneurs, who were on tenterhooks for something that can make them stand out, hyper-local e-commerce has served the purpose. Hyper-local start-ups are looping in more funds, in comparison with other B2C markets. This category of e-commerce industry has become the new favourite segment of experiment for investors. Bunch of entrepreneurs have managed to tighten their position in the mammoth e-commerce domain by blending their ideas with the concept of hyper-local.

In India, all the food-chains and restaurants got a fair chance to push their business in the hyper-local e-commerce. They can easily create a platform to list their food items seeking the services of delivery men for picking and delivering the orders in lieu of registration and service charges. The hyper-local space market in India has largely been steered by soaring number of start-ups and 'on-demand delivery preference' of the shoppers. Collusion with the merchants and buyers through a flexible application endures a business model for hyper-local space enterprises in India. They are predominantly aided by modern technology and are capable enough of conjoining the local retailers with the users in the hyper-local space.

Ken Research in its Report titled "India Hyper-local Market Outlook to 2020—Driven by Rising Start-up Firms and Fluctuating Investments", unfolds that the Indian hyper-local market would grow at a substantial CAGR to reach the level of more than INR 2,306 crore by the close of 2020. Increasing urbanisation, personalisation of affinities along with the competence of carving the goods that appeal to the aesthetic sensibilities or desires of the consumers concerned led to the rise in the Hyper-local market in India. The report covers various aspects of the market size of India hyper-local market, segmentation on the basis of regions, orders and revenue by timely delivery, trends and developments, prerequisites to enter the market and success and failure case studies of various hyper-local organisations in India.

Conclusion

From the foregoing review of the growth of Indian e-commerce Industry since demonetisation, it may be concluded that efficient and effective implementation of various initiatives and policies of the Government of India would bring about better positive outcomes to the industry in the upcoming years. For instance, initiatives invoked, like Digital India, Make in India, Start-up India, Skill India and Innovation Fund, with a view to enhancing production of goods and services in the economy by utilizing internally available human and physical resources would be mutually supportive to the growth of the e-commerce industry. The e-commerce industry has been directly impacting the micro, small and medium enterprises (MSMEs) in India by arranging means of financing, technology and training. Technology enabled innovations like digital payments, hyper-local logistics, analytics driven customer engagement and digital advertisements would amply support to the prosperity of this sector. The growth in e-commerce sector would synchronously promote more employment, export revenues, tax revenues and products and services to the economy. Let us have an optimistic view that the economic crises created internationally by the COVID-19 Virus shall get redeemed soon.

References

Arora, N. & Rahul, M. (2018). "The role of perceived risk in influencing online shopping attitude among women in India", *International Journal of Public Sector Performance Management*, *4*(1), 98-113.

Confederation of Indian Industry (2016). *E-commerce in India: A Game Changer for the Economy*, Retrieved from www.cii.ac.in.

Kalia, P., Kaur, N. & Singh, T. (2017). "E-commerce in India: Evolution and revolution of online retail", *Mobile Commerce: Concepts, Methodologies, Tools and Applications*, 2, 736-758.

http://timesofindia.indiatimes.com/tech/tech-news/India-to-have-519-million-mobile-internet-users-by-FY18-Morgan Stanley/articleshow/36656019.cm Kantar-IMRB All India Mobile Internet Users Estimates, October 2017

https://economictimes.indiatimes.com/small-biz/startups/digital-commerce-market-estimated-to-touch-rs-220330-crore-by-december-2017

https://economictimes.indiatimes.com/tech/internet/internet-users-in-india-to-reach-627-million-in-2019.

Siddegowda, C.J., Ilango, V. & Devi, J. (2016). Analysis of e-commerce challenges in India by using weka tool. *International Journal of Control Theory and Applications*, *9*(36), 363-371.

15

E-Governance

An Indian Experiment with the MyGOV Application

Sudheesh Kumar J.

E-Governance: Meaning

E-governance is regarded as the most effective means to accomplish good governance goals. For quality/smart governance, each country needs the support of an Information and Communication Technology (ICT) enabled administration. E-governance indicates the use by government agencies of ICTs that can transform relations with citizens, business, and various structures of government. It results in better service delivery to citizens, enhanced relations between business and industry, citizen empowerment through information dissemination and efficient management in government. The subsequent benefits it brings in governance are less corruption increased transparency, greater convenience, revenue growth, and cost reductions. The UN agenda of Sustainable Development Goals specifically recognizes the vital role of ICT and e-governance. It observes that the spread of ICT and global networks have great potential to accelerate human progress, bridge the digital divide, develop knowledge societies such as scientific and technological innovation among different sectors (UNDESA, 2020, p. xxiii).

Kettl views e-governance as the impact (from e-government interactions) on government, public service and citizens throughout the political process, policy development, programme design and service delivery (Kettl, 2002, p. 15). The UNESCO interprets e-governance as the public sector's use of Information and Communication Technologies to improve information and service delivery, encouraging citizen participation in the decision-making process and making government more accountable, transparent and effective (UNESCO, 2020). E-governance changes a government in two dimensions: 1. Government business is transformed, i.e., reducing costs, improving service delivery and renewing governance processes; 2. A re-examination of the functions and operations of democracy itself. (Schmutzer, 2000, p. 5). Therefore e-governance is ICT enabled empowerment on the functions of government, capacity building of the citizens, improving democratic processes and re-engineering the government-entrepreneur relations.

The Second Administrative Reforms Commission (ARC) in India states that e-governance needs to transform all levels of government. Still, the focus should be on local governments since local governments are the closest to citizens and constitute for many, the primary interface with government. The relationship of citizens and local authorities tends to be one based on proximity as the interests at stake for both parties are closely entwined concerning issues such as public services, local development, education, etc. Therefore, e-governance based administrative reforms in local governments can have maximum impact on citizens. The Government of India, along with different state governments, have accepted these principles in their actions and policies (Government of India, 2008, pp. ii-iii). In Kerala, for example, the Information Kerala Mission (IKM) has developed an Integrated Local Governance Management System (ILGMS) in 2020 for the local self-governments to deliver electronic services to the people effectively.

E-governance Vs. E-Government

There is an age-long discussion over the consistency of the term e-governance over its conceptual entity. Concerning the ICT enabled projects by different governments there exist an academic conflict whether they follow e-government or e-governance. One could find several studies and researches regarding the ways and means to distinguish them. However, many scholars believe that though these concepts show specific distinct characteristics, they have several points of conjunctions. Though e-government and e-governance are used interchangeably, they have unique interpretations.

E-government deals more with administrative functions for improving the quality of governance while e-governance has a significant role in politics, i.e., in 'citizens-government' relationship. E-government is an instrument through which governments enhance e-services to the citizens. Significant technological reforms within the administration are the inevitable mission of e-government. It involves the vertical and horizontal integration of different agencies within the government. There will be electronic means of communication in the internal affairs of the government.

As such, the governmental functions will be empowered or strengthened by ICT tools. The service delivery function of the government is enhanced with the help of electronic facilities. E-governance, on the other hand, is considered as the first step to reach the complex objective of 'e-democracy'. It means extended participation of people in government. In this context, through e-governance, the government can receive the demands and opinion of the citizens 24 × 7. The feedback sought from the citizens is useful for the government to reform or initiate the policies concerning good governance (Alam, 2005).

E-Governance: Potential Opportunities

Proponents of e-governance suggest that it can provide a variety of opportunities to improve the governance of a country. They believe e-governance offers several overarching benefits that could result, either directly or indirectly, from these initiatives. As with many information technology-related projects, one of the anticipated benefits is improved efficiency. In e-governance projects, efficiency can take many forms. Some projects seek to improve the consistency of outcomes by automating regular tasks. For increasing efficiency, e-government initiatives reduce costs and levels of organizational processes by redesigning and modernizing operating procedures. Similarly, some exponents suggest that reducing the amount of time spent on repetitive tasks allows the government servants to develop new skills and advance their careers (Jeff Breen, 2000, p. 15).

Another opportunity promoted by e-governance supporters is the potential to improve the quality, range, and accessibility of services. Some observers suggest that the quality of services can be improved through quicker transactions, enhanced accountability, and better practices. The emergence of e-government also generates the potential for new services. Along with maintaining existing services, e-government initiatives could contribute to a qualitative change in the conduct of business and citizens' interactions.

A third benefit is increased citizen participation in government. One way this occurs by linking people residing in remote areas of the country so that they can easily send and receive information. Secondly, it increases the participation of younger adults in government processes. The generation of citizens who have grown up with the Internet and digital communications technologies in their everyday lives will be more likely to become participant citizens. By extension, e-government initiatives could also enhance citizen-to-citizen (C2C) interaction by providing opportunities for people with similar interests, opinions, and concerns, which may be geographically separated, to interact and share information.

Improved National Information Infrastructure. A fourth possible benefit of the drive to implement e-government initiatives is the improvement of information infrastructure. It sets up plans that would protect government-operated infrastructures and calls for a dialogue between the government and the private sector to develop the whole governance policy. This heightened awareness with the effort to make many government services available online, could renew interest in the e-governance policies and lead to its further development to accommodate the resource needs of these initiatives. By extension, additional investment e-governance policy could lead to increased attention to information security issues and the development of new technologies (Moteff, 2010).

Principles of E-governance

Clarity of Purpose: There needs to be a clear understanding and appreciation of the purpose and objectives to be achieved through e-governance. An e-governance initiative should not be taken up merely to demonstrate the capacity of existing technology, but the technology should be adopted to solve the existing problem. Citizen centricity should be at the heart of all e-governance initiative (Government of India, 2008, pp. 59-64).

E-Government is about Transformation: It transforms the existing culture of administration by including the ICT tools in relevant phases. Here, it is imperative to manage the mode of change within public institutions. Change management is about managing people in a changing environment so that business changes are successful, and the desired business results are realized. The approach needs to be customer-centric rather than department-centric. At the same time, service orientation, outcome-based assessment and an integrated organizational view are required for enhancing e-governance.

E-governance as an Integral Part of Reform of Governance: E-governance is an integral part of the whole government processes. Thus, every Government organization or entity, every Government programme or policy and every law and regulation would have to integrate e-governance modules within itself rather than brought in as an afterthought or introduced as an adjunct. As governance covers an extensive range of activities in each area, the structures and processes which need to be changed or modified through the use of technology would have to be identified separately.

E-Government Requires a Holistic Approach: Appropriate initiative for managing the data, technology, procurement, resources, processes, the programme is essential. There should be a professional structural reform for managing these elements because these elements constitute the crux of the e-governance projects. The pillars of e-governance are people, process, technology and resources. Correct coordination of these pillars can only bring in desired results for e-governance process.

E-Government Necessitates Capacity Building: For capacity building, both the end-users and the agents are to be empowered to deal with the changes in the administrative procedures. Digital governance requires a smart user as well as an intelligent service provider. Hence, training for the civil servants and alerting the general public on digitized government is the need of the hour (Johannes, 2018).

The Challenges of E-governance

The pillars of e-governance are process, people, resources and technology. A prosperous e-governance system is possible when these four elements are dealt with in a balanced way. When there is a lack of advanced process models, it hinders the overall growth of e-governance in that system. Similarly, the issues like status-quo, inadequate legal frameworks and complex procurement are hindrances to a better e-governance model. The people belong to the system should have sufficient skill in automation. Besides, the lack of political will, official apathy, shortage of champions in the government machinery may adversely affect e-governance. The ample availability of resources is yet another requirement for being a graded e-governance system. The budget constraints and disinterest of the private sector to collabourate in the projects contribute to the shortages in resource management.

Technology, being the most significant element in e-governance, needs to be updated regularly. If there is a lack of architectures, lack of standards, poor communication infrastructure and hardware approach, this will affect the development of e-governance activities (Gouscos, D., 2007).

E-Preparedness

A country needs to be ready for fully adapting to e-governance. E-preparedness for e-governance implementation, or e-readiness, as is generally referred to, means the prerequisites required to be taken care of while formulating digital initiative. As Table 15.1 shows the five-fold preparation is essential for developing and implementing the e-governance initiatives. Technology, institutions, human resources, legal system and a comprehensive data system, are significant in building a digital eco-system. That is, professional and systematic homework is required to institute a powerful digital governmental system.

Table 15.1: Infrastructural Preparedness for E-governance

Sl. No.	Infrastructure	Mode of Change
1	Data System Infrastructure	The core of e-governance is the electronic Management Information System (e-MIS). The whole data manually obtained and preserved should be converted into digital format.
2	Legal Infrastructure	The essential precondition of an e-governance system is the existence of a legal structure to permit and support digital initiatives. Legitimacy for a digital administration is of top priority.
3	Institutional Infrastructure	For any government be with successful digital governance, the institutions should be equipped with sufficient electronic infrastructure.
4	Human Infrastructure	It means the presence of well-trained workforce with expertise in systems analysis, systems design, programming, implementation and documentation.
5	Technological Infrastructure	ICT infrastructure needs to be updated according to the day-to-day changes in technology notwithstanding fiscal and administrative constraints.

Source: ARC Report 2008.

E-governance cannot be introduced in a country across government organization at one go as different organizations are not at the same level of e-preparedness. Hence, there is the need for step-wise approach to e-governance. Therefore, initially, the suitable projects should be identified. Then by setting priority, the existing projects are to be re-engineered to suit the e-governance modality. Subsequently, the technical experts are to develop technological solutions for each task and do the final implementation. E-governance requires a disciplined and systematic way of working in organizations. Most technologies pre-suppose a set of national behaviour on the part of users (Government of India, 2008, p. 1).

Close monitoring of e-governance projects is necessary for both the pilot phase as well as during the actual working of the up-scaled projects. There would also be a need for evaluation of the impact of such initiatives through independent agencies. E-governance represents a paradigm shift in the field of government reforms. Bringing it about would have to be a continuous process which would require many adjustments. It has been well said that e-governance is a journey and not a destination.

Development Stages of E-governance

E-governance is implemented in a country through a number of development stages. Each stage involves certain instinct characteristics. The United Nations has come up with a five-stage development model for e-government. The emerging phase includes creating a government website with limited or static information. The next stage is named enhanced in which the information will be updated regularly. Then there is the interactive phase in which the government provides users with reasonable levels of interaction, enabling them to download forms. The fourth stage is transactional, which empowers the citizens to complete transactions such as obtaining visas, licences, passports, birth and death records online safely and securely. In the final phase of a fully integrated system, there will be provisions of high-level integration across administrative and departmental lines (United Nations, 2002). Silcock gives a six-stage development of e-government. In the first stage is the creation of websites by departments and agencies. There will be just one-way communication here. Then, there is an official two-way transaction, where the users get enabled to have electronic interaction with government services. The next phase will see multi-purpose portals that would allow customers to obtain government services and information from a single point. The portal personalization is the next phase which provides customers with opportunities to customize portals according to their need. The clustering of common services creates portals, which replace government departments in executing the process of service delivery. The final phase is full integration and enterprise transformation by which Government departments will disappear while others will appear; some departments will keep the same names but become entirely different internally (Silcock, 2001).

The countries select these phases according to the available resources and technology. To the final stage of e-governance is e-democracy. In e-government (e-administration), the values included are 'transparency', 'openness' and 'engagement'. Of these, transparency and openness are displayed by the governments during governance. That is, government actions are made transparent and open using ICT tools. Engagement, on the other hand, is exercised by the citizens by interacting with the government online. They register their opinion, feedback and dissent to the public policies. However, even in developed countries, the engagement or demand side of the e-governance system will not be realized. This phase is otherwise called e-democracy. Each country is trying to reach this stage of development (Hu & Wang, 2009, p. 978).

E-Governance: The Indian Experience

In the year 2005, the Government of India has formulated the National E-Governance Plan (NeGP), which consists of 25 Central, State and Integrated Projects to be implemented in Mission Mode along with eight support components for rapid introduction of e-Governance in the country (Rani, 2002). The Plan envisions providing all government services in an integrated manner at the doorstep of the citizen at an affordable cost. It aims to radically change the way governments interact with citizens and businesses and deliver services. The aspiration levels of the government as expressed in the Plan mean that governments at the National, State and local level would have to radically change the way they function and government employees would have to learn a new way of doing business (Pandey, A.B., 2005).

Though the e-governance projects initiated by the National e-Governance Plan were citizen-centric, they never earned desired goals due to their limited features. Most of the projects were less interactive and isolated. Later on, to overcome the shortcomings involved in the NeGP, the Government of India approved e-Kranti programme in March 2015 with the vision of "Transforming e-Governance for Transforming Governance". All-new, ongoing, as well as the existing projects, now follow the key principles of e-Kranti. Many new projects in the social sector such as Women and Child Development, Social Benefits, Financial Inclusion, Urban Governance and e-Bhasha have been added as recent (Mission Mode Projects) MMPs under e-Kranti (Digital India, 2020a).

Along with the National E-governance Plan 2.0 (E-Kranti), the Government of India designed the new IT strategy under the larger entitlement—Digital India. Digital India tends to transform the country not only into a digitally empowered society but to a knowledge economy. As an umbrella programme, it covers different Government Ministries and Departments. It blends several objectives into a single, broader vision. The Government of India implements Digital India with the supervision by the Department of Electronics and Information Technology (DEITY). It aims at providing the much-needed thrust to the nine pillars of growth areas. They are Broadband Highways, Universal Access to Mobile Connectivity, Public Internet Access Programme, e-Governance, i.e., Reforming Government through Technology, e-Kranti-Electronic Delivery of Services, Information for All, Electronics Manufacturing, IT for Jobs and Early Harvest Programmes. Each of these areas is a complex programme in itself and integrates multiple Ministries and Departments (Digital India, 2020).

Government of India has made considerable efforts by the Digital India campaign to reduce the digital divide and ICT has proved to be a tool for its successful implementation. Different initiatives by the government through the advancements in ICT have aided E-governance to take off since the beginning of the millennium. Through projects like increasing literacy rate in rural areas, the Digital India campaign helps in making the rural people more tech-savvy. It encourages them to get in contact with the Indian government through just a click of a button. It is seen that increasing digital literacy will lead to rural development in India. Digital literacy is in the top priority of the government for inclusiveness in the tech-media. Universal digital literacy is proposed in this regard by which the states and union territories are formulating guidelines in their respective domains. The most demanding challenge in the administration of e-governance in India is bridging the digital divide. The services and benefits can reach citizens only when they embrace sufficient digital knowledge (Kiran, 2016, p. 68).

The visions of the Digital India Plan are digital infrastructure as a primary utility to all, governance and services on demand and digital empowerment. For materializing these visions, the government has built a vital infrastructure facility for high-speed Internet. Also, a comprehensive biometric database of the whole residents is prepared. Subsequently, the government initiated the Aadhar, computerized the public offices (e-office) and maintained different channels for information dissemination. Initially, the projects are meant to achieve the objectives of information dissemination and delivery of services through Web portals. Though all the citizens cannot access them due to the existing digital and infrastructural divides, it is accomplished by the intermediaries. There are several providers as e-service agents across the country. In Kerala, for instance, the service delivery is mostly done by the FRIENDS and Akshaya Kendras. The people from remote areas could access government services electronically without any difficulty.

There are m-Government (mobile government) applications which makes it easy to access services and information using the usual gadgets. The provision for e-pay is enabled by the government to avoid intermediaries in service delivery and financial assistant. The national open data-sharing portal (data.gov.in) is a platform which provides the government data and catalogue to the needy without payment. It makes the government more transparent and open to the public. The cloud computing facility is used to enable the portability of official documents and certificates. The digiLocker is an application developed by the government of India to assure portability of credentials and other documents. Besides, there is the provision of integrated service delivery in a unified platform named e-District.

Digital India endeavour aims at multiple and complex administration of digital governance in India. From the initial e-government phase of information dissemination to the intricate point of online political participation, the programme has included whole activities regarding digital empowerment. E-Governance in India is aimed at reducing corruption and making government more accessible. Also, with the use of ICT in service delivery, the process is accomplished in lesser cost and time—E-governance intents to ensure the efficiency, accountability and transparency in the functioning of government. The government has combined the ICT tools with governance goals which result in both efficiency and effectiveness (Joseph, 2001).

Digital India has transformed the traditional approaches in public administration and substituted it with a digital platform. This new paradigm has brought about a revolution in the quality of services delivered to the citizens. It brings in transparency in the governing process, simplifies the procedures, better office and record management, reduces corruption, improves the capacity of the personnel. E-service, in this context, means interactive information service among the service providers, service recipients and agencies. It is different from traditional service, which is based on physical interactive information flow between customers and service providers (Li & Suomi, 2007). Here, in the e-governance process, infrastructural strength is critical for customer satisfaction. E-governance provides essential tools and mechanisms for poor communities within the country to hold both policymakers and service providers accountable for the sustained supply of services (UNDP, 2007).

MyGOV: Triggering E-Democracy in India

The government of India attempts to instil citizen-participatory activities through a web portal called "myGOV" (https://www.mygov.in). It is made available as a mobile application also. This platform provides a forum for discussion, campaign, online survey and poll, blog, podcast etc. It benefits the ordinary citizen to interact, suggest or debate on the policies of the government (Saxena, 2005). These provisions empower the citizens both politically and socially. As discussed at the beginning of the chapter, one of the final phases of good governance is considered as e-democracy. Despite the digital divide, the Government of India is trying to stay on its pledge of 'less government and more governance'. MyGov is a technology-driven platform that would provide people with the opportunity to contribute towards good governance (Verma, 2018).

MyGov is the first-ever citizen engagement platform for participatory governance in India launched in 2014. It aims at facilitating a dialogue between citizens and the Government. It brings citizens and government closer together. The vital elements of MyGov are the 'Discuss', 'Do' and 'Poll/Survey' which help facilitate dialogue, discussion, and engage between Citizens and Government (Fig. 15.1). The significant activities take place are as follows: 'Discuss'—It helps to discuss and debate on various topics with cause-based groups such as Swachh Bharat, Digital India, Caring for Specially-abled etc. The topics of discussion change according to the issues faced by the country from time to time. Each citizen or user can register in the portal to participate in the discussion. The users will be awarded a badge according to the level of participation in the activities. 'Do'—It enables users to set 'to do' tasks and collabourate (with multiple stakeholders) on critical areas of development and governance.

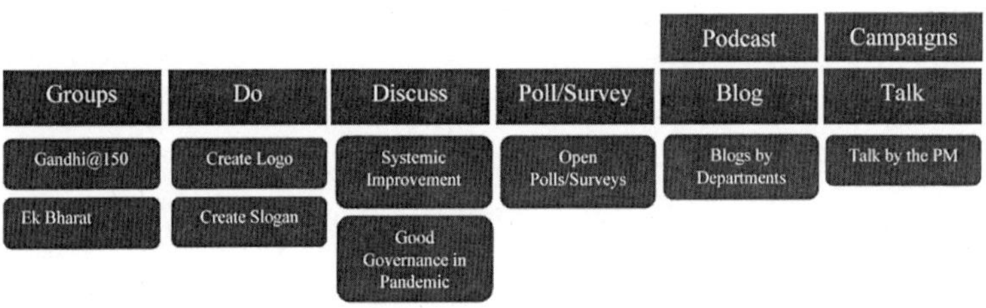

Fig. 15.1: Activities and Pop-downs in the MyGOV Portal.

Source: MyGov.in

'Creative Corner'—To facilitate ministries to organize various contests for creative crowdsourcing ideas such as logo designs and taglines. 'Groups'—There are different groups to which each user can collabourate. Opinion Polls—To gauge the pulse of the citizens through voting over recent issues of public importance online voting is executed in the portal. Besides, there are live surveys organized by different departments to collect user information. 'Talk'—This is the section to solicit topics from citizens for Prime Minister's monthly address. There is a section to hold physical discussions with ministers, senior government officials, top citizen contributors and volunteers, and various domain experts. These discussions are recorded, and videos of such talks are hosted on the portal. 'Blogs'—This section provides update and experiences by different departments on MyGov. It also displays the MyGov impact to the public domain. It gives the user to register comments on the blog-posts. 'Podcasts'—In this section, a series of audio inputs to catch up with the recent activities of MyGov is presented. 'Campaigns'—This section is for announcing various national campaigns to give awareness to the citizens. The MyGov portal not only serves the users with these activities but also engages the citizens. The project, by all means, favours popular consent in administration. The citizens can initiate new policies, participate in discussion and comment on ensuing strategies. The online voting facility is the first step to the electronic franchise. By increasing the participation of citizens in different activities included in the platform, the overall effectiveness of the government can be enhanced.

MyGov is already serving more than 40 lakh users, adding about 20,000 users every week. It is managed by the Ministry of Electronics and Information Technology (MeitY). The National Informatics Centre (NIC) brings about technical support and infrastructure. NIC Data Centre hosts the MyGov website and its associated microsites. Forty-five Ministries are engaged actively on MyGov platform, reaching out to the citizens through the fundamental concepts of Do, Discuss and Dissemination.

The activities involved generating a massive volume of structured, semi-structured and unstructured data which undergo time bound analysis. This analyzed data is sent to the government while taking policy decisions. Moreover, a variety of activities require unique types of analysis. The stakeholders can access a different set of outputs and expect analyzed reports and timelines. The comments and submissions are grouped and analyzed for decision making. The analysis is done by avoiding human error and biases. There is a real-time information dashboard to facilitate an informed and timely decision. Key stakeholders of MyGov are:

Ministry of Electronics and Information Technology (MEITY): The MeitY acts as the nodal Ministry to promote e-Governance to empower citizens. It enables the inclusive and sustainable growth of electronics in the country. The Ministry establishes India's role in e-Governance, by adopting multiple approaches that include the development of human resources, promoting R&D and innovation, enhancing efficiency through digital services and ensuring secure cyberspace.

Central Ministries/Government Bodies: The digital platform is already partnered with all Central Ministries. The government foresees that the MyGOV platform would be leveraged by other Government Institutions, including the PSUs/State Government, etc. (A few State governments have already partnered the platform). The Ministries and Government bodies utilize the platform to reach out to the masses and solicit suggestions and feedback on various planning matters for better governance. The Analytics solution deployed in the forum is used by these Government bodies to conduct intelligent analysis whereby they generate reports and briefings of each group.

Citizens: All the traffic coming to MyGov and its microsites form the user base of MyGov. This platform helps the citizens to engage with the government and act near in policy framework formulation and Government decision making. Citizens are now able to leverage the solution to access a public dashboard (MEITY, 2020).

Conclusion

E-governance is widely used by the countries to materialize the goals of good governance effectively. The operational method stages of development and implementation of e-governance vary in different nations. Because it is the electronic eco-system that decides in each country, in some nations the 'e-government' sector may be in a developed condition. In such states, a healthy system of automated administration persist. Here, the offices will maintain an electronic database and provide maximum e-services to the citizens. In some other countries, most probably in developed ones, not only an advanced e-administrative system but a proper two-way communication of citizens and government exist. Here the 'e-governance' aspect of digital governance is said to be intensified. The functionality of e-governance projects can be optimized only in a society where the whole sectors and stakeholders show preparedness. In India, the initiatives for e-governance started early in the 1990s. Later on, with the expansion of e-infrastructure in the public institutions, information dissemination and service delivery had significantly improved. The e-governance efforts in India are recently managed by the Ministry of Electronics and Information Technology (MEITY) through the Digital India programme. The MeitY has initiated the MyGOV Platform as its flagship project to objectify a resilient interaction between government and the citizens. In line with the 'staged development', the Government of India has managed to enhance the e-governance programmes through different projects. While examining the MyGOV project, it is clear that the Government of India assumes to implement an optimal vision of e-governance. It promotes through MyGOV, the most accepted value of e-governance, i.e., citizen participation. The different segments in this platform empower the citizen by making them the conclusive pillars of policymaking. Thereby, India has gone way forward in realizing the goal of administering e-participation and initiating e-democracy.

References

Alam, M. (2005). E-Government and E-Governance. *Information and Communication System*, 134-136.

Digital India. (2020, October 10). *Digital India*. Retrieved from digitalindia.gov.in: https://digitalindia.gov.in

Digital India. (2020a, October 21). *Digital India*. Retrieved from digitalindia.gov.in: https://digitalindia.gov.in/content/ekranti

Ghosh, S.S., & Antony, J. (2004). Optimization of the Determinants of E service Operation. *Business Process Management Journal, 10(6)*, 616-636.

Gouscos, D.K.M. (2007). A General Model of Performance and Quality for One-stop E-government Service Offerings. *Government Information Quarterly 24(4)*, 860-885.

Government of India. (2008). *Promoting E-Governance: The Smart way forward.* New Delhi: Government of India: Second Administrative Reforms Commission.

Government of India (2008). *Second Adminstrative Reforms Commission—Promoting E Governance: the Smart Way Forward.* New Delhi: Government of India.

Heeks, R. (2001). *Understanding e-governance for development, i-government working paper series.* London: Institute for Development Policy and Management, University of Manchester.

Hu, G.P., & Wang, J. (2009). The widely shared definition of eGovernment: An exploratory study. *The Electronic Library, 27(6)*, 968-985.

Jeff Breen, (2000, October 1). At the Dawn of E-Government: The Citizen as Customer in http://www.cnn.com/2000/TECH/computing/11/13/qna.egov.idg/. *Government Finance Review*, pp. 13-23.

Johannes, V.D. (2018). Introduction to Network Modelling using Exponential Random Graph Models (ERGM): Theory and an Application using R-Project. *Computational Economics,* September, 1-33.

Joseph, S. (2001). Democratic Good Governance: New Agenda for Change. *Economic and Political Weekly, 36* (12), 1009-1016.

Kettl, D. (2002). *The Transformation of Governance.* Baltimore MD: Johns Hopkins University Press.

Kiran Bedi, P., & S. Srivastava (2001). *Government @net.* New Delhi: Sage Publication.

Kiran, C. (2016). Rural Development through E-Governance Initiatives in India at https://www.researchgate.net/publication/324896252. *IOSR Journal of Business and Management,* 61-69.

Lal, B.G., & Manhica, S. (1999). *Information and Communication Technologies for Improved Governance in https://repository.uneca.org/handle/10855/5633.* Addis Ababa: African Development Forum ADF '99.

Li, H., & Suomi, R. (2007). Evaluating Electronic Service quality: a Transaction Process Based Evaluation Model. In D. Remenyi, *Proceedings of ECIME 2007,* pp. 331-240, Montpellier: The European Conference on Information Management and Evaluation.

Meity (2020, October 4). *Selection of Implementation Partner for implementing Analytics Solution for MyGov.* Retrieved from www.meity.gov.in: https:// www.meity.gov.in/writereaddata/files/MyGov%20Analytics%20RFP%20 Vol%201_Final.pdf

Moteff, J.D. (2010). *CRS Report RL30153, Critical Infrastructures: Background, Policy, and Implementation.* Washington DC: Congressional Research Service.

Pandey, A.B. (2005). Core Project should be pushed at National level. *Data Quest,* March 31, 68-73.

Panzardi, R. (2002). *New-Economy Sector Study Electronic Government and Governance: Lessons for Argentina.* Washington DC: World Bank.

Rani, S. (2002). Treasures of the Earth. *Data Quest,* January 31, 62-63.

Saxena, K.B. (2005). Towards excellence in e-governance. *International Journal of Public Sector Management, 18*(6), 498-513.

Schmutzer, G.A. (2000). Organisational, Technological and Regulatory Challenges for Realizing Electronic Government. *ECIS 2000,* pp. 1-9, Vienna: Association for Information System.

Silcock, R. (2001). 'What is e-Government?', Hansard Society for parliamentary Government. *Parliamentary Affairs, 54,* 88-101.

UNDESA. (2020, April). *United Nations Department of Economic and Social Affairs.* Retrieved from publicadministration.un.org: https:// publicadministration.un.org/en/research/un-e-government-surveys

UNDP (2007). *Pro-Poor Public Service Delivery with ICTs : Making local E-governance Work onwards Achieving the Millennium Development Goals.* Washington DC: UNDP.

UNESCO. (2020, September 10). *UNESCO Web archive.* Retrieved from portal. unesco.org: http://portal.unesco.org/ci/en/ev.php-URL_ ID=2179&URL_ DO=DO_TOPIC&URL_SECTION=201.html

United Nations (2002). *Benchmarking E-Government—A Global Perspective* in http://pti.nw.dc.us/links/docs/ASPA_UN_egov_survey.pdf, 2002. Washington DC: Division for Public Economics and Public Administration.

Verma, D. (2018). Governance to Good Governance through e-Governance: A critical review of Concept, Model, Initiatives & Challenges in India. *International Journal of Management, IT & Engineering, 8*(10), 244-269.

16
Exploring Neoliberal Instrumentality in Governance

Arindam Roy

I

Governance has become a popular catch-all phrase. From politician to administrator, to a man on street everybody is taking recluse under this capacious term for his/her possible act of commission and omission. The present chapter unpacks a rather critical discourse on governance. Unlike the much talked about narrative of governance which presents World Bank touted checklist of sound administrative/development management as sacrosanct and to be treated as necessary precondition for availing developmental loans, it talks about the inside story of the birth of governance. If one cares to go through a burgeoning literature on governance, he/she may stumble upon as many as four different connotations of governance: governance as a structure, as a process, as a mechanism; and last but not least as a strategy. Interestingly, there has been a perceptible trade-off between structure and processes in the literature of governance. The importance of structure in defining governance was deliberately downplayed in the Fund-Bank prescriptions to facilitate neoliberal dream of unification of global markets. For, any attempt to strengthen the structure in the conceptualization of governance would derail the project of unification of global markets. Hence, process was foregrounded as the basis of governance in the Bank documents.The present chapter is basically concentrating on the fourth connotation of governance, i.e. it views governance as a strategy for the neoliberals to salvage ailing capitalism from the blues of Keynesianism. It views that the very popularization and maturation of the concept of governance is intrinsically associated with neoliberalism. The chapter has the following sections: section I deals with concept of governance, especially the way it is presented in the World Bank documents.; section II interrogates the conceptualization of governance by bringing in the correlations between governance and neoliberalism; section III finally winds up the chapter with a concluding observation.

This section deals with concept of governance, especially the way it is represented in the World Bank documents. Topicality notwithstanding, it can hardly claim to have a coherent definition. In fact, the concept is notoriously imprecise as it has multiple connotations. Despite a literal mushrooming of literature on the subject, it remains an elusive enterprise. The opening remark of *The Oxford Handbook of Governance* has endorsed the above conceptual confusions. It reads 'governance is an interdisciplinary research agenda on order and disorder, efficiency and legitimacy all in the context of hybridization of modes of control that allow the production of fragmented and multidimensional order within the state, by the state, without the state and beyond the state' (Levi-Faur: 2012). The above statement has identified that the basic puzzle of conceptualizing governance lies in the problem of locating order in the era of increasing hybridization of modes of control. The global interconnectedness has further accentuated the problem of defining governance as the state is often lost in the labyrinth of order marked by a host of national and international non-governmental and civil society organizations operational at the micro, meso and macro levels. The value-loaded slippery adjective 'good', especially its mention in several Fund Bank documents has further confounded the concept. Every government—be it autocratic, democratic or theocratic has been engaged, at least visibly, in this seemingly endless search. Notionally speaking, the concept has always been there with civilized humanity. The etymological root of the term is said to have stemmed from the Greek word *kybernan*, which signifies the act of piloting or steering that is subsequently translated into the Latin word *gobernare*. Hence, the steering metaphor approximates the essence of governance in the contemporary world.

The term secures a permanent berth in the policy discourses since the end of cold war. In the 1950s and 1960s, the topic of governance was very much present, but did not get adequate attention in social science and humanities. The publication of an article by Oliver Williamson, entitled 'Transaction Costs Economics: Governance of Contractual Relations' in 1979 had literally captivated the academic interest in the concept of governance for the first time. Though the focus of the paper was basically the 'law and economics of corporate governance', it received a huge response in terms of citations (Levi-Faur, David:2012). However, the World Bank publications have catapulted the concept from a narrow specialized area of economics and law to a truly public discourse. With an objective of bringing about economic and political reforms in the recipient countries, donor agencies like World Bank, IMF have brought in a series of prescriptions under the rubric of governance. The World Bank had drawn to the issue of governance for the first time in 1989 when a *Long Term Perspective Study on Sub Saharan Africa,* entitled *Sub-Saharan Africa: From Crisis to Sustainable Growth: A Long-Term Perspective Study* (World Bank, 1989) had identified poor governance was at the heart of African crisis. The report had accounted for the crisis of governance with the mounting crisis of population growth, surpassing the GDP growth along with weak agricultural growth, drooping industrial output, deteriorating social indicators and so on. In fact, the said report was instrumental in motivating the Bank's General Counsel to draft a *Legal Memorandum to its Board of Directors* in December 1990, indicating a future roadmap for further analysis on governance (Lateef: 2016). Subsequently, the World Bank had come up with a discussion paper entitled "Managing Development—the Governance Dimension" in 1991, originally meant for the consumption of its board of directors. It was the first ever formal policy statement, issued by the Bank management to lay out the detailed analytical frame for lending work and governance. In 1992, the Bank had set up a task force for spelling out the nuances of governance under the leadership of Sarwar Lateef, which was later published by the Bank as a booklet entitled, *Governance and Development* (1992). Since then there has been a virtual mushrooming of literature on governance. In fact, the World Bank has been grappling with this concept in several of its publications. If one starts browsing through those literatures, he/she would have ended up with a discovery of a prescriptive checklist for sound administrative management, which includes among others, participation, consensus-orientedness, accountability, transparency, responsiveness, effectiveness, equity, inclusiveness, and rule of law. It was projected in such a way that if a country religiously follows that checklist in its administrative deliberations, that country would be considered as 'fit' for availing developmental loans. Otherwise, a country would have been promptly termed as 'failed state' or 'rogue state'. A neoliberal string is said to have been attached with the so-called parameters of governance. Hence, the uncritical compliance of said checklist by the developing countries would sustain the twin objectives of the neoliberalism: on the one hand the compliance to the said checklist would ensure neoliberals with much needed assurance/ guarantee of repayment of loan amount disbursed to the developing countries as developmental loan; and on the other hand, it facilitates neoliberal dreams of unification of global markets by substantially displacing government/state from the social sector. Hence, governance agenda is brought into being by the neoliberals as a necessary precondition for better administrative management.

II

This section intends to understand the supposed correlation between neoliberalism and governance. Before we move into the nuances of this correlation, a brief discussion on the concept of neoliberalism deserves some space here. Neoliberalism, as defined by David Harvey, "is a theory of political economic practices proposing that human well being can best be advanced by maximization of entrepreneurial freedoms within an institutional framework characterized by private property, individual liberty, unencumbered markets and free trade" (Harvey: 2005). Further, neoliberalism wants state to create an institutional framework conducive for the above practices. ...It believes that market dynamism has the potential of realizing individual well-being by unlocking the individual entrepreneurial spirit. Briefly speaking, neoliberalism stands for four fundamental changes, first, trust in small government; secondly, deregulation of the domestic financial systems; thirdly, deregulation of labour market; and the last but not the least facilitating the entry of international capital (Anthony O'Hara, Philip: 2010). However, the adoption of neoliberalism as policy and as populist culture is not spontaneous either. Hence, neoliberalization calls for a thorough construction of consent via microfinance, delegating ownership to the community, poverty alleviation, development, health etc.

The said correlation can be better understood if we put the liberalism into evolutionary matrix. In fact, neoliberalism is an attempt to bail out ailing capitalism which had limped back to life in late 1960s after a brief stint of Keynesianism emerged in the wake of Great Depression of late 1920s. The 'sleight of hand' (invisible hand), howsoever convincing the logic might be, failed to carry forward the project of governance further. The worldwide economic recession or the great depression in 1930s proved the inadequacies of the market model of governance and reiterated the importance of interventionist state in governance via Keynesian macroeconomic remedy of more state. Hence, government or state is brought back in the governance discourse over and over again. However, the danger of a stifling Leviathan with its all encompassing legal formal paraphernalia is often proved to be cumbrous and demotivating. Hence, jettisoning of the spectra of Kenyensian over-statism was necessary. The birth of neoliberalism in 1970 was therefore a natural outcome. However, neoliberalism did not enjoy a smooth tenure. In fact, since its emergence in 1970s till date it has to undergo several ups and downs to stay afloat. In the initial stage (from late 1970s to mid-1980s), neoliberalism was primarily 'structure-dependent', putting a lot of emphasis on strict monetarism and laissez faire and asks for rigorous restructuring of policies which include among others cut in social spending, cut in subsidies, introduction of anti-union laws in order to attract investment and so on. The second phase (from mid-1980s to mid-1990s) was more or less a phase of consolidation for neoliberalism as it has gone past the period of market fundamentalism. The Washington Consensus, a neoliberal 'reform package' gives much more coherence to the policies of neoliberalism. John Williamson has enumerated ten policy prescriptions of the Washington Consensus which was shared by Washington-based institutions like World Bank and IMF along with US congress. They were viz. "(1) fiscal discipline; (2) redirecting public expenditure; (3) tax reform; (4) financial liberalization; (5) adoption of a single, competitive exchange rate; (6) trade liberalization; (7) elimination of barriers to foreign direct investment; (8) privatization of state owned enterprises; (9) deregulation of market entry and competition; and (10) secure property rights" (Lopes, Carlos: 2011). Governance, a well thought out project was born at the second phase of periodization as the ten policy prescriptions of the said consensus have presumably necessitated the birth of it. Consequently, the governing process had transcended the boundaries of government to incorporate a host of agencies and associations involved in the act of governing. For, any amount of Keynesianism was counter-productive for the neoliberal dream of unification of global markets. The third phase of the periodization, also known as the 'post-Washington consensus phase' (from mid-1990s to present) has brought certain modifications in the conceptualization of governance by bringing about humane face in governance with its emphasis on redistribution, social safety net, the targeted poverty reduction, selective health intervention and so on.

The neoliberal policy of moving beyond government/state by manufacturing the concept of governance is also marked by an exponential rise of the third sector along with market. For the rise of third sector was necessary to reclaim the social space, left vacant by the departure of state from the social sector as a part of neoliberal conditionality. Hence, by allowing third sector to grow, neoliberals have supplemented the withdrawal of state from the social sector and paved the way for governance framework. If one tracks the trajectories of governance, he/she may find several changes in the model of governance, primarily brought into being to suit the overarching interest of the neoliberals. The revival of the third sector should not be treated uncritically as a spontaneous growth. In fact, they are the policy artifacts, acted as a conduit of global capital by harnessing community. Moreover, due to 'continuous relocation of authority structures both outward towards supranational entities and inward towards sub-national groups' (Rosenau and Czempiel, 2009), governance model as a neoliberal instrumentality also gets relocated/graduated from global to local via national policy. Interestingly, the neoliberals (as an outcome of Post-Washington consensus) have gone past the phase of financial orthodoxy and its attendant precondition of rampant deinstitutionalization and seemed to have adopted selective institutionalization (institutional reform) in the field of social sector like health, rural development/poverty alleviation etc. In the next section, an attempt will be made to navigate the continuous graduation of governance models across the globe. The varying connotations of the concept of governance from a schematic prescription of sound administrative management by the donor agencies in the early 1990s to its wide spread orchestration in different Fund Bank publications as the panacea for administrative malfunctioning in the late 1990s, to its present modified form of selective re-institutionalization, is indicative of the shifting fortunes of the capital. The neoliberals in a bid to salvaging capital from crises kept on modifying the notion of governance. Hence, it would not be totally out of place to relate the recent renewal of interest in decentralization with neoliberal form of governance.

The emphasis on local governance or call for decentralization/decentralized governance is not an indigenous model of empowering local, rather it is a well thought out neoliberal design of 'spatial fixation of capital'. With an objective of spatializing capital, neoliberals have adopted a couple of policies: first is empowerment of the institutions and processes of local governing by encouraging decentralization and rural development: and second is the creation of exclusive enclaves or Special Economic Zones (SEZs). Depending upon the nature of capitalist development, neoliberals have adopted policies of furthering the reach of capital. For example, the model adopted in a few early liberalized countries in South East Asia like Thailand, Indonesia is markedly different from the rest of Asia. Neoliberals in this part of the world have actively encouraged the creation of SEZ/EPZ for the fixation of FDIs. But they have customized their policy in case of the post-colonial countries like India, where the development of capital is by and large uneven. The neoliberal experimentation in India has taken a different route considering its contextuality. The Indian society has had a long independent tradition of local level governance nestling at the margin for centuries together. The vicissitude of power equations at the centre had rarely touched this pristine traditions of governance, as from Metcalfe to Gandhi all have been very appreciative of these tiny village republics. Neoliberals in India have seized upon this opportunity of capitalizing the tradition of local governance by actively advocating decentralization schemes. For, such attempt would not only stabilize the worldwide crisis of market debacle, but also offer alternative virgin rural market to tap. Hence, the rural development projects received huge patronage from the neoliberals and a flurry of rural development schemes including small scale industries have been introduced in the rural hinterland. Even, the neoliberal modalities have also changed over the years. The modalities of neoliberalism during its consolidation phase (Washington Consensus in 1990s), was primarily based on 'investment-growth equations', which believes investment begets growth. The Structural Adjustment Programme (SAP) was introduced as the guiding principle to stabilize the growth of capital. The state is induced to shed off its responsibility by structurally readjusting itself with a host of other institutions. This phase had a definite deinstitutionalizing focus as processes of governing got utmost priority at the cost of Institution (state). However, within a very short span of time a realization sets in that investment alone cannot ensure growth. In fact, strong institutional structure is equally important to bring about growth. Hence, the importance of institutional reforms was the outcome of the failure of Washington Consensus. The institution building which was almost discouraged at the early phase of neoliberalism, has become mainstay of this phase. Institution building had got a tremendous fillip during this phase as it was encouraged in three different tiers—at the micro level, at the meso level and at the macro level. At the micro level local communities were encouraged to take part in development. Community ownership was also offered to the local and marginal communities. The birth of people's plan, decentralized planning, participatory local resource management were a few such efforts of inducing capital by empowering local communities and giving them a sense of ownership. This is how governance is relocated at the micro level. In the post-1995 onwards, a consensus was reached or what is popularly known as post-Washington consensus that growth without distribution will not be sustainable in nature. Consequently, the neoliberals (as an outcome of Post-Washington consensus) have gone past the phase of financial orthodoxy and its attendant precondition of rampant deinstitutionalization and seemed to have adopted selective institutionalization in the garb of institutional reform in the field of social sector like health, rural development/poverty alleviation etc. However, such shift in governance is not spontaneous either. Neoliberals adopted the so-called humane face of governance for at least two reasons: first, such pro-people, community centric governance approach would act as shock absorber for neoliberals as this bit of providential intervention has mystified the people about the real intention of the neoliberals and bestows much coveted legitimacy to neoliberals and its crony state/ government. Secondly, the said 'humane turn' of governance paradigm, especially its venture in the form of public health initiatives or poverty alleviation programme has a benign political economic dimension. For, allowing concessions to the state to intervene in the health sector or poverty alleviation was anything but the replication Keynesian paradigm of social welfare. In fact, health and poverty proved to be a huge market opportunity for the neoliberals. For, example, selective marketization of health sector by introducing health insurance scheme for the poor without dismantling public health infrastructure may be mentioned. This, selective collabouration between market and state intervention has a legitimizing impact for both the state and market; on the one hand it legitimizes market intervention in social sector; and on the other hand it also brings back a little bit of legitimacy he states in terms of its commitment towards its citizens. Hence, neoliberals allow crony state to facilitate market expansion. The enamoring of C.K. Prahalad's new innovative book by the neoliberals for example has demonstrated how poverty can best be fought with profitability. 'The Fortune at the Bottom of the Pyramid' (2005) could have been an interesting reference point. If one browsing through this book one would invariably stumble upon the rich adulation showered on it. The wide acceptance and readership of the book especially by the chieftain of the industry and market is indicative of the dominant neoliberal perspective towards poverty. Drawing on several cross-country case studies, Prahalad has demonstrated the financial viability of the poverty or what he called BOP market for capital accumulation. Unlike the traditional welfare principle of philanthrophy and providential (ism), a whopping 4/5 billion people at the BOP, as Prahalad viewed, may revolutionize business practices. Hence, the need of the hour is to get out of old prejudices regarding poor. In fact, Prahalad has shown that poor or the BOP could have been a huge market had we customize the market in accordance with the needs of the BOP. Citing the case study of shampoo market, Prahalad had shown that sachet-ization had multiplied the sell of shampoo as BOP people have choices, demands and brand consciousness. Interestingly by new governance paradigm, the millions of marginal people have been roped in the process governing.

III

Concluding observations

In the foregoing analysis an attempt has been made to unearth the inside story of the birth of governance. There is no denying that governance has liberated the notion of governing from the clutches of institutionalization. However, considering governance as a panacea for all kinds administrative evil is a grossly overstatement. In fact, there is a serious neoliberal instrumentality behind the birth of the concept of governance. The neoliberals in a bid to salvaging capitalism from severe economic recession in early 1970s has brought the concept of governance. Hence, the origin, maturation and the ramifications of the concept is intrinsically tied up with neoliberal interest. Hence, the modification of the concept, no matter howsoever delicately constructed smacks of typical capitalist design of manufacturing consent/ legitimacy. The occasional tinkering with the some eternal normative values like equity, justice, inclusivity etc. should be read as various modes. Despite heralding of the triumph of capitalism in the 'End of History' thesis, the above desperation of the part of the neoliberals to project governance indicates a perennial anxiety of capitalism. Hence, the time has come to demystify the concept of governance and interrogate the neoliberal motives before uncritically embracing it as 'the trusted antidote to any type of administrative malfunctioning'.

References

De Angelis, Massimo (2005). "The Political Economy of Global Neoliberal Governance", *Review (Fernand Braudel Center)*, Vol. 28, No. 3.

Harvey, David, *A Brief History of Neoliberalism*, 2005, Oxford: Oxford University Press.

Lateef, K. Sarwar (2016). Background Paper: Governance and Law, Evolution of The World Bank's thinking on Governance, Washington, DC: The International Bank for Reconstruction and Development.

Levi-Faur, David (ed) (2012). *The Oxford Handbook of Governance*, Oxford: Oxford University Press.

Lopes, Carlos (2012). "Economic Growth and Inequality: The New Post-Washington Consensus", *RCCS Annual Review*, 4, October.

O'Hara, Philip Anthony (2010). "After Neoliberalism: A Social Structure of Accumulation or Mode of Regulation for Globalor Regional Performance?", *Journal of Economic Issues*, Vol. 44, No. 2.

Prahalad, C.K. (2005). *The Fortune at the Bottom of The Pyramid*, New Jersey: Wharton School Publishing, Wharton University.

Rosenau, James N. and Ernst-Otto Czempiel (2009). *Governing without Government: Order and Challenge in World Politics*, Cambridge: Cambridge University Press.

World Bank (1989). Sub-Saharan Africa: From Crisis to Sustainable Growth, Washington, DC: The International Bank for Reconstruction and Development.

World Bank (1992). Governance and Development, Washington, DC: The International Bank for Reconstruction and Development.

Index

2030 Agenda for Sustainable Development, 25, 229
74th Constitutional amendment, 35

Agency theory, 64
Agenda for National Human Development Report, 2002, 46
Agricultural Food Processed Products Export Development Authority (APEDA), 138
AMRUT, 36
Armed conflicts, military pollution and its environmental hazards, 154-163
  environmental degradation before wars or conflicts, 157
  environmental degradation during conflicts, 159
  environmental degradation, 155
  environmental security, 155, 161
  exploitation of natural resources, 154
  impact of war on environment, 160
  post-conflict environmental degradation, 160
  threat multiplier, 156
Atal Mission for Rejuvenation and Urban Transformation (AMRUT), 26

Beti Bachao Beti Padhao (BBBP) yojana, 26, 30, 31
  need and rationale for programme, 32
Bharat Interface for Money (BHIM) app, 248
Bilateralism policy, 169
Biological determinism, 120
Build Back Better, 112
Burman Committee, 181

Central Water Commission (CWC), 133, 138
Child Sex Ratio (CSR), 30
Climate change, 155
Climate resilience,
  awareness on and peace building practices in adolescents, 172-178
  awareness of climate resilience of higher secondary school students, 175, 176
  educational implications, 177
  environmental peace building, 174
  peace education for peace building, 173
Community preparedness, 114
Companies (Amendment) Bill, 2019, 19
Companies Act, 2013, 10
Competition Commission Act, 20
Constitution of India, 51
Corporate social responsibility (CSR), 1

and new law & regulations in India, 10
and sustainable development (lessons from India), 1-24
and Sustainable Development in India, 7
conceptualization, 3
issues and challenges, 18
family feuds, 19
government's interference in private sector, 19
inadequate and weak regulatory framework, 20
lack of capacity building, 18
lack of community participation, 19
lack of sufficient funding, 18
methods of implementation, 11
recent private corporates initiatives, 14
understanding CSR in India, 5
Corporate sustainability, 8
COVID-19 Virus, 253
Culture, 214

Decentralisation, 36
Decentralized Waste Management (DWM), 181
Democratic decentralisation and good governance for Indian urban local bodies, 35-53
challenges of MDGs & SDGs before local government, 38
concept of governance, 42
e-governance, good governance & smart governance, 46
good governance, 43
and New Public Management, 48
concept & importance of Good Governance for development, 48
key Indian agencies at work on SDGs, 40
mismatch between functions assigned and available resources, 51
Demonetisation, 244
Digital India Initiatives in transforming governance to achieve SDGs, 224-243
challenges being faced by India in implementing SDGs, 238
solutions to meet these challenges, 240
Digital India Initiatives, 229
Digital India Programme, 230
Broadband Highways, 231
early harvest programmes, 234
E-Kranti, 232
electronics manufacturing, 233
Information for All, 233
IT for jobs, 234
Public Internet Access Programme, 232
Universal Access to Mobile Connectivity, 231
from Millennium Development Goals (MDGs) to Sustainable Development Goals (SDGs), 227
impact of Digital Initiatives in India, 238
tools leading to a transformed Governance in achieving SDGs, 235
Digital India Plan, 264
Digital India, 226
Digital revolution, 229
Disaster Management Act, 2005, 100, 113
Disaster management and good governance, concerns and strategies, 98-118

case study of disaster governance, 113
climatic and geo-spatial conditionalities, 98
disaster governance, 101, 102
international strategies for disaster governance and risk reduction, 103
significance of governance in disaster management, 101
Disaster management, 99

Eco-Marxism, 125
E-Commerce, 244
E-Governance,
an Indian experiment with the MyGOV Application, 254-271
challenges of, 259
development stages of, 261
e-governance Vs. E-Government, 255
e-preparedness, 259
Indian experience, 262
meaning, 254
potential opportunities, 256
principles of, 257
Energy cooperation in Eastern South Asia, 164-171
energy overview of Bangladesh, 165
energy overview of Bhutan, 167
energy overview of India, 165
energy overview of Nepal, 166
prospects for sub-regional energy cooperation, 168
Environment and society, special reference to eco-Marxism, 119-129
eco-Marxism and environmental crisis, 123
economic justice, 123
environmental movement, 122
modern trends in environmental-sociological theory, 126
resources mobilization and relative deprivation in ecological movement, 122
social Darwinism and environmental sociology, 121
Environmental sociology, 119, 127, 128
focus of, 120
Environmental, social, and governance (ESG) and corporate financial performance (CFP), 54-97
ESG perspective, 55
ESG practices, 70
ESG-CFP relationship, 56, 57, 63, 79, 81, 83
implications, 84
practical implications, 85
social implications, 85
theoretical implications, 84
limitations, 86
methodology, 76
PRISMA Protocol, 59
TCCM Framework, 62
characteristics, 68
context, 66
theory, 62
European Commission, 3
EXIM trade basket, 164

FDI Regulations, 247
Fifth Revolution, 238
Food scarcity, 156
Fourth Revolution, 237

Gender-Digital Divide, 239

Global warming, 133
Globalization, 6
Goods and services tax (GST), 250
Governance, 272
exploring neoliberal instrumentality in, 272-282

Human capital index (HCI), 241
Hyogo Framework for Action 2005-2015 (HFA), 107, 108, 110

Inde EA Project, 230, 231
Indian e-commerce industry, upsurge of in era of post-demonetisation, 244-253
hyper-local E-Commerce, 251
logistics, 249
online payments, 247
online retailing, 246
Indian Ocean Tsunami Ready Programme, 114
Information and Communication Technology/ies (ICTs), 36, 46, 212, 225, 254
Information Kerala Mission (IKM), 255
Integrated Local Governance Management System (ILGMS), 255
International Decade for Natural Disaster Reduction (1990-2000), 105, 108
International Girl Child Day, 33
International Strategy for Disaster Reduction (ISDR), 108
Internet and Mobile Association of India (IAMAI), 248

Jawaharlal Nehru Urban Renewal Mission (Jn NURM), 183

Karnataka Municipalities Act, 1964, 183

Local governance, 37
Logistics, 249
LPG, 37

Micro, small and medium enterprises (MSMEs), 252
Military pollution, 158
Millennium Declaration of United Nations, 25, 38
Ministry of Electronics and Information Technology (MEITY), 267
Mobile Banking, 248
MSDGs, 25
Municipal Solid Waste Management (MSWM), 183
MyGOV, triggering E-democracy in India, 265
Mysore City Corporation (MCC), 182
National Disaster Management Authority, India (NDMA), 100, 139
National Disaster Management Institute of India (NDMI), 98
National E-governance Plan 2.0 (E-Kranti), 263
National Electronic Funds Transfer (NEFT) System, 248
National Executive Committee (NEC), 100
National Indicator Framework (NIF), 229
National Institution for Transforming India (NITI Aayog), 26, 40, 226
National Voluntary Guidelines, 10
Neoclassical realist, 207

Neoliberalism, 275
Neorealism, 208
New Economic Policy, 1991, 226
New Public Management (NPM), 48
  according to the Public Management Committee of the OECD (1995), 49
  for local administration in context of issues and problems, 50

Online service index (OSI), 241

Panchayati Raj Institutions (PRIs), 42
Planning Commission, 45
Positive-sum game, 211
Power and soft power, theoretical developments, 194-223
  a power currency approach to soft power, 219
  causes of soft power becoming more prominent in international relations, 212
  criticism on soft power, 217
  different faces of power, 199
  effect of soft power (direct and indirect), 216
  power and its characteristics, 194
  soft power has both material and non-material resources, 213
  Weberian concept of power, 201
Pre-Conception & Pre-Natal Diagnostic Techniques (PC & PNDT) Act, 32
Principles for Responsible Investment (PRI), 54
Public Choice Theory, 47

Real Time Gross Settlement System (RTGS), 248
Realist tradition, 210
Reserve Bank of India, 245
Rice, 130
Rio Earth Summit, 1992, 229
Rising temperatures, 156

SAARC, 164
Second Administrative Reforms Commission (ARC), 255
Second World War, 227
Sendai framework, 111, 112
Smart Cities Mission, 36
Soft power, 212
South East Asia, 278
Special Economic Zones (SEZs), 278
STEM skills, 173
Sustainable Development Goals (SDGs), 15, 36, 224, 226
Sustainable export of water intensive rice in India and climate change and water scarcity, 130-153
  climate change, 130, 132
  contribution of climatic factors on water availability and water usage for exportable rice, 145
  dynamics between climate parameters, 144
  general trend of climate change, 142
  impact of climate variables on quantity of export of rice in India mediated by production, 141
  indirect impact analysis of climate change, 148
  interdependence between climate change, water availability, and water usage for exportable rice, 136

trend analysis, 139
water situation in India and water usage for production of export amount of rice, 144
water situation in India, 133
Sustainable management, 54
Swachh Bharat Mission, 179

Technology and Capacity-Building, 240
Telecommunication Infrastructure Index (TII), 241

UN Agenda for Peace, 173
UNDP, 101
UNESCO, 172
UNESCO's Education for Sustainable Development (ESD) programme, 175
UNESCO-Intergovernmental Oceanographic Commission, 113
UNICEF Programme Report, 2016, 173
United Nations Development Programme (UNDP), 36, 44
Urban local bodies (ULBs), 42
Urbanization and economic development, 35

Voluntarism, 22

Washington Consensus, 276
Wilcoxon Signed Rank Test (WST), 139
Women empowerment through quality education, agenda for (a case study of Beti Bachao Beti Padhao scheme in India), 25-34
conceptualizing empowerment of women, 27
determinants of empowerment, 27
World Bank, 1, 42, 45, 272
World Business Council for Sustainable Development, 3
World Conference on Natural Disaster Reduction, 105, 107

Yokohama Strategy, 105

Zero Waste City, 192
Zero Waste Management (ZWM), a key to sustainable development, 179-193
cost benefit of ZWM,191
in Mysore City, 182
MCC's new initiatives, 191
municipal solid waste (MSW), 180
need of the 21st century, 181
occupational safety, 189
problems involved, 191
processes, 185
composting, 185
dry leaves compost beds, 188
liquid resource management, 188
special project of wet waste management at Pinjrapole, 189
vermi cast, 186
vermi composting, 185
vermi culture, 186
vermi tank, 186
waste to energy, 187
SHGs/community participation, 191
solid Waste (SW), 180
waste management (WM), 180